SOUND THE TRUMPET

BEAT THE DRUMS

SOUND THE TRUMPET

BEAT THE DRUMS

Horse-Mounted Bands of the U.S. Army
1820–1940

BRUCE P. GLEASON

University of Oklahoma Press ⬦ Norman

LIBRARY OF CONGRESS CATALOGING-IN-PUBLICATION DATA

Name: Gleason, Bruce P., 1958– author.

Title: Sound the trumpet, beat the drums : horse-mounted bands of the U.S. Army, 1820–1940 / Bruce P. Gleason.

Description: First edition. | Norman : University of Oklahoma Press, [2016] | © 2016 | Includes bibliographical references and index.

Identifiers: LCCN 2016004193 | ISBN 978-0-8061-5479-4 (hardcover : alk. paper)

Subjects: LCSH: United States. Army. Cavalry—Bands. | Bands (Music)—History. | United States. Army. Cavalry—History—19th century. | United States. Army. Cavalry—History—20th century. | Military music—United States—19th century—History and criticism. | Military music—United States—20th century—History and criticism.

Classification: LCC ML1311.4 .G54 2016 | DDC 784.8/40973—dc23

LC record available at http://lccn.loc.gov/2016004193

To the memory and collected works of

HENRY GEORGE FARMER,

EDGAR M. TURRENTINE,

and

JEROME S. GATEHOUSE.

Thank you all for looking over my shoulder.

ॐ

Contents

Illustrations

Preface

AT THE TIME OF THIS WRITING, THE U.S. DEPARTMENT OF DEFENSE is the largest employer of musicians in the country with nearly 6,500 musicians serving in active duty, reserve, and National Guard bands. The jobs of today's military musicians are similar to mine when I played for the reunification ceremonies of Germany with the 298th U.S. Army Band more than twenty years ago—and like that of military musicians of centuries past—supporting soldiers, sailors, marines, airmen, and civilians in times of warfare and peace in ceremonies, parades, concerts, dances, and other performances. As a euphonium and trombone player, I have had a long interest in military music playing the marches, waltzes, and suites of Sousa, King, Teike, Alford, Fučík, Holst, and Vaughan Williams—long before I was a soldier-musician myself. The beginnings of a love for this music began with high school and with my band director, Richard Foley, who was also a veteran army musician.

Within this arena of military music, my interest in horse-mounted bands can be traced to an exact point in time. One day after a brass sectional with the University of Minnesota Golden Gophers Marching Band, one of the mellophone players was showing us band members a recent purchase from the Coffman Memorial Union bookstore—a framed photograph of a horse-mounted euphonium player dressed in what I recognized years later as the uniform of the band of the Life Guards of the Queen's Household Cavalry. The photo of a well-trained musician serving in the historic traditions, uniforms, gallant music, and well-bred horses of a mounted band planted itself in my mind, where it has stayed for more than three decades. Several years later, in searching for a thesis topic in conclusion of my master of arts degree, I recalled the photo and began reading everything I could about military music in general and the little I could find on mounted bands in particular. This led to a 1985 trip to the United Kingdom and projects of interviewing men who had played with the Royal Artillery Mounted Band in the 1920s, '30s, and '40s, and in studying documents at the Royal Artillery Barracks and Government House and the Henry George Farmer papers at the University of Glasgow.

Although I left this line of research for a while during my doctoral studies, I came back to it at Gordon College, when an open-format grant was offered to faculty. With this, I resumed my mounted band research, but, rather than focusing only on the United Kingdom, I decided that I would travel to the countries having the last three or four remaining horse-mounted bands in the world, gather some information about the tradition in general—including that of the United States—and put a book together within a couple of years. My naivety has served me well.

Now these eighteen years later, I have visited nine of the current mounted bands in England, France, Denmark, Sweden, Belgium, and Oman with leads on another dozen or so around the world and have collected nearly a thousand images—scans, slides, paintings, photographs, tapestries, and drawings—of eight hundred years of horse-mounted musicians. While my initial and over-arching interest in mounted bands has been worldwide, my foray into seeking information about those in the United States sent me on several tangents. When I collected a few photographs from the Smithsonian Institution in addition to a few from several military museums, I thought this would be the extent of my U.S. research and I would be free to traverse the world. As I proceeded to collect information from documents and photographs about mounted bands in the U.S. Cavalry, I also found that those in the artillery would show themselves as well, along with nearly twenty in the Army National Guard. I had always assumed that I would be able to assemble a book of some kind, but I thought it would be about the bands of the United Kingdom and the European Continent where the tradition continues to this day after centuries of development. However, as my research has grown, it has become apparent that the first story I need to tell is the one attached closer to home—but one that was birthed long before there was a United States of America. While I bring field trumpets into the discussion throughout the present work, especially in early chapters where I discuss their service as forerunners of mounted bands, interested readers should delve into this topic in works by true experts.

In closing this preface, an attempt to thank all of the people who have helped along the way would be futile, so I will keep the list short with three equal categories. I mention in further detail the veteran U.S. Cavalry musicians I was able to interview in the appendix, and am thankful that by word of mouth over the years, I found each of you. Second, a listing of the staff members with the numerous organizations who have helped in countless capacities would be endless. However, I am compelled to mention the following organizations to which I am indebted: 1st Cavalry Division Museum, Fort Hood, Texas; 1st Troop Philadelphia City Cavalry, Philadelphia; 3rd Cavalry Museum, Fort Hood, Texas; Ancestry.com; Anne S. K. Brown Military Collection, Brown University Library; Bibliothèque nationale de France; Buffalo Soldiers National Museum, Houston, Texas; Chicago History Museum; College of Arms, London, England; Fort Bliss and Old Ironsides Museums, Fort Bliss, Texas; Fort Huachuca Museum, Fort Huachuca, Arizona; Fort Sam Houston Museum, San Antonio, Texas; Fort Sill Museum, Fort Sill, Oklahoma; Friends of Jefferson Barracks, St. Louis, Missouri; Harold Washington Library Center, Chicago, Illinois; House of Lords, London, England; Illinois State Military Museum, Springfield, Illinois; Jefferson National Expansion Memorial, St. Louis, Missouri; Kentucky Historical Society, Frankfort, Kentucky; Kentucky Military History Museum, Frankfort, Kentucky; Kremlin Museum, Moscow, Russia; Kunglinga Arméemuseum, Stockholm, Sweden; Library of Congress, Washington, D.C.; Minnesota Historical Society, St. Paul, Minnesota; Museum of Missouri Military History, Jefferson City, Missouri; The Museum of the Confederacy, Richmond, Virginia; National Archives and Records Administration, Washington, D.C.; National Guard Militia Museum of New Jersey, Sea Girt, New Jersey; New York State Military Museum and Veterans Research Center, Saratoga Springs, New York; Old Guard Museum, Fort Myer, Virginia; Pennsylvania National Guard Military Museum; The Queen's Dragoon Guards Regimental Museum, Cardiff Castle, Cardiff, Wales; Royal Military School of Music, Twickenham, England; Smithsonian Institution, Washington, D.C.; Tøjhusmuseets, Copenhagen, Denmark; University of Kansas Libraries, Lawrence, Kansas; U.S. Army Military History Institute, Carlisle, Pennsylvania; U.S. Army Quartermaster Museum, Fort Lee, Virginia; U.S. Cavalry Association, Fort Riley, Kansas; U.S. Cavalry Museum, Fort Riley, Kansas; U.S. Army Field Artillery Museum; and West Point Museum, West Point, New York. The third group, and by no means least, consists of Faith Bonitz, JoAnn Toussaint and Lindsey Loree of the interlibrary loan staff at the University of St. Thomas. Their aid over the years has been immeasurable.

SOUND THE TRUMPET

BEAT THE DRUMS

FIGURE 1.1. Image depicting hajj, the Islamic pilgrimage to Mecca, appearing in *Maqamat al-Hariri,* by Abu Muhammad al Qasim ibn Ali al-Hariri (1054–1122), illustrated by Yahya ibn Mahmud al-Wasiti and published in 1237. *Courtesy of the Bibliothèque Nationale de France, ms. Arabe 5847, fol. 94.*

CHAPTER I

Middle Eastern and European Traditions and the Birth of the Mounted Band

Stemming from the practice of giving direction to one's troops—and taunting those of the enemy—music has been an integral part of warfare for millennia. Horses and other animals have played prominent roles in battle for the past three to four thousand years as well,[1] and coupling them with military music has resulted in a tradition of horse-mounted military musicians, initially as signalers and motivators (and enemy frighteners) and later as members of bands. This practice was common with several cultures including the ancient Celts, who used seventy-centimeter-long metal cones with cavalry troops in Germany, and with the Romans, who inspired their cavalry troops with several different styles of horns.[2] However, a more direct connection with later mounted bands was the practice of mounting kettledrummers and trumpeters on elephants during the Sassanian period in Iran (224–651 A.D.).[3] This practice spread to donkeys, camels, and horses, and became central to mounted bands during war and peacetime—a tradition that crossed Europe and finally spread to the Americas. It was this Middle Eastern tradition that European crusaders found upon their arrival to the Holy Land—a varied culture

1. Phil Livingston and Ed Roberts, *War Horse: Mounting the Cavalry with America's Finest Horses* (Albany, Tex.: Bright Sky Press, 2003), 20; Louis A. DiMarco, *War Horse: A History of the Military Horse and Rider* (Yardley, Pa.: Westholme Publishing, 2008), 1.

2. Renato Meucci, "Roman Military Instruments and the Lituus," *Galpin Society Journal* 42 (August 1989): 90.

3. David Nicolle, *Medieval Warfare Source Book: Christian Europe and Its Neighbors* (London: Brockhampton Press, 1998), 265.

of military musical instruments—trumpets (*anafir/al* or *nafir/añafil*), horns (*buqat/buq*), shawms (*zumur*), kettledrums (*kusat, nakers*), drums (*tubul*), and cymbals (*kasat*)—all of which were used on horseback (see figure 1.1).[4]

Through these encounters, the returning crusaders introduced kettledrums into Europe, which came to be used at court and in the military—including on horseback. Initially called "nakers" from the Arabian *naqqara* and varying from four to twelve inches in diameter,[5] kettledrums became larger throughout the fifteenth century and, rather than simply giving two different dull or clear sounds, were moving to the idea of "high" and "low"—as music theoretical tonal concepts of tonic-dominant harmony (first and fifth pitches of a scale) were making headway in Western music.[6] The probable advent of these larger instruments in Western Europe was 1457 when a pair of "tabourins like great kettles" were described by the archbishop of Cologne as a novelty seen in an embassy from Ladislaus of Hungary to France to seek the hand of Madeleine, daughter of King Charles VII.[7]

Along with mounted kettledrums, records indicate that trumpets and other wind instruments were also part of the European court picture. One such source is a Bologna statute of 1405 that concerns the hiring of trumpeters for ceremonies celebrating students completing doctoral degrees. The document states that, along with trumpeters needing to be ready for the ceremonies, they were to be paid more if on horseback.[8] A problem of holding these long trumpets at court, on the march and on horseback, was alleviated shortly before 1400 when instrument makers began taking advantage of the various melting points of different metals and learned to bend tubing effectively—resulting in S- or folded-shaped instruments—reducing instruments' lengths by about two thirds

---

4. The terms *buqat* and *buq* are probably derived from the Latin word *bucina*, a Roman trumpetlike instrument. Edward Tarr, *The Trumpet* (London: Batsford, 1988), 36–37. Various forms of the word "naker" appear throughout Arabic and European texts. Titcomb indicates that "the Saracen origin of the new kettledrum is borne out in the names given it by the Europeans. Difficulties of transliteration, the lack of systematized orthography in the Middle Ages, and the carelessness of copyists resulted in a plethora of forms, but they all clearly betray a common root." Caldwell Titcomb, "The Kettledrums in Western Europe: Their History Outside the Orchestra" (PhD diss., Harvard University, 1952), 8. Bruce P. Gleason, "Cavalry Trumpet and Kettledrum Practice from the Time of the Celts and Romans to the Renaissance," *Galpin Society Journal* 61 (2008): 233.

5. Jeremy Montagu, *Timpani and Percussion* (New Haven, Conn.: Yale University Press, 2002), 26.

6. Ibid., 27.

7. Henry George Farmer, "Turkish Influence in Military Music," in *Handel's Kettledrums and Other Papers on Military Music* (London: Hinrichsen, 1950), 42; Montagu, *Timpani and Percussion*, 43. Wathier indicates that Ladislaus's successor, Mathias Corvinus (r. 1458–90) introduced a kettledrummer into each band of five trumpets of his army: R. Wathier, *Les Timbaliers de la Grande Armée* (Paris: Editions de la Sabretache, 1951), 3.

8. Nan Cooke Carpenter, *Music in the Medieval and Renaissance Universities* (Norman: University of Oklahoma Press, 1958), 35–37.

FIGURE 1.2. *Der Zug der Drei Könige—ein Festzug mit Trompeten und Fanfaren (Procession of the Three Kings—A Parade with Trumpets and Drums)* from the Chapel of Saint Agatha (Kapelle Sontga Gada) in the village of Disentis, Graubünden, Switzerland, ca. 1450, by brothers Cristoforo and Nicolao da Seregno. Historian Dieter Matti sees this procession as an allusion to similar festival processions by Italian rulers of the period. Dieter Matti, *Alte Bilder—neu gedeutet, Kirchliche Kunst im Passland*, vol. 3 (Chur, Switzerland: Casanova Druck und Verlag AG, 2010), 51–54. *Photograph of original painting taken by the author.*

(see figure 1.2).[9] These advancements, compounded by the facts that battles were becoming larger and more complicated; the human voice was no longer discernible in battle; and the advent of gunpowder was further increasing the decibel levels of warfare, the trumpet found a permanent place in Western armies.[10]

---

9. Tarr, *Trumpet*, 53; Don L. Smithers, *The Music and History of the Baroque Trumpet before 1721* (Carbondale: Southern Illinois University Press), 35–36.

10. In his *The Dawn of Modern Warfare*, vol. 4 of *History of the Art of War*, trans. Walter J. Renfroe, Jr. (Lincoln: University of Nebraska Press, 1990), Hans Delbrück suggests that "the first historically confirmed use of firearms in warfare in Europe took place in 1331 at the time of Louis the Bavarian, in the Italo-German border area in Friuli, when the two knights de Cruspergo and de Spilimbergo attacked the town of Cividale" (25). See also Leonard Digges and Thomas Digges, *An Arithmetical Warlike Treatise . . .* (London: Richard Field, 1590), 86.

While trumpeters served both with cavalry and infantry units, gradually the latter began replacing them with side drummers, fifers, and in some instances, bagpipers—with trumpeters and kettledrummers remaining with the cavalry, taking their cue from court trumpeters, who served on horseback.[11]

As warfare methods progressed, quick-moving cavalry units began appearing with the demise of armored knights. These advancements coupled with the sixteenth- and seventeenth-century idea of retaining standing armies of ordered units of officers and rank soldiers between wars resulted in structural advancements, including the coding of signals and training of musicians—which heretofore had apparently been agreed upon for each battle.[12] Writing in 1639, Gervase Markham lists the main cavalry signals of the time, "which we generally call Poynts of Warre," as "Butte Sella, or Clap on your Saddles";[13] "Mounte Cavallo, or Mount on Horsebacke"; "Al'a Standardo, or Goe to your Colours"; "Tucquet, or March"; "Carga, Carga, or an Alarme, Charge, Charge"; "Auquet, or the Watch," as well as several "other Soundings . . . as, Tende Hoe, for listening, a Call for Summons, a Senet for State, and the like."[14] While early calls are lost in history, those of later years, which varied by country, era, and military unit, appear in Georges Kastner's *Général de Musique Militaire*.[15]

Governing the use of these signals, and of trumpet and kettledrum practice in general on and off the battlefield in the lands of the Holy Roman Empire—which in turn influenced use in other countries for several centuries—was the robust trumpeters' and kettledrummers' guild.[16] The subsequent status of these instruments ensured that their playing by anyone other than members of the guild—who were obliged by oath not to reveal the secrets of their techniques—was forbidden.

---

11. Farmer, *The Rise and Development of Military Music* (London: W. Reeves, 1912), 17; Farmer, "Turkish Influence," 43.

12. Edward H. Tarr, "Further Mandate against the Unauthorized Playing of Trumpets (Dresden: 1736): Introduction and Translation," *Historic Brass Society Journal* 13 (2001): 67.

13. Many of the names of signals are corruptions, or similar-sounding replacements, of the Italian versions, such as the English signal, "Boots and Saddles," meaning to put on the saddles, which is derived from the Italian, "Butte Sella." Lilla Fox, *Instruments of Processional Music* (London: Lutterworth Press, 1967), 65.

14. Gervase Markham, "The Souldier's Accidence," in *The Souldiers Exercise, in Three Bookes*, The English Experience, No. 677 (Amsterdam: Theatrum Orbis Terrarum, 1974; facsimile of Gervase Markham, "The Souldier's Accidence," in *The Souldiers Exercise: In Three Bookes* [London: Printed by John Norton, for John Bellamy, Hugh Perry, and Henry Overton, 1639]), 60–61. Francis Markham gives a similar list of signals in his *Five Decades of Epistles of Warre* (London: Augustine Matthewes, 1622), 83, all of which he says "are most necessary for euery Souldier both to know and obey."

15. Georges Kastner, *Manuel Général de Musique Militaire* (Paris: Typ. F. Didot frères, 1848), appending pages, 1–55.

16. John Wallace and Alexander McGrattan, *The Trumpet* (New Haven, Conn.: Yale University Press, 2011), 101; Johann Heinrich Zedler, *Grosses vollständiges Universal-Lexicon* (Halle, Ger., 1732–54), xii, "Trompeter," col. 1118, cited in Smithers, *Music and History of the Baroque Trumpet*, 112.

On the march, trumpeters rode at the head of the troops, and, in addition to sounding the many calls in camp and on the battlefield, they performed the confidential tasks of carrying messages and secret letters and conducting parleys and negotiations with the enemy. In these duties, the kettledrummers, where available, would supplement the trumpeters or sometimes substitute for them. Because of these crucial responsibilities, as well as the stringent guild considerations and rigorous apprenticeship-training period of field trumpeters and kettledrummers, when captured and imprisoned by the enemy, they were exchanged only for other officers (noncommissioned officers by the nineteenth century)—or other equal-standing personnel depending on the era.[17]

Kettledrummers and trumpeters were a "protected species"—typically remaining near the commander in camp and riding in front of him during parades and to the rear of the action in wartime—safely conveying various orders through signals.[18] As tradition dictated the honor of these musicians being noncombatants, writing in 1622 in his *Five Decades of Epistles of Warre*, Francis Markham indicates that a drummer was to be regarded as "rather a man of Peace than of the sword, and it is most dishonourable in any man wittingly and out of his knowledge to strike him or wound him."[19] Similarly for trumpets, Gervase Markham, in his "The Souldier's Accidence," asserts, "The Trumpeter is not bound to any Armes at all, more than his Sword, which in former times was not allowed, but with the point broken," showing that trumpeters were noncombatants and were to be revered in battle.[20]

Because of this status, the employment of kettledrums signified a certain stature and rank within military units and were reserved for cavalry units and initially then only within a king's troops. Cavalry units at this point did not include dragoon units, which, although they traveled by horseback, fought on foot and were not comprised of gentlemen—and were thus relegated to side drums and hautbois (double-reed instrument that was a predecessor of the oboe but more related to the ancient shawm). Lesser units were allowed to have kettledrums when the drums were captured in battle—a custom borrowed from the Saracens—as indicated

---

17. Titcomb, "Kettledrums in Western Europe," 268, citing Leonhard Fronsperger, *Baron of Mindelheim, Von kayserlichem Kriegsrechten Malefitz und Schuldhändlen* (Frankfurt-am-Main, 1564–65), fol. 130a; Peter Panoff, *Militärmusik in Geschichte und Gegenwart* (Berlin: Karl Siegismund Verlag, 1938), 35.

18. David Whitwell, *The Baroque Wind Band and Wind Ensemble*, The History and Literature of the Wind Band and Wind Ensemble, vol. 3 (Northridge, Calif.: Winds, 1983), 128; Wilhelm Stephan, "German Military Music: An Outline of its Development," *Journal of Band Research* 9, no. 2 (Spring 1973): 12; Kastner, *Manuel Général de Musique Militaire*, 107–108.

19. Markham, *Five Decades of Epistles*, 59.

20. Markham, "Souldier's Accidence," 44–45.

by Altenburg when writing of the Prussian cavalry in 1795: "Kettledrums are looked upon as a great decoration for [any] regiment. If they have been lost in an encounter, the regiment is not allowed to carry any again, according to the rules of war, until it has acquired another pair by conquest from the enemy."[21] Accordingly, they were prized trophies of war up through the nineteenth century. Thus, while official policy and gentlemen's agreements protected kettledrummers on the battlefield, Manesson Mallet felt it necessary to include in his *Les Travaux de Mars* of 1691 an exhortation for kettledrummers to be courageous soldiers as well as good musicians: "The kettledrum player should be a man of courage, preferring to perish in the fight, than allow himself and his drums to be captured."[22]

---

21. Farmer, "Turkish Influence," 41; Titcomb, "Kettledrums in Western Europe," 301; Johann Ernst Altenburg, *Versuch einer Anleitung zur heroisch-musikalischen Trompeter- und Pauker-Kunst (Essay on an Introduction to the Heroic and Musical Trumpeters' and Kettledrummers' Art)*, trans. Edward Tarr (1795; repr., Nashville: Brass Press, 1974), 122; James Turner, *Pallas Armata: Military Essays of the Ancient Grecian, Roman, and Modern Art of War. Written in the Years 1670 and 1671* (London: Printed by M. W. for Richard Chiswell, 1683), 236.

22. Farmer, *Rise and Development*, 43, citing Manesson Mallet, *Les Travaux de Mars ou l'Art de la guerre* (Paris, 1691), n.p.

FIGURE 1.3. Kettledrummers and trumpeters, shown leading Count Ladislas Ignace de Bercheny's French hussar regiment, ca. 1752–63. Late nineteenth- or early twentieth-century painting, after the original anonymous painting in the Cottereau collection. Oil on canvas, 66 × 152 cm. 5857; Ec116. © Musée de l'Armée / Dist. RMN-Grand Palais / Art Resource, New York.

The threat of losing kettledrums warranted serious precautions so that it became customary for four cavaliers to precede the kettledrummer at port arms when traveling through enemy territory and into battle. Frederick the Great pushed this idea even further and instructed all mounted units to store their kettledrums in strongholds until the particular war was over.[23] They were also safely guarded when the troops were in garrison.[24]

Along with playing in battle and in camp, trumpeters of a cavalry squadron would have ridden together at the front of the unit between, to, and from battles, giving signals together in unison (see figure 1.3).[25] Sometimes accompanied by a pair of kettledrums, they would have also enlivened the march with a few memorized tunes—signals, fanfares, marches, and flourishes—birthing

23. Panoff, Militärmusik, 123–24.

24. Titcomb, "Kettledrums in Western Europe," 307.

25. J. A. Kappey, Military Music: A History of Wind-Instrumental Bands (London: Boosey, 1894), 79; Emir Bukhari, Napoleon's Line Chasseurs (London: Osprey, 1977), 28–29; Emir Bukhari, Napoleon's Dragoons and Lancers (London: Osprey, 1976), 10.

the idea of a trumpeter corps numbering between twelve and fourteen men under the direction of a trumpet major.[26]

Trumpeter corps music would have gradually involved harmony—especially during the second half of the eighteenth century, when trumpets in other pitches were added to the E♭ or D trumpets.[27] While the trumpet parts for signals and marches were set, kettledrummers were expected to supply a rhythmic bass part and to fill this in with improvisations. Moreover, since they were symbolic of nobility and wealth, they were thus expected to show extravagance in their playing.[28] This display was described by Altenburg as "artful figures, turns, and movements of their bodies" by Manesson Mallet, who stated that a kettle-drummer "should have a pleasing motion of the arm, an accurate ear, and take a delight in diverting his master by agreeable airs,"[29] and by Johann Heinrich Zedler, writing in 1735 (a little less respectfully), "which elsewhere would seem ridiculous."[30] Like that of trumpeters, kettledrum playing technique was therefore passed down from generation to generation with students learning by rote from masters, all of whom played by memory throughout their careers.

Toward the close of the eighteenth century, cavalry regiments began expand-ing music for mounted purposes by extending trumpeter corps. According to Farmer, the initial addition to British cavalry bands (and presumably to those of other countries) was the horn,[31] which had been used mounted for the hunt for centuries, and was already in use in some dragoon units and had been found

26. Gleason, "Cavalry and Court Trumpeters and Kettledrummers from the Renaissance to the Nine-teenth Century," *Galpin Society Journal* 62 (2009): 47; Farmer, *Rise and Development*, 40; Kappey, *Military Music*, 79; Caldwell Titcomb, "Baroque Court and Military Trumpets and Kettledrums: Technique and Music," *Galpin Society Journal* 9 (June 1956): 69; Johannes Reschke, "Studie zur Geschichte der brandenburgisch-preussischen Herremusik" (PhD diss., Friedrich-Wilhelms Universität, Berlin, 1936), 38.

27. Kappey, *Military Music*, 79. A discourse on the keys and pitch of cavalry and court trumpets, which varied through the years and by country, is outside the parameters of the present study. Qualified authors, including Anthony Baines, delve deeper into this topic. Anthony Baines, *Brass Instruments: Their History and Development* (New York: Dover, 1993), 120, 124, 129.

28. Titcomb, "Baroque Court," 61.

29. Farmer, *Rise and Development*, 43, citing Mallet, *Les Travaux de Mars*, 98: "*Il doit avoir un beau mouvement de bras et l'oreille juste, et se faire un plaisir de divertir son Maître par des airs agréables dans les actions de réjouissances.*"

30. Altenburg, *Versuch einer Anleitung zur heroisch-musikalischen Trompeter-und Pauker-Kunst*, 124; Zedler, *Grosses vollständiges*, xii, col. 1092–93, quoted in Titcomb, "Baroque Court," 60, and Curt Sachs, *The History of Musical Instruments* (New York: Norton, 1940), 330.

31. Farmer, *Rise and Development*, 85–86. Farmer suggests that mounted dragoon bands already were available for both mounted and dismounted duties and traditionally employed bands of hautbois. To these were added bassoons and "French" horns (54). As Farmer, like any historian, was a part and product of his times, he used the term "French horn," when referring to the orchestral horn, although there was really nothing French about it. Current word usage among musicians often deletes the "French" in the name. Historians in the future may question our dropping the term, and in fact this entire footnote.

useful in sounding more elaborate signals like the "retreat." Farmer indicates that "combined with the trumpet, some 'showy' flourishes could be obtained, and the authorities were not slow to observe the excellent results."[32]

An addition of a bass of some kind was another early acquisition, initially found in the trombone, the natural complement to the trumpet. Several Russian cavalry bands, including those of the 2nd Ukrainian Cossack Regiment and the Siberian Uhlan Regiment, were comprised exclusively of silver trumpets and trombones (apparently with varying instrumentation), made by an anonymous German instrument maker between 1812 and 1816 living in St. Petersburg. Edward Tarr indicates that these instruments were gifts from Tsar Alexander I to the regiments who had displayed particular bravery in repelling Napoleon.[33] A German newspaper account of a Russian cuirassier trumpeter corps in 1813 during the Russian occupation of Paris confirms the existence and ambience of these cavalry trumpet-trombone bands and recounts,

The heavy cuirassier regiment with large horses had . . . its own music corps, [which was] not only beautiful and most effective, but also completely appropriate to and most characteristic of such a choir of soldiers. It consisted only of six trumpets and six trombones. The musical pieces were also completely as they should have been for their warlike destination in general and their character in particular, also as far as the nature and the most powerful effect of these very instruments were concerned. The tempo was moderate.[34]

Ludwig Degele, writing in 1937, lists ten trumpets (four in G, four in F, and two in low C), with three trombones for German cavalry bands in 1805.[35] In France as well, cavalry bands began encompassing broader instrumentation after a brief suppression by Napoleon (in 1802 because they were

---

32. Farmer, Rise and Development, 85–86.

33. Edward H. Tarr, East Meets West: The Russian Trumpet Tradition from the Time of Peter the Great to the October Revolution, Bucina: Historical Brass Society Press, no. 4 (Hillsdale, N.Y.: Pendragon Press, 2003), 33.

34. Ibid., 34, citing Allgemeine Musikalische Zeitung, 15, no. 44 (3 November 1813): 713–18: "Das schwere Kürassierregiment mit grossen Pferden, hatte . . . eine ganz eigene, nicht nur an sich schöne und äusserst effectvolle, sondern auch vollkommen zweckmässige, und, eben für solch ein Kriegerchor, ganz charakteristische Musik. Sie bestand blos aus sechs Trompeten und sechs Posaunen. Die musikstücke waren ebenfalls ganz, was und wie sie seyn mussten für ihre allgemeine kriegerische und für ihre besondere Bestimmung, und auch für die Natur und den mächtigsten Effect eben dieser Instrumente. Das Tempo war gemässigt."

35. Ludwig Degele, Die Militärmusik, ihr Werden und Wesen, ihre kulturelle und nationale Bedeutung (Wolfenbüttel: Verlag für musikalische Kultur und Wissenschaft, 1937), 143; David Whitwell, The Nineteenth Century Wind Band and Wind Ensemble in Western Europe, The History and Literature of the Wind Band and Wind Ensemble, vol. 5 (Northridge, Calif.: Winds, 1984), 17.

FIGURE 1.4. *1724. Louis XV. Dragons: Tambour et Hautbois*, lithograph no. 151 (ca. 1854) by Gustave David (1824–91), after Alfred de Marbot (1812–65), *Régiment de Bauffremont* [drummer], *Régiment d'Orléans* [hautboist]. *Author's Collection.*

monopolizing horses and equipment). Kastner states that they were soon rein-stated and were instrumented with sixteen trumpets, six horns, and three trombones.[36]

Further developments in instrumentation came to the cavalry through infan-try bands, which by this point were based on *Harmoniemusik*—a combination of pairs of hautbois, clarinets, horns, and bassoons, to which were initially added the regimental drums, which had been typically reserved for marching and signaling. Further percussion instruments had been added to bands with the addition of "Turkish" music of bass drum, cymbals, tambourine, and triangle, a practice that spread through Europe after the power of the Ottoman Empire began to diminish at the beginning of the eighteenth century, and which, along with military music, influenced classical and folk genres.[37] Moreover, Mameluke mounted bands captured by General Jean Baptiste Kléber during the Siege of Acre in 1799 served as a model for Western mounted bands, and in addition to trumpets, as they had continued with their Middle Eastern background, included timpani, chapeaux chinois, and cymbals.[38]

While more common in infantry bands, by the 1770s, woodwinds and added percussion were also being adopted by those in British cavalry regi-ments—with trumpeters often doing double duty on these instruments for dismounted duties.[39] This instrumentation was generally not part of mounted performances—except for dragoon units, which had traditionally utilized hautbois and side drums (see figure 1.4) and gradually horns and bassoons.[40]

---

36. Kastner, *Manuel Général de Musique Militaire*, 169. Farmer, *Rise and Development*, 80–81.

37. Raoul Camus, *Military Music of the American Revolution* (Chapel Hill: University of North Carolina Press, 1976), 24–25.

38. Mamelukes were members of an Arabic military class, originally composed of slaves. The chapeau chinois was a musical instrument of central Asian origin consisting of an upright wooden pole ornamented with a canopy, a crescent, and other shapes from which bells and metal jingling objects were hung—often with horsetail plumes suspended from one of the crescents—"Jingling Johnny" or "Turkish Crescent" in English; "*Schellenbaum*" in German. Emir Bukhari, *Napoleon's Guard Cavalry* (London: Osprey, 1978), 29. Bukhari shows an elaborate illustration of a parade headed by a "kettledrummer, followed by the *brigadier-trompette* with four trumpeters and six musicians in tail, including two cymbalists, two *chapeau-chinois* players ('Jingling Johnnies') and two timpani drummers."

39. Gordon Turner and Alwyn Turner, *Cavalry and Corps*, vol. 1 of *The History of British Military Bands* (Staplehurst, UK: Spellmount, 1994), 101. Harmoniemusik ensembles probably stemmed from Janissary bands of Turkish origin, comprised of zarnas (shawms), large shawms, kettledrums, bass drum, cymbals, triangles, and the crescent, with Western instruments gradually supplanting Eastern ones. One of the first connections between East and West with Janissary bands was through the gift of an entire band from the Turkish sultan Ahmed III to August II, King of Poland and Elector of Saxony (d. 1733); Kappey, *Military Music*, 82; Robert Hinde, *The Discipline of the Light Horse* (London: Printed for W. Owen, 1778), 206–207.

40. Farmer, *Rise and Development*, 54.

As dragoon regiments became regarded as full-fledged cavalry,[41] in some units trumpets and kettledrums replaced hautbois and side drums, and, consequently, the "bands of music" of hautbois, horns, and bassoons were superseded by trumpeter bands—mounted and dismounted—like other cavalry units.

French cavalry bands seem to have utilized woodwinds on a more regular basis—hearkening back to Middle Eastern uses of shawms and other instruments of the Crusades. Instead of brass superseding hautbois, they were simply added to variations of harmoniemusik—but again this varied by the year and probably by the regiment. One image that depicts these cavalry woodwinds is *Musiciens de Dragons, 4ᵉ Régiment* (see figure 1.5), rendered in the early twentieth century by Charles Brun (1825–1908) after Christoph Bommer (b. 1790).[42] As Bommer was an eyewitness to Napoleon's army in Saxony during the armistice of 1813, the depiction, which also includes a bass horn, trombone (reversed bell to the rear), side drum (rather than kettledrums, thus continuing with the dragoon tradition), cymbals, and chapeau chinois, is likely accurate. Of his original, Bommer specifies that each dragoon regiment had, as in the infantry, a full band of around twenty men: "Among these 20 men, the brass and woodwind musicians rode at the front of their group, whereas the Janissarics [Turkish music (percussion)] rode at the rear of this group behind the music. All musicians, as well as the trumpeters, rode on white horses."[43]

Bommer's quote bears examination on two accounts. Separating the percussionists from the woodwind and brass musicians was not unusual at the time, as drummers had traditionally been regarded as utility signaling musicians who gradually undertook appended duty involving band work. As well, field trumpeters on parade within cavalry regiments typically rode behind (but separate from) the band. The second issue concerns the color of the horses. Descriptions differ throughout the nineteenth century of the color of cavalry band horses—even between records addressing the same horses. Gray was the traditional color for trumpeters' horses throughout Europe and the United Kingdom—a tradition that stems from the custom of mounting battlefield trumpeters on

---

41. Interestingly, as dragoon regiments struggled for centuries to be regarded with equal stature as other horse-mounted units, by the late nineteenth century, William Carter suggests that, by serving both mounted and dismounted, dragoons were setting an example rather than following one: "The cavalry of all great powers has, for all practical purposes, assumed the role of dragoons." William H. Carter, *The U.S. Cavalry Horse* (1895; repr., Guildford, Conn.: Lyon's Press, 2003), 159.

42. Alfred Umhey, *Napoleon's Last Grande Armée* (Berkeley, Calif.: Military History Press, 2005), plate 134, 288–89. Brun's original plate no. 48, rendered after Bonner II. 20 (4 and 1).

43. Ibid.

FIGURE 1.5. *Musiciens de Dragons. 4ᵉ Régiment*, by Charles Brun (early twentieth century), after Christoph Bommer (ca. 1813). *Courtesy of the Red Lancer, Inc.*

gray horses (in contrast to blacks and roans) for quick identification. As we shall see in following chapters, both Custer and Sheridan followed this custom with their mounted bands, and several present-day mounted bands, including the Band of the Household Cavalry in London and Windsor, continue the tradition of mounting trumpeters on "greys." While several records refer to European and U.S. mounted bands on white horses, most were probably technically gray, but to untrained observers appeared white. (The difference between gray and white horses has to do with the color of the horse's skin. Gray horses have black skin—white horses have pink skin.)[44]

44. David Kleinendorst, Roseville, Minn., president of the Minnesota Farriers Association, e-mail message to author, 27 February 2003.

Military bandsmen along with their orchestral counterparts were recipients of instrumental mechanical advancements during the early nineteenth century, with key systems (e.g., the Kent bugle or Kenthorn) and later with valves widening brass capabilities to play chromatically and diatonically rather than being limited to an instrument's overtone series. Likewise, woodwinds went through a series of developments, including the Boehm system, which, when adapted to several instrument families, resulted in mechanics whereby tone holes were located at optimal pitch points on the body of the instrument, rather than at locations conveniently covered by the player's fingers.

Of these inventions, the valve—developed through the independent efforts of Friedrich Blümel and Heinrich David Stölzel in the 1810s in Pless, Upper Silesia, and Berlin, Prussia—may have also been an initial catalyst that separated signaling trumpets from those in bands. Taken up by various Prussian cavalry and jäger[45] regiments, the invention finally reached the mainstream through the efforts of Wilhelm Wieprecht, who applied it around 1828 to a family of brass instruments, which included an E♭ soprano cornet (three valves), an E♭ trumpet (two valves), a B♭ tenor horn (three valves), and a B♭ euphonium (three valves). Seven years later, he designed the bombardon (an early bass brass instrument) also with three valves.[46] Commenting on these initial valves, the purpose of which was to divert the air stream through additional tubing, thereby lowering the fundamental tone and associated harmonics, Wieprecht explained that they "were then used in my chromatic brass instruments for army bands, especially cavalry bands."[47] While an in-depth account of the invention and development of brass instruments is outside the parameters of this study, it should be mentioned that conically bored valved instruments were being developed simultaneously by Wieprecht in Prussia and by Adolphe Sax (saxhorns) in Belgium and France. Valved instruments spread to the military bands of other countries as well.

Moreover, military trumpeters continued to use natural instruments on the battlefield, and bandsmen continued to play them in bands alongside valved and keyed brass instruments for several decades. Moreover, military trumpeters

45. The term "jägers" (hunters)—or "chasseurs" in French—referred to light infantry *(chasseurs à pied)* or light cavalry *(chasseurs à cheval)*—troops trained for rapid response.

46. Farmer, *Rise and Development*, 103. While I give basic information about the invention of the valve here, a thorough discussion is outside the parameters of the present study. An excellent chronicle of these events can be found in Christian Ahrens, *Valved Brass: The History of an Invention*, trans. Steven Plank, Bucina: Historical Brass Society Press, no. 7 (Hillsdale, N.Y.: Pendragon Press, 2008).

47. Cited in Baines, *Brass Instruments*, 211–12.

continued using valveless instruments up through the adoption of the bugle, and then up until the time of World War II in some armies, when militaries stopped using trumpeters and buglers for signaling altogether.[48] The valve was soon adapted to horns, some of which were right handed with the adjacent piston valves located near the bell, which worked well in mounted cavalry work—as the bell was away from the ear of the horse, and the left hand, unencumbered with the valves, was free to hold the reins.[49] Instrument manufacturers were quick to adapt the valve to trombones as well, the invention of which was welcomed in cavalry bands where players were relieved to be able to hold and operate an instrument with one hand, leaving the other hand for holding horses' reins. Anthony Baines suggests that the first of these instruments were made in Prague or Vienna in the later 1820s.[50]

It appears that by the 1820s, uniform instrumentation in any nation's army for cavalry bands was still decades away, with a regimental band's instrumentation corresponding to availability, to the tastes of the officers (especially the commander), and to current popularity. David Whitwell gives several instrumentation lists by year, country, and type of unit, as do Kastner and Degele.[51] The following is an example of an instrument lineup of Prussian cavalry bands of the 1820s, which shows a period when trumpeter corps instrumentation could include natural, keyed, and valved brass instruments:

> 2 first trumpets
> 1 second trumpet
> 2 first Principal-trumpets
> 2 second Principal-trumpets
> 2 Kenthorns
> 1 chromatic trumpet [valved]
> 1 trumpet in (high) E♭
> 1 trumpet in F
> 1 trumpet in G
> 4 trombones (alto, tenor, bass, bass)[52]

---

48. Tarr, *Trumpet*, 46.

49. Richard J. Martz, "Reversed Chirality in Horns, or is Left Right? The Horn, on the Other Hand," *Historic Brass Society Journal* 15 (2003): 198.

50. Baines, *Brass Instruments*, 248.

51. Whitwell, *Nineteenth Century Wind Band*, 29, 30, 42, 43, 61, 85, 88. Kastner, *Manuel Général de Musique Militaire*, 195–293 passim; Degele, *Militärmusik*, 143–46.

52. Whitwell, *Nineteenth Century Wind Band*, 29.

"Principal" here refers to the lowest-sounding trumpets, which were typically playing tonic-dominant functions. Because the trombone evolved from the slide trumpet, its presence here is not unusual.

Mounted bands developed across Europe and Britain in cavalry units as well as within some artillery units where numerous horses were employed for hauling the large guns. Some mounted bands within both services began including woodwinds along the lines of infantry bands, like that of Britain's Royal Horse Artillery Band, which Farmer indicates by 1876 hosted a full complement:

1 Piccolo	2 French Horns
1 Flute	2 Baritones
1 Oboe	2 Euphoniums
8 Clarionets	3 Trombones
1 Bassoon	3 Bombardons
7 Cornets	2 Kettledrums[53]

THE MUSIC

Throughout the Baroque and Classical eras, trumpeter corps marches were learned aurally, as per control of what Whitwell terms "the quasi-secret aristocratic trumpet guilds," and therefore were typically not written down.[54] As the guild lessened its grip and finally disappeared, marches were gradually scribed and given wider distribution. What must have been a unifying event among trumpeter corps took place in 1753, when Ferdinand Hase of the Saxon court in Dresden, the chief court field trumpeter at the time,[55] after amassing a collection of these *Trompetenmärsche* from various historic sources, sent this collection—*Heroischen Trompetenmärsche*—to all the cavalry regiments in the Holy Roman Empire.[56] Several decades later, the idea of a march collection was furthered when Friedrich Wilhelm III of Prussia ordered that a collection of marches be compiled so "troops will thus be in possession of good music [and

---

53. Henry George Farmer, "The Royal Artillery Mounted Band," in *Handel's Kettledrums*, 79.

54. Whitwell, *Nineteenth Century Wind Band*, 23.

55. The Saxon court held a place of prominence for trumpeters beginning in 1528 when the Holy Roman emperor appointed the elector of Saxony as hereditary master of the Guild of Court Trumpeters.

56. Joachim Toeche-Mittler, *Armeemärsche*, vol. 3, *Die Geschichte unserer Marschmusik* (Neckargemünd: Kurt Vowinckel Verlag, 1975), 19, 91–93. Ian Smart, "Music on Horseback," unpublished manuscript (2000), 4.

so] that in all parades and reviews, and especially when I am in attendance no other marches will be played."[57] The result of this order, comprised of officially sanctioned parade music beginning in 1817, was *Die Königlich Preussischen Armee-Märsche Sammlung*,[58] a set of three volumes from which regiments could choose their regimental march. Volumes one (slow infantry marches) and two (quick-step parade marches) initially were comprised primarily of marches borrowed from a similar Russian collection—albeit composed by German-Bohemian Anton Dörffeld, the director of music for the Russian Guard in St. Petersburg.

In 1817, without the aid of the valve, cavalry bands comprised of natural instruments would not have had much use for volumes one and two, and were still playing open-tone fanfares and simpler marches. However, by 1825, enough Prussian cavalry bands were utilizing valved instruments, so a third volume—again initiated by Friedrich Wilhelm III and compiled by Johann Heinrich Krause, a trumpet player who had served with the Garde-Jäger-Bataillon in Potsdam before becoming solo trumpet with the Berlin Opera—was added to the collection and contained music intended for mounted bands within cavalry regiments.[59]

Many of these cavalry marches were typically in compound time (6/8) to accompany a horse's gait, as opposed to the simple time (2/4 or 2/2) of infantry marches, and, with the adaptation of the valve, had become more complex than the traditional natural-trumpet marches. Over the years, these marches were arranged by different individuals for various instrument combinations,[60] typically for *Trompeterkorps*: six to eight trumpets of different pitches and positions, mainly E♭; one or two cornets in E♭ or B♭; two Kent horns; and tenor

57. Whitwell, *Nineteenth Century Wind Band*, 23, citing *Allerhöcheste Kabinetts-Order*, 10 February 1817. It is perhaps not surprising that while other countries had strong military music traditions, Prussia would be the one to regiment and prescribe a collection of marches, as military regimental society was a dominant culture of Prussia. As Anthony Dean of Eagle and Lyre Military Music CDs and Publications states, "No other country developed their march collection in such a rigorous way over so many years, and enforced it by Royal Decree, and then imposed such strict rules that only tunes from it could be adopted by regiments, and that only marches from the collection could be played at parades. It takes Prussian-German thoroughness to go to these lengths." Anthony Dean, e-mail message to author, 19 February 2009.

58. Th. A. Kalkbrenner, *Die Koniglich Preussischen Armee-Märsche* (Leipzig, Ger.: Breitkopf and Härtel, 1896); Joachim Toeche-Mittler, *Armeemärsche* (Neckargemünd: Kurt Vowinckel Verlag, 1966), 58–59.

59. It appears that, unlike the infantry volumes, volume three—mounted music—was never comprehensive or all-inclusive; thus, cavalry bands incorporated music from outside volume three into their repertoires as well.

60. Anthony Dean states, "The 'collection' was in reality just an official list of approved marches which the Prussian king called his *Königliches Preussischen Armee-Marsch Sammlung*. It was not a book of arrangements. Arrangements of items from the 'collection' were actually by different people at different times." Anthony Dean, personal communication, 12 March 2010.

and bass horns. Additions of original marches and selections from opera and ballet arranged as trots, walk marches, gallops, polkas, and slow marches by *Stabstrompeters*, bandmasters, directors of music, and civilian musicians were made to all of the volumes over the years, including the third volume. Many of these pieces were borrowed from the other volumes and arranged for mounted bands. Others, like No. 10, *Gallopmarsch* by Eduard Havn, combined natural trumpet fanfares with a brass ensemble, a combination that would characterize German cavalry music for the next century.[61]

With this collection, each Prussian cavalry regiment had its own official march (or marches)—a practice similar to that of British cavalry regiments, each of which had a slow march and a quick march as well as various trots and gallops.[62] Austrian, French, and Russian regiments had similar traditions.[63]

Early nineteenth-century cavalry music consisted of field musicians—attired and accoutered splendidly and in distinction from other troops as they had been for centuries—playing signals on the battlefield, as well as trumpeter corps performing fanfares, flourishes, marches, and other pieces. Through the demise of the trumpeters' and kettledrummers' guilds, the dissolution of courts, and the raising of dragoon units to that of full cavalry, the way was gradually paved for freer use of trumpets and kettledrums as well as instrumentation additions and instrument development, resulting in bands of brass in addition to trumpets, as well as those that included woodwinds. These developments in turn increased the variety of music that mounted cavalry bands were able to perform. Moreover, these advancements resulted in the establishment of signal and march collections, which further spread the idea of notated cavalry music, leading to the establishment of mounted bands throughout much of Europe—and across the Atlantic.

---

61. Kalkbrenner, *Koniglich Preussischen Armee-Märsche*; Toeche-Mittler, *Armeemärsche*, 70.

62. Turner and Turner, *Cavalry and Corps*, 21–29, 32–51, 55–76, 81–99, 103–12, 123, 141, 154–89 passim; Trevor Herbert and Helen Barlowe, *Music and the British Military in the Long Nineteenth Century* (New York: Oxford University Press, 2013), 220–22.

63. Eugen Brixel, Gunther Martin, and Gottfried Pils, *Das ist Österreiches Militärmusik* (Graz, Aus.: Kaleidoskop, 1982), 324, 352–69ff.

CHAPTER 2

American Revolutionary War and 1812 to Mexico

As indicated in the preceding chapter, horse-mounted military music developed over centuries across Europe and had its roots in Middle Eastern traditions. Some of this tradition crossed the Atlantic intact, but as horse-mounted warfare figured differently in New World conflicts due to geographic and social differences, cavalry music differed as well—especially during the late eighteenth century and the first quarter of the nineteenth.

Generating workable and useable cavalry regiments in colonial America was complicated. Cavalry was more a social than a military institution, with the few cavalry troops being volunteer organizations in which members furnished their own mounts and were exempt from service in the territorial militia companies. Writing for the *Cavalry Journal* in 1938, Frederic Bauer suggests that the issues were further compounded since many of those of the leisure class who had the time and means to cultivate advanced equitation skills were royalists. They also knew that the chances of cavalry, which were often little more than social clubs, being called out to serve against the French and Indians were negligible. Thus, as it had been for hundreds of years in Europe, cavalry, although in new environs, was still "a rich man's game."[1]

Bauer also makes the argument that while horses were common throughout various areas of the colonies—especially Virginia—there were other areas in the North where horses were not so prevalent, and where the common classes traveled on foot and used oxen for draft. And, when they did use horses, they were far different than those used by the upper classes, as the horse and

---

1. Frederic Bauer, "Notes on the Use of Cavalry in the American Revolution," *Cavalry Journal* 47 (March–April 1938): 138.

horsemanship required for a farmer and his wife to ride to market or to church at a walk or jog trot "on saddle and pillion" differed dramatically from that required in equestrian or cavalry work. Weaponry was another issue, and one that propelled infantry rather than cavalry to the fore, as infantrymen—particularly from the more sparsely settled regions—used the same familiar firelock in battle they had grown up with in hunting game, whereas cavalrymen had no need in civilian life to learn the use of the horse pistol, sword, lance, musketoon, or carbine.[2] Also, cavalry was an expensive branch of the service with perennial shortages—with mounts needing to be purchased and horse furniture and special weapons needing to be procured. Therefore, there was little to induce cavalry as a main component of colonial warfare.

While George Washington as a member of the Virginian gentry was an accomplished horseman, he, along with other colonial military leaders, initially felt that the use of cavalry during the Revolutionary War would be limited. Bauer concurs and suggests that since early British Americans had learned tactics from fighting American Indians, they had come to realize that troopers crashing through forests gave ample warnings of approaches and provided swell targets. Evidence suggests, however, that when independent militias, including Captain John Leary's Light Horse Troop of New York City, the Virginia Light Horse, the Connecticut Light Horse, the Philadelphia City Troop of Light Horse, and other units, offered their services over varied periods of time, Washington was happy to accommodate them—although he dismissed the initial four hundred to five hundred Connecticut Light Horse troopers who showed up because of their refusal to perform some of the more menial soldier tasks.[3]

An official approach to cavalry came on 14 March 1777 with Congress approving for the Continental Army the organization of four cavalry regiments (the formation of which Congress had authorized on 24 December 1776)—formally designated as light dragoons—with each regiment being allotted a colonel, lieutenant colonel, major, quartermaster, surgeon, surgeon's mate, paymaster, adjutant, saddler, trumpet major, four supernumeraries, and six troops, each consisting of a captain, lieutenant, cornet, quartermaster sergeant, orderly or drill sergeant, trumpeter, farrier, armorer, four corporals, and thirty-two

---

2. Ibid.

3. Gregory J. W. Urwin, *The United States Cavalry: An Illustrated History* (Poole, UK: Blandford Press, 1983), 9–12. A detailed chronicle of cavalry involvement and units during this period is outside the parameters of this study but makes for interesting reading. Along with Urwin, readers should consult Jim Piecuch, ed., *Cavalry of the American Revolution* (Yardley, Pa.: Westholme Publishing, 2012).

privates, for a total of 279 men to a regiment.[4] These four dragoon regiments however, were disbanded at the conclusion of the Revolutionary War in 1783 with the last of the troops being discharged in 1784. Because a large standing army was one of the instruments of tyranny that the Revolution was fought to shed, only a skeletal force was retained to guard military stores at West Point and Fort Pitt, with added soldiers from New York, New Jersey, Connecticut, and Pennsylvania to serve in a regiment to protect the western frontier.[5]

The music within these regiments seems to have consisted only of trumpeters.[6] Therefore, the first mounted military musicians in the United States were the same as those in the histories of other parts of the world—battlefield trumpeters (field musicians) who served in horse units. Like their European counterparts, these musicians played signals on the battlefield and within camp (see figure 2.1)—providing direction, stimulation, and ambience—through various "soundings" as Epaphras Hoyt writing in 1811 indicates, which included "reveille," "stable-call," "boots and saddles," "to horse," "draw swords," "return swords," "parade-march," "parade-call," "officers-call," "sergeants-call," "trumpeters-call," "orders," "dinner-call," "watering-call," "setting the watch," "march," "trot," "gallop," "charge," "halt," "retreat," "rally," "turn out skirmishers," "call in skirmishers," and "skirmishers cease firing."[7]

While signals were standardized for British forces by 1798 with the publication of *The Sounds for Duty and Exercise for the Trumpet and Bugle Horn*,[8] the United States was not at the same point. Raoul Camus points out that the United States had not yet developed standardized bugle calls by 1811 when Hoyt recommended that "these signals must be concealed from the enemy, and may frequently be changed by the commander, to prevent their gaining a knowledge of them."[9] Camus explains, "It would have been impossible to change the signals at will if

4. Bauer, "Notes on the Use of Cavalry," 138. Due to the expense and logistics involved, it is doubtful that any Continental cavalry regiments were ever at full strength.

5. Urwin, *United States Cavalry*, 30. Urwin indicates that, "thanks to the weak Articles of Confederation, under which the new nation was governed until 1789, Congress had little power to do more. Indeed, only Pennsylvania filled its quota of enlistments for the 1st American Regiment, and the unit never achieved full strength."

6. Camus, *Military Music*, 19, 20, 25–28, 56–81.

7. Epaphras Hoyt, *Practical Instructions for Military Officers . . . To Which is Annexed, a New Military Dictionary . . .* (Greenfield, Mass.: John Denio, 1811), 462.

8. Great Britain, Army, *The Sounds for Duty and Exercise for the Trumpet and Bugle Horn* (London: Broderip and Wilkinson, 1798); Raoul Camus, "The Military Band in the United States Army Prior to 1834" (PhD diss., New York University, 1969), 383.

9. Hoyt, *Practical Instructions*, 226.

they had been standardized through the army."[10] Following the British model, military signals were gradually standardized in American military units, with training often provided by "teachers of music."[11] Along with federal enterprises, this training was sometimes offered at the state level as suggested in the 1829 *Laws of the State of Delaware*, which refer to "teachers of music for the troops of cavalry, to be procured by their respective commanding officers, which expense shall also be paid out of the fines of the brigade to which such troop shall belong."[12]

The earliest American military music, however, was that of musicians on foot—rather than horseback—with drummers and fifers carrying out signaling duties. As in Europe, the hautbois soon took hold as evidenced in a *New England: The Boston News-Letter* article of 11 October 1714, which reported on the New York celebrations of the coronation of King George I, the first Hanoverian to the British throne, after the death of Queen Anne, the last of the reigning Stuarts: "New York, October 11. . . . The Regular Forces Marching after his Excellency, and the Corporation, with Hoboys [hautbois] and Trumpets before them. The Militia making a double Guard for Him from the Fort to the City Hall, all the Guns of the Garrison made a Triple Discharge, the Regular Forces and Militia Twice Three Volleys, with Huzza's and great Acclamations of Joy."[13] A later military band in the colonies was the one attached to Benjamin Franklin's Regiment and Artillery Company of Philadelphia in 1756. This ensemble would have numbered between four and eight musicians, and was probably based on harmoniemusik[14]—the paired combination of instruments common throughout European infantry bands—which also became common throughout the colonies. Conversely, early mounted bands when they did appear were probably simply groupings of trumpeters gathered from troops within a regiment playing together in the European tradition of accompanying mounted troops riding to or from battle.[15] It appears that mounted kettledrums were not regularly part

10. Camus, "Military Band," 383.

11. U.S. War Department, *An Act, Establishing Rules and Articles for the Government of the Armies of the United States; with the Regulations of the War Department Respecting the Same. . . .* (Albany, N.Y.: Printed by Websters and Skinners, 1812), 50, 60.

12. Delaware General Assembly, *Laws of the State of Delaware; From the Second Day of January, One Thousand Eight Hundred and Twenty-Seven, to the Sixteenth Day of February, One Thousand Eight Hundred and Twenty-Nine*, vol. 7 (Dover: Published by Authority, 1829), 6.

13. *New England: The Boston News-Letter, Published by Authority*, no. 548 (Monday, October 11–Monday, October 18, 1714).

14. Camus, *Military Music*, 29, 43.

15. Gleason, "Cavalry and Court Trumpeters," 46.

FIGURE 2.1. *Trumpeter, First Troop Philadelphia Light Cavalry*, ca. 1812–15. Watercolor by Eugène Lelièpvre (mid-twentieth century). *Courtesy of Sylvie Lelièpvre Botton.*

of early American cavalry units—probably for several reasons including cost, which would have been considerable. Also, by the end of the eighteenth century when the colonies were coming into their own, the kettledrum tradition in Europe, although hundreds of years old, was changing due to the demise of the guild and because kettledrum use was concluding on the battlefield. As Titcomb states, "Despite the sporadic use of kettledrums throughout the nineteenth century, I think it is fair to say that what could in any way be called a widespread use ended around 1815 after Napoleon was out of the picture. This by no means implies that cavalry bands were rare after this date. . . . The point is that the instrumentation of these military bands did not often include kettledrums."[16] While this may have been the case, kettledrums were probably still coveted during this period in Europe, and were probably used when they could be acquired and afforded. However, while the tradition had not died out completely in Europe, there was no strong thrust for it to start in the Americas—as American forces were birthed out of necessity and task rather than of ancient tradition. However, their place within cavalry regiments was still known in the United States, as indicated by Hoyt in the "Kettle Drums" entry in his "A New Military Dictionary" section of *Practical Instructions for Military Officers*, which was published in 1811 in Massachusetts: "Kettle DRUMS are large basons [basins] of copper or brass, rounded at the bottom, and covered with vellum or goatskin, which is kept fast by a circle of iron and several holes, fastened to the body of the drum, and a like number of screws to stretch it at pleasure. They are used by the cavalry."[17] As a major general in the Massachusetts militia, Hoyt published various military and genealogical works and thus would have had a knowledgeable understanding of U.S. military practice. For British and/or European terms, Hoyt identifies them as such throughout the dictionary, and as he makes no disclaimers about the kettledrum, he perhaps knew—or *thought*—that they were known to be used in the United States.

Another consideration for the success of military music is that bands have typically had some kind of connection with the general populace, especially in the United Kingdom and on the Continent, where connections among a regiment and its band as well as with the local population and a monarch, were often close. As the backdrop for warfare within early America consisted of wilderness rather than the urban and sometimes overpopulated areas of European

16. Titcomb, "Kettledrums in Western Europe," 349.
17. Hoyt, *Practical Instructions*, 393.

battle zones, the audience for military music in the colonies was simply limited. With a restricted audience, funds, and tradition, a delay in a system of developed military music—especially horse-mounted music—is hardly a surprise, even though at the time of the War of 1812 mounted musicians were common throughout European areas involved in warfare.

The same could probably be said for the use of kettledrums by British forces serving in the Americas. It is doubtful that British forces incorporated mounted kettledrums during their visits to the colonies.[18] During the War of 1812, neither of the two British regular cavalry units—the 14th and the 19th Light Dragoons—serving in North America during the War of 1812 included mounted kettledrums. The 14th only had two (rather than five) squadrons and served dismounted in New Orleans. The 19th served south of Montreal with horses procured in Lower Canada until August 1816 when the regiment was sent back to England.[19] As a dragoon unit, it may have included a mounted side drummer and hautboists.

Other military music considerations when reviewing the War of 1812 revolve around the fact that the North American battle stage was merely another front of a much larger arena for the British. Engaged in warfare with France and its allies since 1793, with a small period of truce between 1801 and 1803, Britain's military resources were engaged in Spain, the central Mediterranean, and in the East Indies. Consequently, massive reinforcements were not available to be sent to Canada.[20] Thus, due to other concerns, using/developing/flaunting its rich cavalry music heritage was probably not a major British consideration.

Over the next several decades, numerous U.S. horse-mounted regiments were initiated but were all disbanded at the end of the War of 1812, when the two regiments of U.S. Light Dragoons were reduced to one in 1814 and finally disbanded altogether on 3 March 1815—once again leaving the country without a viable mounted military force.[21] As a tradition of cavalry had a difficult time

---

18. However, at least one infantry unit utilized at least a single kettledrum as evidenced by an extant one belonging to the British IXth Regiment of Foot (the Royal Norfolk Regiment), which surrendered to American forces after the Battle of Saratoga in 1777. Along with several pieces of artillery and colors, this drum, which was probably part of a band of musick, was one of the first trophies in the West Point collection, which eventually became the museum collection.

19. René Chartrand, *A Scarlet Coat: Uniforms, Flags and Equipment of the British in the War of 1812* (Ontario: Service Publications, 2011), 23.

20. Ibid., 10.

21. Urwin, *United States Cavalry*, 49; Francis B. Heitman, *Historical Register and Dictionary of the United States Army, from its Organization, September 29, 1789, to March 2, 1903* (Washington, D.C.: Government Printing Office, 1903), 1:79.

of being developed and maintained, cavalry music did as well. Thus, records of early U.S. mounted bands are sketchy with various reports simply indicating "mounted band" without giving the name of the unit, which could have been a federal, volunteer, militia, or private unit or enterprise. Indeed, the distinction between some of these was at times hazy.

One of the first mentions of an actual mounted band in the United States was in 1824 when Revolutionary War hero General Marquis de Lafayette returned to tour all twenty-four states. A. A. Parker indicates that the reception Lafayette received in Philadelphia was especially warm and was launched by a military review outside the city followed by a procession—5,500-people strong—which included infantry, artillery, civilian, and governmental participation in a procession more than three miles long and which was headed by a cavalcade of one hundred citizens, one hundred mounted field and staff officers, five hundred cavalry troops, and a "mounted band of music."[22]

Another early U.S. mounted band, this one identified, was that of the National Lancers of Boston, a volunteer militia troop. Originally organized as the governor's mounted ceremonial unit, not an unusual endeavor of the time, the National Lancers were equipped and uniformed similarly to the Polish Lancers of the Napoleonic army and included a mounted band for their first parade on 14 June 1837, when they rode through the streets of Boston.[23] While the instrumentation of neither the Lafayette and National Lancer accounts is given, both are referred to as "mounted bands" rather than mounted trumpets or bugles; thus, they were probably comprised of either valved brass instruments, keyed brass instruments, and/or woodwinds.

While mounted and foot bands would continue to appear through the nineteenth and twentieth centuries within U.S. volunteer and militia units, in the long run, it would be those within federal and National Guard units where the tradition would develop the most and last the longest. This could not happen though until a permanent standing army in general, and a mounted arm in particular, was initiated and maintained.

With American settlers flooding into the Mississippi River valley after the

22. A. A. Parker, *Recollections of General Lafayette on His Visit to the United States in 1824 and 1825; with the Most Remarkable Incidents of His Life, from His Birth to the Day of His Death* (Keene, N.H.: Sentinel Printing, 1879), 112. Lafayette was well known for his horsemanship, having received the nickname "Kayewla" from the Oneida tribe, which he had recruited to the American side during the Revolutionary War.

23. John Stuart Barrows, "The National Lancers," *New England Magazine, An Illustrated Monthly*, n.s., 34 (March 1906–August 1906): 403.

U.S. Senate ratified the Louisiana Purchase Treaty on 20 October 1803, thereby doubling the size of the country and paving the way for westward expansion, friction with the extant Indian population continued, culminating in the Winnebago outbreak of 1827 and the Black Hawk War of 1832. This situation, combined with the Mexican overthrow of Spain in 1821, inducing commerce and settlement westward through the blazing of the Santa Fe Trail to New Mexico— as well as the Indian Removal Act of 28 May 1830 as an effort toward moving Indian tribes living east of the Mississippi River on their ancestral homelands to west of the river—resulted in a call for the U.S. Army to raise a cavalry regiment that would remain with a standing army—and not just in times of war.

However, even with a clear necessity at hand, Congress hesitated. As Francis Paul Prucha states, "The old bugaboo of a standing army was not easily dispelled, and an aristocratic mounted arm seemed a special threat to American life."[24] Consequently, on 15 June 1832 Congress authorized a halfway measure—the formation of a six-hundred-man Battalion of Mounted Rangers, which, because of its men's one-year commitments as volunteers and the provision that each man furnish his own arms and horse, was classified as a special type of militia rather than as a unit of regular troops.[25]

While the new unit demonstrated that mounted troops were essential for western defense and expansion, the one-year arrangement of rangers and regulars working together proved inefficient, as the two groups had been trained differently and had singular attitudes about military discipline. Therefore, continued pressure to efficiently streamline western defense moved the House Committee on Military Affairs to introduce an Act for the More Perfect Defense of the Frontiers on 28 December 1832—essentially changing the corps of rangers, with the addition of more recruits and officers, into a regiment of dragoons.[26] The result was the United States Regiment of Dragoons, constituted on 2 March 1833 at Jefferson Barracks, Missouri. On 15 May 1836, the regiment was redesignated as the 1st Regiment of Dragoons with the formation of the U.S. 2nd Regiment of Dragoons following on 23 May 1836 to augment the

24. Francis Paul Prucha, *The Sword of the Republic: The United States Army on the Frontier, 1783–1846* (Lincoln: University of Nebraska Press, 1969), 240.

25. Ibid., 240–41; Otis E. Young, "The United States Mounted Ranger Battalion, 1832–1833," *Mississippi Valley Historical Review* 41, no. 3 (December 1954): 453–70; Heitman, *Historical Register and Dictionary*, 1:141.

26. U.S. Congress, House of Representatives, Report of House Committee on Military Affairs, 28 December 1832, *American State Papers: Military Affairs* 5:126; U.S. Congress, "Statues at Large, 1879–1875, Vol. 4, 18th–23rd, 1823–1835," *Library of Congress, American Memory*, https://memory.loc.gov/ammem/amlaw/lwsllink.html, 652; Prucha, *Sword of the Republic*, 245.

force being assembled to fight in the Second Seminole War in Florida, which had been ceded to the United States by Spain in 1821.[27]

Army regulations for 1832 provided for sergeants to act as masters of ten-member bands, and while this was a year prior to the formation of the first permanent federal dragoon unit, it is likely that the same provision was extended for dragoon bands. This was an initial regulation that provided for a position as a master of a band and also separated this position from the junior principal musician of field music units.[28] By 1839, the 2nd Dragoons hosted one of the earliest bands attached to a U.S. federal mounted unit, and, like many nineteenth-century military bands, this band was well respected by the surrounding community, which by this point was Baltimore, as indicated by a *Baltimore American* article of the time:

> The corps of U.S. Dragoons now quartered at Fort McHenry [Baltimore] is said to have attached to it a band of musicians which for number and masterly performance is not exceeded by any other in the country. The reputation which this band has attained has caused numerous parties of ladies and gentlemen to visit the post, and these have lately become so frequent that it is found impossible to gratify the wishes of all. We are happy to learn, however, that in order to prevent disappointment, Lieutenant Asheton has in the kindest manner offered to send the musicians to the city every Friday afternoon—when the weather permits—during their stay in their present quarters, for the purpose of affording the citizens generally an opportunity of hearing them.[29]

By this point, this 2nd Dragoon Band along with other federal bands would have typically been aligned with the 1834 *General Regulations for the Army*, which specified that "in regiments that have bands of music, ten privates are allowed to act as musicians, in addition to the Chief Musician authorized by

27. James A. Sawicki, *Cavalry Regiments of the U.S. Army* (Dumfries, Va.: Wyvern Publications, 1985), 151–54.

28. Randy Steffen, *The Revolution, the War of 1812, the Early Frontier, 1776–1850*, vol. 1 of *The Horse Soldier 1776–1943: The United States Cavalryman: His Uniforms, Arms, Accoutrements, and Equipment* (Norman: University of Oklahoma Press, 1977), 174; *A History of U.S. Army Bands, Subcourse Number MU0010*, edition D (Norfolk, Va.: U.S. Army Element, School of Music, October 2005), 18; "Organization of the Army under the acts of April 5 and June 15 and 28, 1832" in Heitman, *Historical Register and Dictionary*, 2:582.

29. *Baltimore American*, ca. 1839, cited in Theophilus F. Rodenbough, *From Everglade to Cañon with the Second Dragoons (Second United States Cavalry), An Authentic Account of Service in Florida, Mexico, Virginia, and the Indian Country, Including the Personal Recollections of Prominent Officers, with an Appendix Containing Orders, Reports and Correspondence, Military Records, Etc., etc., etc. 1836–1875* (New York: D. Van Nostrand, 1875), 41.

law."[30] Apparently, officials felt that bands were becoming too large, as this regulation was initiated to reduce the number of musicians allowed in bands, which were often numbering twenty or more.[31] With reduced numbers, both infantry and cavalry bands may have unofficially added field music (trumpets and drums) to their ensembles, at least periodically to overcome the limiting regulation.[32]

Military bands accompanied the U.S. Army as the nation grew westward, and records indicate that among these musical units were mounted bands accompanying forces as the country became involved in the Mexican-American War—the United States' and Mexico's embroilment over Texas's status as a U.S. state as well as the validity of the Rio Grande as an international border. Henry Libenau of Hackensack, New Jersey refers to one of these ensembles in a record dated 23 July 1847 and thanks "Capt. Jagels and his Troop of Hussars, together with his mounted band," for participating in the funeral ceremonies of his friend, Captain Jacob W. Zabriskie,[33] who had been killed on 23 February 1847 serving with the 1st Illinois Volunteer Infantry at the Battle of Buena Vista.[34] This band is likely to have been comprised of all brass instruments like that of many European cavalry bands. As federal regimental commanders had gained the authority to increase the number of privates serving in their bands from ten to twelve in 1841 with another increase in 1845 to sixteen,[35] Jagel's mounted band probably figured somewhere between these two numbers.[36]

---

30. Raoul Camus indicates that, prior to this regulation, several infantry and artillery bands numbered more musicians (some more than doubled) than the ten prescribed in this 1834 regulation, and he indicates that the regulations "were not meant to initiate bands in the army, but rather to limit their size"; Camus, "Military Band," 488. U.S. War Department, *General Regulations for the Army*, 19, article 10, paras. 24, 25, and 26 (Washington, D.C.: Printed by Francis P. Blair, 1834), 19.

31. Camus, "Military Band," 478, 488, 489.

32. Ibid., 489.

33. Heitman, *Historical Register and Dictionary*, 2:73.

34. *Honor to the Brave, An Account of the Funeral Obsequies of the Late Captain J. W. Zabriskie, of the 1st Illinois Regiment, Who Was Slain at the Battle of Buena Vista, on the 23d Day of February, 1847* (New Brunswick, N.J.: Published by the Committee, 1847), copy in possession of author. Samuel Chamberlain indicates that in this battle there were 272 killed, 388 wounded, and 6 missing, out of 4,691 engaged. Samuel E. Chamberlain, *My Confession* (New York: Harper and Brothers, 1956), 130. He states further that Zabriskie, "a Polish exhile [sic], and a gentlemen [sic] of remarkable literary and scientific attainments, lost his life, and the world a rare scholar, while Liberty lost a devoted worshiper, and Illinoise [sic] a valued citizen" (132).

35. U.S. War Department, *General Regulations for the Army of the United States* (Washington, D.C.: J. and G. S. Gideon, 1841), 13, article 15, para. 70; U.S. War Department, General Order 32, 8 July 1845, General Orders, Records of the Adjutant General, National Archives and Records Administration (hereafter NARA), RG 94, College Park, Md.

36. This 1845 regulation was a turning point for U.S. military music as band members now would be "mustered as privates in a separate squad under the serjeant [sic] or Chief Musician," rather than being mustered with other troops, a practice that eventually set the band apart as a separate unit from the other troops.

Mexico had its own cavalry music practices as well by this point. Describing the Mexican military procession on the morning of this same battle in which Captain Zabriskie was killed, eyewitness Samuel Chamberlain describes what he terms a "brilliant spectacle" and what must have been reminiscent of the splendor of an Old World Spanish army complete with a musical contingent: "Their Cavalry was magnificent—some six thousand cavaliers richly capari-soned in uniforms of blue faced with red, with waving plumes and glittering weapons. . . . They formed in one long line with their massed bands in front, and then a procession of ecclesiastical dignitaries with all the gorgeous parapher-nalia of the Catholic Church advanced along the lines, preceded by the bands playing a solemn anthem."[37] While Chamberlain does not indicate as such, as the bands were part of a six-thousand-man cavalry contingency, it would seem that they would have been mounted.

Another reference to a mounted band during the Mexican War is that of J. Jacob Oswandel of the 1st Regiment Pennsylvania Volunteers, who later found himself serving with the Volunteer Division of General Winfield Scott's army in the push for Mexico City. Remaining with the main garrison of Puebla, Mexico, for several months to gather supplies and reinforcements after the city's capitulation on 1 May, Oswandel wrote that when cheering for General David Twiggs and his 2nd Division of Regulars as they were leaving Puebla for Mexico City on the morning of Saturday, 7 August 1847, he envied their departure: "The mounted band on their splendid white horses, struck up the 'Star Spangled Banner,' and 'Yankee Doodle,' etc. Oh! didn't I wish I was with that crowd."[38] Oswandel indicates that the division was composed of "the whole cavalry brigade of dragoons and mounted riflemen," which along with various infantry and artillery units, included the 1st Dragoons, 2nd Dragoons, 3rd Rifle Dragoons, and Mounted Rifle Regiment. Of these units, Rodenbough indicates that it was the mounted band of the 2nd Dragoons that was part of the escort of General Scott's entry into Mexico City a month later following the Battles of Chapultepec and Molino del Rey and the Battle for Mexico City:

At eight o'clock [14 September 1847], General Scott and staff, in full dress, escorted by Major Sumner and command, entered the city of Mexico amidst the most intense enthusiasm on the part of his troops. As he arrived at the Plaza, the band of the

---

37. Chamberlain, *My Confession*, 118.

38. J. Jacob Oswandel, *Notes of the Mexican War, 1846–47–48* (Philadelphia, 1885), 45, 245. The publish-ers indicate Sunday, 7 August 1847 followed by Sunday, 8 August 1847. August 7 was a Saturday in 1847.

Second Dragoons (mounted) played with much spirit the appropriate air of "Hail Columbia," and while the escort was coming into line discoursed with much effect upon the susceptible soldiery the patriotic strains of "Yankee Doodle."[39]

The three pieces of music mentioned by Oswandel and Rodenbough are an interesting comment on the times. Because the Revolutionary War was recent enough to this occasion, *Yankee Doodle* was still popular with the general public as well as with military bands to be a natural part of the proceedings. While Francis Scott Key and John Stafford Smith's *Star-Spangled Banner* was certainly well known throughout the United States, it would be another eighty-four years before it achieved national-anthem status. Thus, playing it on the march alongside other patriotic and military fare, rather than reserving it for special occasions, was not unusual. *Hail Columbia*, on the other hand, written in 1789 by Philip Phile with lyrics by Joseph Hopkinson added in 1798, served as the unofficial U.S. national anthem for much of the nineteenth century, and thus Rodenbough's terminology of "appropriate air," is indeed appropriate. As this was the first time in history that the U.S. flag was flown over a foreign capital, the event and subsequent accompanying music were particularly momentous.

With the Treaty of Guadalupe Hidalgo, signed on 2 February 1848, acknowledging the surrender of Mexico and the conclusion of the Mexican-American War—coupled with the Oregon Treaty (signed on 15 June 1846), which established the border between the United States and British North America at the 49th parallel (with the exception of Vancouver Island)—nearly 1.2 million square miles were added to the United States, encompassing all or parts of the present states of Oregon, Washington, Idaho, Wyoming, Montana, California, New Mexico, Arizona, Nevada, Utah, and Colorado—doubling the size of the country again. With this new vision for western expansion, President James K. Polk voiced the sentiments of many by pronouncing that as volunteers had proven themselves in Mexico, so they would on the western frontier. This however, is not how things went, and along with Congress's creation of the Department of the Interior in 1849, there began a strengthened presence of the Regular Army—signifying a renewed attitude toward the benefits of using federal troops as, what Robert Wooster terms, "constabularies in blue."[40]

A series of American presidencies and their administrations continued to

---

39. Rodenbough, *From Everglade to Cañon*, 158.

40. Robert Wooster, *The American Military Frontiers: The United States Army in the West, 1783–1900* (Albuquerque: University of New Mexico Press, 2009), 122.

further a strong Regular Army. Zachary Taylor, who had become a national hero as a result of his victories as a major general in the Mexican-American War was elected to the U.S. presidency in 1849 and was successful in increasing the size of army companies stationed in frontier garrisons. Taylor's death in 1850 brought Millard Fillmore to office along with Secretary of War Charles M. Conrad, who supported army increases, including adding to the number of cavalrymen. Then, in 1852 with Franklin Pierce's election, Jefferson Davis, another Mexican-American War hero and West Point graduate, came to the war office and made further efforts to invigorate and reform the army, including the establishment of the 1st and 2nd Cavalry Regiments, which were constituted on 3 March 1855.

Through these years and initiatives, by building posts and roads and working through a combination of establishing and moving Indians to reservations, protecting Indians from one another as well as from white settlers, and of course fighting Indians directly, federal troops established a strong presence in the trans-Mississippi area.[41] As white settlers moved west over the Sante Fe and Oregon-California Trails, calamitous encounters occurred between them and the Indians who had lived there for centuries, as well as with tribes who had been newly relocated, totaling some 200,000—not to mention the 85,000 Hispanics, some of whom had been living in the Mexican Cession for several generations.[42]

In 1857, led by future Civil War leaders Edwin Vose Sumner, John Sedgewick, and J. E. B. Stuart, the 1st Cavalry was called in to settle matters initially with the Cheyennes—and brought its mounted band with it. As cavalry bands would do in the 1860s and '70s, William Chalfant explains that the band of the 1st Cavalry played a significant role in troop movements:

> On May 18, 1857, the Cheyenne Expedition began. Breaking camp at 9:00 A.M., the four companies of Major Sedgwick's command started their march, four men abreast. Company E, mounted on roan horses and with Captain Sturgis, the senior captain, at their head, led the way. They left the bluegrass pasture where they had been encamped and met the mounted band, then marched proudly through the garrison with carbines slung, sabers drawn, and guidons flying. The band, in the lead, played the traditional piece for such occasions, "The Girl I Left Behind Me."

---

41. Prucha, *Sword of the Republic*, 342. The complexities of the history of western U.S. expansion are considerable—especially in terms of the roles of settling pioneers, the U.S. military, and the various Indian tribes—and largely fall outside the parameters of the present study. See Prucha and Wooster for further information.

42. Wooster, *American Military Frontiers*, 119.

As they crossed the old drill ground southwest of the post, the band wheeled off to the north side of the road and struck up "Goodby, John." Colonel Sumner and his staff sat on their horses nearby, taking the salute of the passing companies.[43]

Leading an expedition of this nature seems to have been typical duty for cavalry bands, which were often documented to be playing this same *The Girl I Left Behind Me*, an Irish folksong adopted throughout the U.S. military.[44] While this song was old by this point—stemming from the early nineteenth or late eighteenth centuries—the ageless theme of warfare involving loved ones left behind continued to resonate with soldiers. While U.S. Army bands would not officially number sixteen personnel until four years later, the band of the 1st Cavalry may likely have been this size already by 1857.

In addition to these battle-connected performances, there are several 1850s accounts indicating mounted bands in various official and military capacities. In reference to Hungarian journalist and political leader Louis Kossuth's December 1851 visit to New York City from Hungary, an unidentified writer for an issue of *Kate Field's Washington*, simply referred to as "E. L. N.," recalls, "I was a mere child when Louis Kossuth visited this country in the winter of 1851–52, but I remember his triumphal reception in New York as well as if it were yesterday." The writer states further that it was an unidentified mounted band that had captured her/his attention rather than the presence of Kossuth, and within the band, it was the bass drummer who was the focal point and who had apparently taken on the aura of European mounted kettledrummers, who for centuries were expected to show extravagance in their playing:[45]

I stood at the window and watched the procession pass our house. I had been much interested in what had been told me about Kossuth, but what impressed itself most vividly upon my mind at the time was not the face and figure of the Magyar hero as he rose and doffed his hat in response to the plaudits of the crowd, but the antics of a member of the mounted band which accompanied the cavalry escort. This man

43. William Y. Chalfant, *Cheyennes and Horse Soldiers: The 1857 Expedition and the Battle of Solomon's Fork* (Norman: University of Oklahoma Press, 1989), 72.

44. *The Girl I Left behind Me* has many different versions of lyrics. One verse that was well known during the mid-nineteenth century in the United States was, "I'm lonesome since I crossed the hill, and o'er the moorland sedgy. / Such heavy thoughts my heart do fill, since parting with my Betsey. / I seek for one as fair and gay, but find none to remind me; / how sweet the hours I passed away, with the girl I left behind me."

45. Gleason, "Cavalry and Court Trumpeters," 41.

was the first bass-drummer I had ever seen on horseback. His drum was rested on the neck of the horse and the pommel of the saddle, and he pounded it with such vigor that the steed had to be led by grooms on foot to prevent its bolting and breaking up the display. The drummer was placed in the procession quite near Kossuth's carriage, and each crowd of spectators would begin its cheering for the city's guest about the time that the band came fully abreast of it. This demonstration the drummer evidently accepted as a tribute to himself, and between the vehemence of his blows, his nervous efforts to keep himself from being unseated by his restless horse, and his effort to indicate to the populace his appreciation of their greeting, the poor fellow was almost beside himself. I dare say it was the proudest day of his professional career, and that he never forgot the incident as long as he lived. I can say positively that one of the on-lookers never will forget it.[46]

The following year, the mounted band of the Boston National Lancers made the news again—this time in Danvers, Massachusetts, for "the One Hundredth Anniversary of the Separation of Danvers from Salem, and its existence as a distinct Municipal Corporation, [which] was celebrated by the citizens, in a spirited and patriotic manner, on Wednesday, the 16th day of June, 1852."[47] The account indicates that the procession for the event headed for Old South Church and included a cavalcade "of nearly 300 horsemen, led by the Mounted Band of the Boston Lancers, [which] terminated the grand programme of the pageant."[48] Perhaps it was this same band that led a "Cavalcade of Gentlemen" and is listed along with Gilmore's Brass Band, and two other groups referenced as "Band[s]" as participants several years later in the 1856 procession "at the reception of George Peabody, Esq., of London, at South Danvers, his native place, in old Danvers, Thursday, Oct. 9, 1856." The writer of the same account does us a favor several pages later and specifies the basic instrumentation and number of the band as well as the flavor of the ambience, indicating that "the Cavalcade was preceded by a mounted Band of eighteen brass instruments, and, as the cortege took its line of march, the scene was lively and animating."[49]

The midwestern section of the country boasted its mounted bands as well.

---

46. E. L. N. "Some Interesting Incidents," in "Louis Kossuth: The Hungarian Patriot in the United States," *Kate Field's Washington*, 9, no. 14 (Washington, D.C., 4 April 1894): 214–15.

47. *Celebration, at Danvers, Mass. June 16, 1852* (Boston: Dutton and Wentworth, 1852), 97.

48. Ibid., 111.

49. *Proceedings at the Reception and Dinner in Honor of George Peabody, Esq., of London, by the Citizens of the Old Town of Danvers, October 9, 1856* (Boston: Henry W. Dutton, 1856), 23, 27.

Another example of what was probably a militia mounted band appears in a record of the one hundredth birthday of Robert Burns (25 January 1859), which, as a nationwide holiday in Scotland, was celebrated in various places around the world including the United States, where there were at least sixty-one separate celebrations across the country including one in Chicago. There, a large parade marching down Lake Street was put into motion by "a salute of one hundred guns . . . being fired from the Lake shore, at the foot of Randolph Street." Of what must have been a sizeable contingency, which included six groupings of militia, fraternal, and civic organizations, were interspersed four bands: "Mounted Band," "Light Guard Band," "Garden City Band," and the "Great Western Band." Placed between the Chicago Artillery, which led the parade under the command of Captain Charles Barker, and the Chicago Dragoons, the mounted band may have been part of one of these organizations.[50]

Stemming from utilitarian music of the colonial period, cavalry music in the United States developed over the turn of the nineteenth century to full mounted bands emulating those in Britain and the European Continent by the middle of the century. As a main component of the popular music of their day, infantry and cavalry bands played current marches and other popular tunes, including patriotic airs. Mounted bands, as they had for centuries in Europe, could not help but attract attention—and mixing the visual with audial aspects made them favorites with the general public as well as with military personnel. However, this popularity was only a glimpse of what was coming as the country verged on the next all-consuming war.

---

50. James Ballantine, ed., *Chronicle of the Hundredth Birthday of Robert Burns* (Edinburgh: A. Fullarton, 1859), 564. Lake Street at this point was the main thoroughfare, and thus the main street of honor for major occasions in downtown Chicago, and ran (and still does) east and west—as opposed to the present-day north-south thoroughfares of State Street and Michigan Avenue.

FIGURE 3.1. *Reception of General Michael Corcoran, by the Mayor and Citizens of New York City, August 22d, 1862, On his release from the Confederate Prison, in which he had been confined one year,* from the series "The Soldier in Our Civil War," *Frank Leslie's Illustrated Newspaper* (6 September 1862): 374–75. *Author's Collection.*

CHAPTER 3

Civil War and the 1860s

ON THE EVE OF THE CIVIL WAR, THE REGULAR ARMY HAD FIVE mounted regiments: the 1st and 2nd Regiments of Dragoons,[1] the Regiment of Mounted Riflemen (constituted 19 May 1846), and the 1st and 2nd Cavalry Regiments (both constituted 3 March 1855). Seeing the need for more mounted troops, Congress authorized a 3rd Cavalry Regiment on 4 May 1861—and, to help with tighter and more uniform organization, redesignated all six regiments as cavalry regiments on 3 August 1861 with the 1st Dragoons becoming the new 1st Cavalry and the other units redesignated in order of seniority as the 2nd, 3rd, 4th, 5th, and 6th Cavalry Regiments.[2] As it was apparent that six cavalry regiments would be insufficient for serving on a thousand-mile front, Adjutant General Lorenzo Thomas issued a call to the state governors for raising 40,000 cavalrymen on 19 February 1862. On 31 December 1861, cavalrymen in the Union numbered 4,744 in the Regular Army and another 54,654 volunteers—each regiment having three battalions of two squadrons each, which were divided into two companies—for a total minimum strength of 997 officers and enlisted men per regiment. By 13 February 1865, 160,237 cavalrymen were on Cavalry Bureau rolls, of which 105,434 were present and fit for duty. Of the 154,000 horses purchased the year previously, 77,847 were considered serviceable.[3]

Added to these volunteer cavalry numbers were thousands of infantrymen, to the point that of the three million Americans who saw military service during the Civil War, the vast majority were volunteers, many of whom saw service

---

1. The U.S. Regiment of Dragoons was constituted on 2 March 1833 at Jefferson Barracks. On 15 May 1836, the regiment was redesignated as the 1st Regiment of Dragoons with the formation of the U.S. 2nd Regiment of Dragoons following on 23 May 1836. Sawicki, *Cavalry Regiments*, 151–54.

2. Ibid., 151–64; Heitman, *Historical Register and Dictionary*, 1:65, 66, 68, 70, 71, 72.

3. Philip Katcher, *Union Cavalryman, 1861–1865* (Oxford: Osprey, 1995): 3–4.

in the West and Southwest as Confederate and Union forces recognized the potential in the new territories—as well as in the never-ending Indian Wars.[4] Also, with these numbers, military music continued to develop in hundreds of bands through the efforts of thousands of musicians,[5] who by this point were separate entities from field musicians. While European tradition in the seventeenth and eighteenth centuries had elevated field trumpeting to a high skill and art that included years of apprenticeship training,[6] U.S. Civil War buglers often had no musical experience before enlisting, were not part of the band, and could seldom read music. They simply learned by rote in camp—and probably on the job.[7] A case in point was George Sargent, an eighteen-year-old from Charlestown, Massachusetts, who was a mounted bugler and eventually a mounted cymbal player with the bands of the 1st New England Cavalry, 1st Rhode Island Cavalry, and the 1st New Hampshire Cavalry.[8] Enlisting on 30 November 1861, Sargent's Monday, 2 December 1861, diary entry reads,

> In the afternoon we got our bugles and went down to a pond about half a mile distant to practice. I have heard it remarked that music hath charms to split a rock, but I think the music that afternoon was enough to split a whole stone quarry. It was the first time I ever undertook to blow a wind instrument, but before night I felt competent to act as clerk to a fish peddler, that is I could do the blowing part.[9]

---

4. Wooster, *American Military Frontiers*, 163–87.

5. While Public Law 165, which Congress passed on 17 July 1862, abolished regimental bands in the volunteer army—replacing them with brigade bands (one band for every four regiments)—this only applied to bands in the volunteer service and not to bands in the Regular Army or in state militia units. Consequently, thousands of musicians still served.

6. Gleason, "Cavalry and Court Trumpeters," 35–37.

7. *History of U.S. Army Bands*, 25.

8. The First New England Cavalry was formed on 22 January 1861 with battalions from Rhode Island and New Hampshire. On 31 March 1862, the name of the regiment was changed from the First New England Cavalry to the First Rhode Island Cavalry by order of the War Department. In January 1864, the New Hampshire battalion separated from the First Rhode Island Cavalry, and became the nucleus of the new First New Hampshire Cavalry. The New Hampshire regiment fought with General Philip Sheridan's forces as part of the Army of the Shenandoah (which Sheridan commanded from 6 August to 16 October 1864, and from 19 October 1864 to 28 February 1865) and for a time served as Sheridan's escort and bodyguard, with the First New Hampshire Cavalry Band serving as Sheridan's headquarters' band. By January 1865, George Custer was the commander of the 3rd Cavalry Division of the Army of the Shenandoah, of which the First New Hampshire Regiment was a part.

9. George Sargent, "Diary of a Bugler with Company C of the 1st Rhode Island Cavalry and Musician in the Regimental Band from His Enlistment in November 1861 to the Final Confederate Surrender in April 1865," 2 December 1861, unpublished manuscript, accessed from Huntington Library, Art Collections, and Botanical Gardens, San Marino, Calif.

The distinction between field musicians and band musicians became more apparent on 21 July 1861 with the passage of an Act to Increase the Present Military Establishment of the United States. Section 2 deals with field and staff commissioned and non-commissioned officers, and among other issues, authorized two principal musicians (trumpeters) per cavalry troop and sixteen musicians per cavalry band—with twenty-four being allotted to infantry and artillery bands.[10] Article 12, numbers 81 and 82 of the *Revised United States Army Regulations of 1861* gives a little more detail indicating that regiments were authorized (rather than simply allowed as in previous acts) sixteen privates to act as musicians in addition to the chief musician. Moreover, while they would be dropped from company muster rolls from where they had been transferred (no more than two per company), they would continue to be instructed as soldiers, and would be liable to serve in the ranks on any occasion. However, as band members, they would be "mustered in a separate squad under the chief musician, with the non-commissioned staff, and be included in the aggregate in all regimental returns."[11] It appears that the army wanted bandsmen to be treated as special, but not too special.

Chauncy Norton, serving with the 15th New York Cavalry, indicates in a 13 March 1864 diary entry that these regulations were the practice with bands being comprised of men from various companies of a regiment, and that mounted bands were not everyday occurrences: "March 13th [1864].—Colonel Richardson arrives and assumes command of the regiment for the 1st time since we left Syracuse. A novelty to be seen in camp is a brass band mounted. The members composing it were taken from the different companies, and after a little practice rendered some excellent music."[12] The station of the band was also addressed in the regulations, indicating that the band would remain with the headquarters company if the regiment occupied several stations. Field musicians, however, remained with their companies. The authorizations regarding field musicians seem to have stayed in place at least until the 1890s, although Sargent

---

10. U.S. War Department, General Orders, No. 48, *General Orders of the War Department Embracing the Years 1861, 1862 & 1863, Adapted Specially for the Use of the Army and Navy of the United States, Chronologically Arranged in Two Volumes. With a Full Alphabetical Index, by Thos. M. O'Brien & Oliver Diefendorf, Military Attorneys, Leavenworth, Kansas,* vol. 1 (New York: Derby and Miller, 1864), 86.

11. U.S. Army, *Revised United States Army Regulations of 1861. With an Appendix Containing the Changes and Laws Affecting Army Regulations and Articles of War to June 25, 1863,* 19, article 12, nos. 81 and 82.

12. Chauncey S. Norton, *"The Red Neck Ties," or History of the Fifteenth New York Volunteer Cavalry* (Ithaca, N.Y.: Journal Book and Job Print House, 1891), 28.

maintains that sometime in the fall of 1862, "The order was issued from the War Department allowing but one chief bugler to a regiment. Two was the number until then."[13] The record is not apparent as to how long this order was in effect, or if in fact it was carried out. By 1876 and the Battle of the Little Big Horn, Custer's 7th Cavalry had two trumpeters per company—but as established in prior years, they were distinct from the sixteen-plus-one band musicians.[14]

Along with the distinction between field music and bands, there was also a difference between bugles and trumpets. Although the two instruments served in similar capacities, and later on, in the same functions, they are different instruments. A natural trumpet (valveless) has two-thirds of its length in the form of a cylindrical tube, whereas a bugle has a conical shape throughout, and has its basis in the hunting horn—not in the military trumpet. Moreover, differences in mouthpieces—cup-shaped for the trumpet, and funnel-shaped for the bugle—result in the trumpet having a bright, strident, brash sound, while the bugle is known for its darker and mellower tone. Confusion between the two instruments arises because the terms have been used interchangeably. The natural trumpet used with kettledrums in court and military music was typically pitched in D (although sometimes with a crook was lowered to C) until the last half of the eighteenth century (when cavalry units moved to trumpets in Eb), and was pitched a sixth below the present-day Bb trumpet. Eb has traditionally remained the key of cavalry trumpets and consequently of cavalry bands.[15] Bugles however, have traditionally been in G, and field trumpets by the end of the nineteenth century were related more to the bugle than to the historic field trumpet.

All of this is not to say that bugles were not used as musical instruments. Elizabeth Custer, the widow of General George Custer, wrote of the postwar era, years after her husband's death, "In large posts, like Fort Leavenworth or Fort Lincoln, there was a corps of trained buglers, and it was a surprise to strangers that such good music could be evolved from instruments with so few notes."[16] Stemming from the European custom of mounted bands of valveless trumpets, one of these bugle bands is mentioned by Walt Whitman

---

13. Sargent, "Diary of a Bugler," 14 December 1862.

14. Kenneth Hammer, *Biographies of the 7th Cavalry, June 25th 1876* (Fort Collins, Colo.: Old Army Press, 1972), 44, 74.

15. Titcomb, "Baroque Court," 66; Caldwell Titcomb, "Carrousel Music at the Court of Louis XIV," in *Essays on Music in Honor of Archibald Thompson Davison by His Associates* (Cambridge, Mass.: Department of Music, Harvard University, 1957), 210. At the time of this writing, several contemporary mounted musical units continue to play valveless instruments in Eb, including the Danish Gardehusarregimentets Hesteskadron Trompeterkorps and the French La Fanfare de Cavalerie de la Garde Républicaine.

16. Elizabeth B. Custer, *Following the Guidon* (New York: Harper Brothers, 1890), vi.

in his Washington, D.C., 29 June 1863 war memoranda entry, in which he also describes the aura that seems to regularly accompany such units:

Just before sundown this evening a very large cavalry force went by—a fine sight. The men evidently had seen service. First came a mounted band of sixteen bugles, drums and cymbals, playing wild martial tunes—made my heart jump. Then the principal officers, then company after company, with their officers at their heads, making of course the main part of the cavalcade; then a long train of men with led horses [pack horses], lots of mounted negroes with special horses—and a long string of baggage-wagons, each drawn by four horses—and then a motley rear guard. It was a pronouncedly warlike and gay show; the sabres clank'd, the men look'd young and healthy and strong; the electric tramping of so many horses on the hard road, and the gallant bearing, fine seat, and bright faced appearance of a thousand and more handsome young American men, were so good to see.[17]

Whether Whitman meant that this band really was comprised of valveless bugles in the traditional model of European trumpeter bands (see chapter 1), or whether he was simply using "bugle" in referring to brass instruments, is not clear. It is clear, however, that since the band included cymbals, the group was a formed, intentional band and not simply a grouping of field musicians from various companies.

Whitman also makes it clear that military music was continuing to serve as a great public relations tool as it had for centuries—connecting the public with military personnel in feelings of spirit, conquest, justice, and teamwork. With this in mind, Civil War military bands, especially at the beginning of the war, were often professional or community bands whose members enlisted en masse, or who were hired by a regiment. While these bands were not often attached to cavalry units, Prof. Carl Colby's Silver Cornet Band, which served with the 1st Regiment West Virginia Cavalry Volunteers, was an exception: "When the regiment entered the field mounted and equipped, with its complement of field, staff and line officers, and led by Prof. Carl Colby's famous silver cornet band, all mounted on milk-white horses, the regiment well caparisoned, with jingling and flapping trappings, the riders all young and handsome, it was as beautiful and inspiring an organization as ever graced the armies of the United States."[18]

17. Walt Whitman, *Complete Poetry and Collected Prose*, ed. Justin Kaplan (New York: Library of America, 1982), 728.

18. Theodore F. Lang, Major 6th W.Va., Cavalry and Brevet Colonel, *Loyal West Virginia from 1861 to 1865* (Baltimore: Deutsch Publishing, 1895), 163.

Serving in one of the most musical wars in history, these U.S. Civil War musicians, whether they had enlisted en masse, had been recruited as musicians, or had never played anything prior, were popular with officers and enlisted ranks as well as with the general public.[19] Moreover, the custom of bands on horseback was akin to other cavalry practices that stemmed from centuries of tradition as evidenced by the 70th Pennsylvania Regiment (6th Cavalry)—an elite unit commanded by Colonel Richard H. Rush, which not only included a mounted band, but also had ten companies of cavalrymen who, in the Renaissance fashion of tournaments, jousts, and carrousels,[20] were initially equipped with nine-foot Norway fir lances with eleven-inch, three-edged blades. After an imposing display on 4 December 1861 in a street parade (in which five infantry units also participated), the unit became known as Rush's Lancers, and with their active-service departure for Washington, D.C., on 10 December, the Lancers were accompanied by their band, as recorded by Frank H. Taylor: "On December 10th Companies A, B, C and F proceeded to Washington, and the balance of the command followed within a few days. The regiment was encamped at Camp Barclay, north of the city. On January 1st, 1862, to the music of their splendid mounted band, the Lancers, nearly 1,000 strong, paraded through the Capital City."[21]

As military bands gained in popularity during Civil War years, valved brass instruments developed in several different styles, including bell front (typical trumpets, cornets, and trombones), upright, and over-the-shoulder saxhorn models (patented by Allen Dodworth in 1838; see figures 3.1 and 3.2). These latter instruments are the ones often associated with Civil War bands, used to point the sound to the rear to the troops marching or riding behind the band with instrumentation varying from band to band but typically adhering to that indicated in Dodworth's *Brass Band School* and Friederich's *Brass Band Journal*:

---

19. One interesting mounted band influx into popular culture of the time was through several romance novels by Robert W. Chambers, who was born in 1865 as the Civil War was ending. A Union Army mounted band and bandmaster figure heavily in his *Special Messenger* (1904; repr., New York: D. Appleton, 1909), and, in his *Lorraine* (New York: Harper and Brothers, 1898), 93, a French hussar mounted band appears journeying toward Saarbrücken during the Franco-Prussian War playing "a gay air with plenty of trombone and kettle-drum in it," resulting in "the horses ambl[ing] and danc[ing] in sympathy, with an accompaniment of rattling carbines and clinking, clashing sabre-scabbards" (93).

20. Gleason, "Cavalry and Court Trumpeters," 50–51.

21. Frank H. Taylor, *Philadelphia in the Civil War, 1861–1865: Illustrated from Contemporary Prints and Photographs and from Drawings by the Author* (Philadelphia: The City [of Philadelphia], 1913), 163.

Dodworth	*Friederich*
E♭ Soprano (first)	E♭ Soprano (first)
E♭ Soprano (second)	E♭ Soprano (second)
B♭ Alto (first)	B♭ Alto (first)
B♭ Alto (second)	B♭ Alto (second)
E♭ Tenor (first)	E♭ Tenor (first)
E♭ Tenor (second)	E♭ Tenor (second)
Baritone	Baritone
Bass (first)	Basso (first)
Bass (second)	Basso (second)
E♭ Trumpet	E♭ Trumpet
Trombone (first)	. . . .
Trombone (second)	. . . .
Snare Drum	Small Drum
Bass Drum	Bass Drum[22]

These "voiced" brass instruments were in the line of conical-bored instruments developed earlier in the century by Wieprecht and Sax and mentioned in chapter 1.

While some Civil War bands included woodwinds, most, including mounted ones, typically consisted of twelve to sixteen brass instruments.[23] The question of what to do about percussion by this point seems to have been answered by utilizing mounted bass and snare drums. Already mentioned in chapter 1 are the side drums used in dragoon units, and Farmer also makes a case for mounted bass drums (also mentioned in reference to the Kossuth parade in chapter 2): "Against the use of the latter [bass drum] at the battle of Waterloo one writer has urged, that as the Seventh Hussars were mounted at the battle, a bass drum would have been no use to a mounted band. This is quite an error. Mounted bands of the period carried the bass drum on horseback (see Kastner), and even in recent years a similar custom was in vogue in Austria."[24]

In fact, the majority of photographs of North American mounted bands of the late nineteenth century show bass drums with kettledrums as being

---

22. Allen Dodworth, *Brass Band School* (New York: H. B. Dodworth, 1853); G. W. E. Friederich, *The Brass Band Journal* (New York: Firth, Pond, 1853).

23. Robert Garofalo and Mark Elrod, *A Pictorial History of Civil War Era Musical Instruments and Military Bands* (Charleston, W.Va.: Pictorial Histories Publishing, 1985), 56.

24. Farmer, *Rise and Development*, 90.

rare—probably, as mentioned in chapter 2, as a result of expense and lack of tradition. Nonetheless, kettledrums in U.S. Cavalry bands were not unheard of.[25] Writing in 1875, Theophilus F. Rodenbough indicates that the band of the 2nd U.S. Cavalry (2nd Dragoons 1836–61), included kettledrums and a bass drum in 1861.[26]

On the Southern front, several records refer to mounted bands within Confederate units as well. Colonel James Gordon, commander of the 2nd Regiment of Mississippi Cavalry, Armstrong's Brigade indicates that, as magnificent as mounted bands appeared and sounded, they were still susceptible to the infringements of warfare:

> As we marched gaily forward Gen. Price's Mounted Band kept well up in front of our column, just in rear of our skirmish line, yet out of range of the retreating Federal cavalry. In the rosy realm of childhood my fancy had pictured the bands discoursing martial music while the soldiers were fighting. Old Pap Price's band soon disabused my mind of this fairy tale. The woods resounded with that popular air "Listen to the Mockingbird." When we came in sight of the entrenchments one of those big guns opened with a terrific roar and a huge shell came humming overhead and struck an oak where it forked, about twenty feet above us, splitting it in two, scattering fragments of limbs, bark and splinters among the musicians. The Mockingbird hushed its dulcet strain and the boys shouted with glee as the band and Negro camp followers "*skedaddled*" to the rear. The ball had opened and it was a different tune we danced to the rest of the day.[27]

Gordon portrays an accurate picture of mixing tranquil strains of music with the realities of warfare. *Listen to the Mockingbird* with lyrics by Septimus Winner (pseudonym Alice Hawthorne) and music by Richard Milburn by this point was a well-known song—growing in popularity to sell more than twenty million copies of sheet music.[28] Like those of *The Girl I Left Behind Me*, the lyrics express grief over a woman left behind, albeit in the latter song with "Hally" being left behind in a grave rather than simply at home—early deaths being not uncommon in nineteenth-century real life or in popular songs. The song's

---

25. Kettledrums were also used in U.S. foot regiments. See Camus, "Military Band," 468–69.

26. Rodenbough, *From Everglade to Cañon*, 250.

27. Col. James Gordon, "The Battle and Retreat from Corinth," *Publications of the Mississippi Historical Society* 4 (1901): 65.

28. David Ewen, *All the Years of American Popular Music* (New York: Prentice Hall, 1977), 54.

performance by a military band indicates its popularity, as listeners, upon hearing the melody, filled in the words themselves. The song's popularity as a band piece indicates the enormous popularity of the military band as a genre of the people during the Civil War.

As with Union units, Confederate cavalry bands were often referred to simply as belonging to a particular unit by name of the commander rather than the actual unit—a noticeable holdover from the privatized militia tradition as well as the days when newly commissioned officers recruited men to serve under them resulting in companies being referred to by the commanding officers' names.[29] Jennings Cropper Wise refers to one of these bands, which was apparently part of Hampton's Brigade, commanded by Brigadier General Wade Hampton: "The Horse Artillery, which was continuously engaged in the cavalry operations during the months of September, October, November, and December [1863], was ordered into winter quarters at Charlottesville, on December 21st. Gen. Lee and Governor Letcher had reviewed the infantry and Stuart's command at Culpeper Courthouse on November 5, when again Beckham's Battalion passed before the great soldier at the head of the cavalry, to the tune of Hampton's mounted band."[30]

Likewise, a mounted band that must have been part of the 7th, 11th, or 12th Virginia Cavalry Regiments or the 35th Virginia Cavalry Battalion, all of which comprised Rosser's Brigade, appears in John Sergeant Wise's (father of Jennings Cropper Wise) memoirs:

In the spring of 1864, I was still a cadet at the Virginia Military Institute. . . . Rosser's brigade had wintered in Rockbridge, but a few miles from the Institute. Lexington and the Institute were constantly visited by [General Thomas L.] Rosser, his staff, and the officers of his brigade. They brought us in touch with the war, and the world beyond, more than anything else we had seen. They jangled their spurs through the archway, laughed loudly in the officers' quarters, and rode off as if they carried the world in a sling. In March, they broke camp, and came ambling, trotting, galloping, prancing past the Institute, their mounted band playing, their little guidons fluttering, bound once more to active duty in the lower valley.[31]

---

29. Edward M. Coffman, *The Old Army: A Portrait of the American Army in Peacetime, 1784–1898* (New York: Oxford University Press, 1986), 13.

30. Jennings Cropper Wise, *The Long Arm of Lee, or the History of the Artillery of the Army of Northern Virginia, with a Brief Account of the Confederate Bureau of Ordnance*, vol. 2 (Lynchburg, Va.: J. P. Bell, 1915), 717

31. John S. Wise, *The End of an Era* (Boston: Houghton, Mifflin, 1899), 285.

Other records mention civilian recollections of observing Union mounted bands in Confederate territory including those of Mary Rawson, who recorded the following in her diary on 11 September 1864 when she heard the painful reminder proclaimed by one of Sherman's bands that Atlanta had been captured and would soon be no more:

> This afternoon on hearing martial music, we looked up from the front porch where we were sitting to see the street filled with cavalry and infantry pack mules and army wagons and cattle crowded promiscously [sic] together, the cavalry and infantry ensigns floating in unison together. The musicians all riding on white horses. After making the signal for the march to commence they rode silently along until they passed in front of Gen. Gearys [sic] headquarters when simultaneously they broke into the old soul stirring "Hail Columbia"; the suddenness of the music startled me. They then, (after finishing the piece) slowly and silently marched through the city.[32]

Again, *Hail Columbia* shows up, this time perhaps carrying separate and distinct feelings for Southern listeners about to witness the burning of one of their premier cities in comparison with those of Northern musicians and the soldiers who would be burning it.

While extant records describe more Union than Confederate mounted bands, even then, they were still probably a rarity in comparison with the total number of Civil War military bands, as suggested in Norton's previous 15th New York Cavalry quote (page 41), and by George Sargent who by this point was a part of the 1st New Hampshire Cavalry Mounted Band: "Jefferson [Maryland] is quite a pretty place, passing through it just as the people were coming out of church. I guess that there have not been many troops through here before, because they seemed to be very much surprised and pleased to see a band on horseback, and all white horses, too."[33]

With no courts of nobility or royalty as bases, U.S. mounted bands relied on larger-than-life military personalities for their propulsion during the Civil War.

---

32. Katharine M. Jones, ed., *Heroines of Dixie: Winter of Desperation* (St. Simons, Ga.: Mockingbird Books, 1988), 150. Rawson was the youngest daughter of E. E. Rawson, one of the city council members, who—along with S. C. Wells and Mayor James M. Calhoun—wrote a letter, also on 11 September 1864, to Major General Sherman, asking him to rescind his order for Atlanta's citizens to evacuate the city. General Sherman denied their request in a letter on the following day.

33. Sargent, "Diary of a Bugler," 6 August 1864.

FIGURE 3.2. *Music on Sheridan's Line of Battle*. From Robert Johnson and Clarence Buel, eds., *Battles and Leaders of the Civil War*, vol. 4 (1887; repr., New York: Castle Books, Thomas Yoseloff, 1956), 4:708. *Author's Collection.*

Among these bands were those within units under the command of General Philip H. Sheridan, whose members found themselves reliving a Saracen custom of playing under fire by leading troops into battle while controlling their horses with their knees (see figure 3.2). Also General Horace Porter, writing in 1897 of his Civil War experiences when he was acting as a courier for General Grant to General Sheridan, who was leading union troops in the Battle of Dinwiddie Courthouse, recalls:

> I turned the corner of the Brooks cross-road and the Five Forks road just as the rear of the latter body of cavalry was passing it, and found one of Sheridan's bands with his rear-guard playing "Nellie Bly" as cheerfully as if furnishing music for a country picnic. Sheridan always made an effective use of his bands. They were usually mounted on gray horses, and instead of being relegated to the usual duty of carrying off the wounded and assisting the surgeons, they were brought out to the front and made to play the liveliest airs in their repertory, which produced

excellent results in buoying up the spirits of the men. After having several of their instruments pierced by bullets, however, and the drums crushed by shells, as often happened, it must be admitted that the music, viewed purely in the light of an artistic performance, was open to adverse criticism.[34]

Interestingly, Porter was by the time of this writing more used to the spelling of "Nellie Bly," the penname of Elizabeth Jane Cochran, rather than "Nelly Bly," the title of the Stephen Foster song from which she borrowed the name. Published in 1850, *Nelly Bly* was a top-of-the-charts tune as Foster's other songs were—although it is doubtful that Foster ever envisioned his lyrics praising domestic bliss would ever serve as military fare.

Performances under fire were apparently not uncommon in Sheridan's command. An order given by the general to mass his musicians on the firing line, recorded in another account of the Battle of Dinwiddie Courthouse, serves as a vivid reminder of the tenuous circumstances that military musicians could find themselves in when they were ordered to "play the gayest tunes in their books—play them loud and keep on playing them, and never mind if a bullet goes through a trombone, or even a trombonist, now and then."[35]

Likewise, taking his cue from Sheridan under whom he had served, Brigadier General George Custer ordered the mounted band of the Michigan Cavalry Brigade to lead the unit into battle playing *Yankee Doodle* near James City, Virginia, against a contingency of Confederate Cavalry led by Major General Fitzhugh Lee on 9 October 1863. Similarly, at Columbia Furnace, Virginia, on 16 April 1862, Custer's band led the cavalry charge.[36] Another utilization of bands under Custer's watch is revealed in one of his reports during the Virginia campaign: "I have caused fires to be built along the edge of the woods and my band to play at different points since dark, to give the impression that a strong force of infantry is here."[37]

Cavalry bandsmen themselves recall battlefield experiences, or attempts to

34. Horace Porter, *Campaigning With Grant*, ed. Wayne C. Temple (1897; repr., Bloomington: Indiana University Press, 1961), 431. This campaign was against Confederate forces led by Major General George A. Pickett, southwest of Petersburg, Virginia, on 31 March 1865 during the Appomattox campaign—a day before the Battle of Five Forks.

35. Bruce Catton, *A Stillness at Appomattox* (Garden City, N.Y.: Doubleday, 1954), 347.

36. Kenneth E. Olson, *Music and Musket: Bands and Bandsmen of the American Civil War* (Westport, Conn.: Greenwood Press, 1981), 207.

37. George A. Custer, Report No. 4, Mine Run, Virginia, 26 November 1863, in *Custer in the Civil War: His Unfinished Memoirs*, comp. and ed. John M. Carroll (San Rafael, Calif.: Presidio Press, 1977), 15.

avoid them as indicated by Sargent, who by the time of this 20 July 1862 diary entry had moved from being a field bugler to a cymbal player with the mounted band of the 1st New England Cavalry at Manassas Junction near Bull Run Stream: "I was well pleased with the change for several reasons: I was very fond of music, besides my duty would be lighter; and in the case of a fight I would not be in so much danger. All we had to do besides taking care of our horses was to play at Guard Mounting in the morning, dress parade in the afternoon, and before the Colonel's quarters in the evening."[38]

Serving under Sheridan, as part of the Army of the Shenandoah in the Shenandoah Valley campaign, Sargent's entry for 25 August 1864 suggests that by this point he may have had some change of thoughts:

> The whole corps went out on a reconnaissance in force towards Martinsburg [West Virginia], but before reaching there we drove in the Reb pickets, and soon came to the main force, where skirmishers were sent out and a line of battle formed. . . . Presently, the Rebs made a charge, smoke and dust. I saw men and horses fall, officers shouting for the men to keep cool and steady, and presently one of our batteries opened from a small hill but a stone's throw behind us, throwing the shells over our heads; we fell back and took a position behind the battery and struck up "Star Spangled Banner," while the battery boys were dealing death and destruction among the Reb's ranks. . . . Although the balls whizzed over our heads and under our horses, none of our crowd got hurt, but some from another regiment got killed in a barnyard next to us. . . . This was the first time the band ever played on the battlefield and I don't care about repeating it very often. Although I liked the excitement, I didn't like the music of those lead pills that were flying about so carelessly.[39]

The practice of bands playing in battle however, sometimes backfired, with the ensuing music serving as an excellent alarm for the unintended recipient—as Confederate soldier, and son of General Alexander Wise, John Sergeant Wise, found:

> "Plague take you, be quiet!" I said to the mare, slapping her impatiently on the neck; for at that moment she lifted her head, pointed her ears, and, raising her ribs, gave a loud whinny. By good luck, almost at the same instant the sound of clashing

---

38. Sargent, "Diary of a Bugler," 20 July 1862.
39. Ibid., 25 August 1864.

cymbals and the music of a mounted band came through the forest. The hostile forces were but a few hundred yards away. As I soon learned, they were moving on a road leading to the ford, but entering the road that I was traveling just beyond the spot where I first heard them. The hill on my left ran down to a point where the advancing column was coming into the road on which I was. The summit of the hill was covered by a thick growth of laurel and pine. I sprang from the saddle, led the mare up the hillside, tied her, and, reflecting that she might whinny again, left her, ran along the hill-crest as near to the enemy as I dared go, lay down behind an old log, covered myself with leaves and bushes, and was within a hundred yards of the spot which the enemy passed. I could see them from behind the end of my log.

"Hurrah! hurrah!" they shouted, as the band played "Johnny Comes Marching Home." They were elated and full of enthusiasm, for the Johnnies were on the run, and the pursuit was now little more than a foot-race. The band struck up "Captain Jenks [Jinks] of the Horse Marines" as they swept on to the ford, walking, trotting, ambling, pacing, their guidons fluttering in the spring breeze. "Hurrah! hurrah! hurrah!" How different was the cheering from the wild yell to which I was accustomed! I lay there, with my pistol in my hand, watching them, really interested in contrasting their good equipment and their ardor with the wretched scenes that I had left behind.[40]

Wise makes several keen observations, one of which was simply the psychological role that military music had played for centuries. *When Johnny Comes Marching Home*, with lyrics written by Irish American bandleader Patrick Gilmore, in this context was presumably being played as a taunt—to any Confederate "Johnny Reb" soldiers who may have been within earshot. With lyrics by William Horace Lingard, and music attributed to T. Maclagan, *Captain Jinks of the Horse Marines* was a popular song throughout the 1860s and '70s, written in a lilting 6/8 meter reminiscent of a horse's step—a favorite tactic of cavalry march composers.[41]

While cavalry bands in some cases led the way into battle and performed concerts in forward positions during the fighting, with the martial and patriotic music startling the enemy and rallying soldiers to victory, these accounts of musicians performing in the midst of combat probably reflect unusual incidents. When band musicians did find themselves on the battlefield, work typically consisted of non-musical duties, as Sargent reports on 29 July 1864 when facing

40. Wise, *End of an Era*, 440–41.

41. Lingard was a nineteenth-century English comic singer who often appeared in drag on stage. *Captain Jinks of the Horse Marines* continued to be popular over the next decades and was the basis of a stage comedy of the same title by Clyde Fitch, starring Ethel Barrymore, in 1901.

a Confederate contingent: "The cavalry had orders to prepare to fight on foot, every number four to hold the horses. Four of the band (myself included) were ordered to stay behind to take care of the horses and instruments, the rest proceeding to the front with the regiment to take care of the wounded."[42]

Band duty off the battlefield typically consisted of performing under less threatening circumstances of military and civilian parades, drills, reviews, guard mounts and other ceremonies for encamped troops, and troop movements. Additionally, like infantry bands, cavalry bands also drummed soldiers out of the army and performed for funerals and executions. And Rodenbough indicates that listening to music was a pleasant way to conclude a cavalryman's day, "When, after a wearisome march under the dispiriting effect of heavy casualties, the trooper would come in to a pleasant camp and his day's work done, be refreshed by the light melodies of Strauss or the lighter Offenbach, the musical 'Stable-call Waltz,' the 'Feast of Roses,' and the inevitable 'Star-Spangled'; gloomy forebodings would vanish, and in a cheerful frame of mind, strengthened in body, the soldier would seek his blankets."[43] Not relegated only to marches, folk songs, and other military fare and popular tunes, military and civilian bands of the time were also playing light classics as Rodenbough indicates. As well, Sargent indicates that as the 1st New Hampshire Cavalry was passing by Mount Vernon, along with *The Star-Spangled Banner*, they also played "Dead March" (probably from Handel's *Saul*) and *Plays Hymn*.[44]

Another important aspect of Civil War military bands was to perform for the war weary in back areas including military hospitals—lifting the morale of suffering soldiers, as Sargent recalls in his 20 May 1863 diary entry: "Went and played for the wounded soldiers again. One of the doctors told us that when we played there before, some of the men left their beds for the first time since the battle and have not taken to them since. He said it done them more good than all the medicine he could give them. So you see we are doing something for our beloved country."[45]

Since bands were considered essential for troop morale, cavalry musicians, like those in the infantry, also performed dismounted at balls and other dances and parties and formal and informal concerts at concert halls and forts, as well as in battlefield and expedition camps and for church calls and services. In this vein,

---

42. Sargent, "Diary of a Bugler," 29 July 1864.
43. Rodenbough, *From Everglade to Cañon*, 250–51.
44. Sargent, "Diary of a Bugler," 3 August 1864.
45. Ibid., 20 May 1863.

Sargent explains that the band of the 1st New England Cavalry, in addition to brass instruments, had "a full set of quadrille instruments, consisting of a harp, violins, clarinets, piccolo, guitar, and bass viol," which were used in camp. He continues, "Most every evening, we would have music, and sometimes dancing . . . the only thing we lacked was partners of the female persuasion."[46]

Life for Civil War cavalry bandsmen varied. Like soldiers in the rest of the army, band members often lived off the land but sometimes were able to find enjoyment even amidst hardship, as Sargent recalls in his 2 August 1862 entry: "Arrived at Rappahannock town this afternoon. . . . As soon as camp was established, five of the band went out foraging for the whole band, bringing in corn and hay for the horses and turkeys and chickens for ourselves. Coming back, I had a race with the fastest horse in the regiment."[47] Sargent's diary entries of 5 and 13 January 1865 when he was serving in the 1st New Hampshire Cavalry in the 3rd Cavalry Division under George Custer indicate that the survival involved in serving as soldier-musicians was not all fun:

> We cleared a space of the snow and pitched our shelter tent, which we lived in for the next three or four days, being nearly frozen during that time. We came to the conclusion we would stand it no longer, so George and I started off on a tour of observation after building material. After travelling nearly a mile, we came to a farm house with barns and outbuildings. On one of these barns were some loose boards. How to get them off without attracting the attention of the guard at the house was the next question, but it was finally done.[48]

Several U.S. mounted bands serving at the time of the Civil War served away from the front in other theaters with their units or at home in official or community functions, or traveling among the isolated outposts manned by various regiments. While the 2nd Minnesota Cavalry was headed for Civil War duty in New Orleans in the spring of 1864, the order was rescinded, and members of the regiment found themselves as members of the 8th Minnesota Regiment, "mounted for the purpose of taking part in an expedition against the Sioux" and commencing a march westward on the 5th of June with 2,100 mounted men, 106 mule teams loaded with supplies and equipment, 2 six-pounder brass smoothbore cannon, two mountain howitzers, and twelve ambulances making up

---

46. Ibid., 8 December 1861.
47. Ibid., 2 August 1862.
48. Ibid., 5 and 13 January 1865.

the force.[49] Musicians in the 2nd Minnesota Cavalry Band thus found themselves serving in Dakota Territory rather than in the Southeast, and, according to the front page of the 19 May 1864 *St. Paul Press*, were part of a highly regarded unit:

> Within the last few weeks the 2d Cavalry have organized a splendid Band which is mounted upon beautiful white horses and furnished with a magnificent set of silver instruments, from Munger Brothers, St. Paul. They daily and nightly discourse "sweet music" to us, which helps revive the weary soul, and relieve the dull monotony during this sleepy, stupid weather. They gave the remaining members of the noble First a handsome serenade the evening previous to their departure, which was duly responded to by speeches and cheers from the officers and men.[50]

Even farther west, a "Band of Music—Mounted" is listed in the parade entries in Sacramento for the Grand Celebration of the 87th Anniversary of National Independence: Fourth of July, 1863, following "Three Policemen—Mounted" and preceding the Sacramento Hussars, a privately funded volunteer militia, commanded by Captain J. Marten in Sacramento, California. Also in the parade were troops of the 1st and 2nd Cavalry, California Volunteers. Presumably, the mounted band was part of the Sacramento Hussars or one of the cavalry units.[51]

Two mounted band records of note during this era are connected with Abraham Lincoln—one with Gettysburg and one with the president's funeral. One of these documented bands was attached to the dedication ceremonies for the Gettysburg cemetery on 19 November 1863 and was described in 1938 by William V. Rathvon, who attended the dedication ceremonies as a nine-year-old boy: "At the head of the procession preceded by a mounted military band, the first I had ever seen, rode the president. He was mounted on a grey horse of medium size, which accentuated his unusual height. . . . The president was escorted to the cemetery by many distinguished officers of the army, representatives of foreign countries, military and civic organizations, and the surging crowds of patriotic citizens estimated at 20,000."[52]

---

49. Hon. William H. Houlton, "Narrative of the Eighth Regiment," in *Minnesota in the Civil and Indian Wars, 1861–1865* (St. Paul, Minn.: Board of Commissioners, Legislature of Minnesota, Electrotyped and Printed for the State by the Pioneer Press Company, 1890), 387–89.

50. Venice, "The Second Cavalry Band," Fort Snelling Items, *St. Paul Press*, 22 May 1864, 1.

51. "Fourth of July," *Sacramento Daily Union*, Friday, 3 July 1863, 1.

52. William V. Rathvon "Eyewitness at Gettysburg," *All Things Considered*, 15 February 1999, http://www.npr.org/templates/story/story.php?storyId=1045619. A family in Pallatine, Illinois, related to Rathvon had possession of the recording.

Records of the period indicate that there were four military bands in the procession leading to the Gettysburg dedication ceremony, and that the entire entourage, as indicated by Orton Carmichael, was sizeable:

> The procession was made up of several bands of music, including the Marine Band of Washington, the Second U.S. Artillery Band of Baltimore, the Birgfield Band of Philadelphia, the band of the Fifth New York Heavy Artillery, several military organizations, various officers of the army and their staffs. Immediately behind the Fifth New York Heavy Artillery came President Lincoln and the visiting members of his Cabinet on horseback, escorted by Marshal Ward B. Lamon with his aids and their staffs. . . . The line of march was up Baltimore Street, along which three months before the Union Army had retreated on the evening of the first day's fight, leaving the street strewn with their wounded and dead.[53]

It is not clear from Rathvon's record which band he is referring to, and, indeed, there is of course the question of his memory being accurate. If it was, the mounted band was presumably one of the artillery bands, and if it was the band preceding the president, and if Carmichael's account is accurate, it would have been the New York unit, which would not have been unusual to be mounted.

Another New York mounted band was part of Lincoln's Washington, D.C., funeral procession just days after Lee's surrender at Appomattox Court House during the final devastating months of the Civil War. On 19 April 1865, along with the United States Marine Band and a "Drum Corps of fifteen drums and ten fifes," the "13th New York Mounted Band" provided music in Abraham Lincoln's funeral procession. This immense entourage, carrying the body of the slain president in a horse-drawn hearse, followed by the president's riderless horse led by a groom from the White House to the Capitol Rotunda down Pennsylvania Avenue, was comprised of hundreds of foot and mounted soldiers, carriages of dignitaries, and various other military, diplomatic, and civilian contingencies and was of course organized within a few days.[54]

---

53. Orton H. Carmichael, *Lincoln's Gettysburg Address* (New York: Abingdon Press, 1917), 53–54.

54. Barclay and Co., *The Terrible Tragedy at Washington: The Assassination of President Lincoln* (Philadelphia: Barclay, 1865), 51. Of this event, the editors note, "At least thirty thousand men assisted in the grand proof that the Union is not dead in the hearts of the people."

TRAINING MUSICIANS

Training of bandsmen and field musicians during the Civil War differed between the two groups. Official training was probably negligible and/or site based for bandsmen, and training for field musicians (who were often children and adolescents with no musical experience) seems to have varied as well. With many Civil War bands being intact professional and town bands whose members enlisted together when the war began, musical training was probably seen as unnecessary. Further, because many military bands were unofficial, they received their support from the officers of the regiment—a custom borrowed from Europe and the United Kingdom. Because of this status, there was no central training point for bandsmen and bandleaders, and official musical training consisted mainly of training for infantry field musicians (fifers and drummers) from some years prior to 1860 to the end of the war at Fort Columbus (later renamed Fort Jay), Governors Island, New York.[55] This training however, was for regular federal army field musicians; musicians of volunteer regiments were expected to learn their duties and craft on the job (e.g., George Sargent). Official training for band musicians apparently did not begin in the U.S. Army until Congress authorized a school for bandleaders in 1911 at the same site—with bandsmen training beginning ten years later.[56]

Above musical training, however, and of more probable concern to band members, would have been attaining the crucial skill of riding a horse and playing an instrument—and then, in the case of Sheridan's and Custer's bands, learning to accomplish this at the trot or gallop under gunfire. While the horse was a primary means of transportation and power throughout the country at the time—with over 650,000 horses being employed by both armies during the Civil War[57]—universal equestrian experience was by no means the case, with plenty of people not being riders. This is exemplified by an 1861 account given by John C. Linehan of the Penacook, New Hampshire, Fisherville Cornet Band, when its members were selected to perform service for the Governor's Horse Guards, a stylish military organization of the time: "Their engagement . . . although a

---

55. Augustus Meyers, *Ten Years in the Ranks, U.S. Army* (1914; repr., London: Forgotten Books, 2012). Writing in 1913, Meyers chronicled his ten years in the U.S. Army, beginning in 1854 as an apprentice musician (fifer) at Governors Island. His work serves as a vivid lens for investigating field music training during this period as well as military life in general.

56. Olson, *Music and Musket*, 84–87.

57. Livingston and Roberts, *War Horse*, 28. Livingston and Roberts indicate that the Union Army had some 370 volunteer cavalry regiments and 6 regular regiments and that the Confederacy utilized 137 volunteer cavalry regiments.

matter of pride, was nevertheless an occasion of dismay, for the boys for the first time in their lives had to play on horseback. As nearly all of them were novices in this direction the outlook was serious, for it is a question if there were half a dozen of the number that had ever straddled a horse."[58]

Methods of riding and playing used by musicians probably varied between bands—but especially differed according to the instrument played. Little hint has been recorded about horse guidance in cavalry bands during the Civil War, but accounts of U.S. mounted bands of the 1930s and 1940s, as well as those of contemporary British and European bands, indicate that well-trained horses can be guided by the musicians' knees as well as by following and relying on horses in front of them during parades. Additionally, trumpeters and other valved and valveless brass instrument players have often played with the right hand while guiding the horse with the left. Trombonists have devised ways of playing and riding using a system of double reins with a runner on them, whereby the rider put his arm in the loop, and tightened or loosened it as he moved the slide. Woodwind players, when they were added to the mix, typically wrapped the reins around their arms. Drummers devised different methods of attaching the drum to the saddle, or mounting kettledrums in special harnesses, and play- ing with one or both hands while guiding the horse with waist or foot reins.[59]

Horsemanship was probably an individual concern among band members— as was the training of horses to become accustomed to the sounds of musical instruments. While little evidence of the period addresses cavalry band horse training, accounts of other bands of other places and times do. The 1930s train- ing techniques of the Royal Artillery Mounted Band of Woolwich, England, illustrate a procedure of acclimating horses to loud abrupt sounds—a method that may have been used in the United States during the nineteenth century: "To do this, boys were instructed to go up into the gallery (loft) to make as much noise as possible with dustbin lids, pots, pans and cymbals . . . eventually horses became less frightened and gradually no loud or sudden sound, including music, startled or disoriented them."[60]

---

58. John C. Linehan, "The Fisherville Cornet Band," in *History of Penacook, New Hampshire*, comp. David Arthur Brown (Concord, N.H.: Rumford Press, 1902), 248–49.

59. Bruce P. Gleason, "A History of the Royal Artillery Mounted Band, 1878–1939" (master's thesis, University of Minnesota, Minneapolis, 1985), 12–13; Dr. Hubert Henderson, Louisville, Ky., e-mail message to author, 21 March 2004. Henderson played trumpet and cornet with the 3rd Cavalry Band at Fort Myer, Virginia (1941–42). He later served as the director of bands at the University of Maryland for ten years and then went to the University of Kentucky in 1965 as the chair of the music department, retiring in 1989.

60. Gleason, "History of the Royal Artillery Mounted Band," 14–16.

With this equine music education in mind, Sargent's entry of 31 December 1862 describes what has probably been a problem in all mounted bands at one time or another: "We got a few new horses while here, and for the first few times playing on them they acted wild, but soon got used to it, going as steady as old veterans."[61] Even though horses became accustomed to the sounds of musical instruments, all mounted bandsmen had to be careful of frightening their horses—especially cymbal players, who could easily find themselves thrown or quickly back in the stables or across a field if they played their cymbals unexpectedly or too loudly for their mounts' tastes. Likewise, Rodenbough gives an 1861 2nd Cavalry account that was perhaps not unusual with any unit attempting to mount a band on horses unaccustomed to music:

> On one occasion, however, a new supply of horses was received at the depot, and it was decided to remount the band. Fifteen symmetrical blacks were selected, and their musical riders, under charge of the dignified old Sergeant-Major, mounted and went through a few simple and silent evolutions, in order to accustom the green "remounts" to the jingling of sabres, the sight of polished brass, etc. Finding that the horses went very quietly, the Sergeant-Major requested the leader to try the effect of a little music. "Play something *very softly*," said he. The first wail of the "Miserere" was heard, and then—a brief pawing of the air, some fine posing on the part of the equines, some less picturesque human attitudes, and away swept the cavalcade in wild disorder, the frantic kettle-drum leading, closely followed by the cornet and trombone, the others making good time, and the big drum (for which a fat and lazy beast had been taken) leisurely bringing up the rear with elephantine strides. Not until the barracks had been twice circled were the runaways all captured, the battered instruments picked up, and band-practice for that day at an end.[62]

If Gregorio Allegri's plaintive, inspirational, and prayerful seventeenth-century setting of Psalm 51, *Miserere mei, Deus* (Have mercy on me, O God), initially composed for use in the Sistine Chapel during matins, caused this much calamity, a strong program of training was indeed in order.

Cavalry music was indeed a specialized profession, and, along with being accomplished musicians, bandsmen needed to be skilled horsemen because of the unpredictable nature of their mounts. Of prime concern for all active

---

61. Sargent, "Diary of a Bugler," 13 December 1862.
62. Rodenbough, *From Everglade to Cañon*, 250.

cavalry units throughout the Civil War was the training and care of horses, which, along with their riders, often lived in squalid conditions for months at a time, distanced from adequate food and shelter. On campaigns, bandsmen, along with other cavalrymen, attempted to provide for their steeds, foraging for themselves as well as their horses, with men and animals living together in the open during much of the year. While cavalry soldier-musicians worked to keep their operations running smoothly for horses and themselves, combining soldiering and foraging with the unlikely addition of performing on musical instruments and living with horses in the countryside, resulted in issues that could not always be planned or trained for, as Sargent indicates in his 16 August 1864 diary entry: "A few days later, the bass tuba player had his instrument (costing $110) stepped on by a horse, squashing it so that it had to be sent to Boston to be repaired. But we never saw it afterwards, and this reduced the band down considerably, but we managed to keep in playing condition."[63]

Employing tens of thousands of musicians, typically utilizing brass and percussion instruments, the Civil War was one of the most musical wars in history. Being called upon to perform in battle, in camp, and in parade and concert became everyday occurrences for mounted military musicians, providing a foretaste of what was to come. After the war, U.S. military music continued to develop along with military tactics, strategies, and technology—especially with renewed attention westward, where mounted bands were about to make an even stronger statement within cavalry and artillery units.

----

63. Sargent, "Diary of a Bugler," 16 August 1864.

CHAPTER 4

The 1860s and Plains Indian Wars

AFTER THE CIVIL WAR, THE COUNTRY'S UNIFIED MILITARY MOVED to concern itself with coastal defense and reconstruction—as well as with supporting efforts in western expansion, which had been heightened with the Homestead Act of 1862. As a means of populating the territory acquired sixty years earlier in the Louisiana Purchase, the act granted 160 acres to individuals willing to settle on and farm the land for at least five years. Of course, the land that the federal government was giving away consisted of ancestral Indian lands, resulting in further treaties, skirmishes, and battles with American Indians that had been occurring since the seventeenth century—before there was a federal government.[1]

Toward these efforts—although general sentiment continued to be wary of the idea of a standing army during peacetime—the army constituted four new cavalry regiments—7th, 8th, 9th, and 10th—on 28 July 1866.[2] Concerning these units, Major General William T. Sherman stated to Lieutenant General Ulysses S. Grant, that "as soon as the Indians see that we have Regular Cavalry among them they will realize that we are in condition to punish them for any murders or robberies."[3] Other statements supporting the apparent consensus view included those of Captain William T. H. Brooks of the 3rd U.S. Infantry, who wrote, "It is only a question of time. In the end, they are bound to be exterminated,"[4] and of Captain Thomas Williams, who, in favoring strong measures against the Cheyennes and Sioux, concurred, "I'm not sure that good

---

1. DiMarco, *War Horse*, 271; Larry Sklenar, *To Hell with Honor: Custer and the Little Bighorn* (Norman: University of Oklahoma Press, 2000), 5.

2. Sawicki, *Cavalry Regiments*, 164, 166, 169, 171.

3. William T. Sherman to Ulysses S. Grant, 6 November 1865, as cited in Wooster, *American Military Frontiers*, 188.

4. William T. H. Brooks to unknown, 29 October 1854, as cited in Wooster, *American Military Frontiers*, 104.

FIGURE 4.1. *The Hancock Expedition at Fort Harker*, 1867, with the 7th Cavalry Band on the left. Photograph by Alexander Gardner. *Courtesy of the Kansas State Historical Society.*

policy would not decide they should receive a sound thrashing first, & peace afterwards. The Indians of the Plains are all alike, in, that, they have to be flogged into decency."[5]

With these sentiments toward continued "manifest destiny"[6] in moving

5. Captain Thomas Williams to Mary Williams, July 11, 1858, as cited in Skelton, *American Profession of Arms*, 319.

6. Coined by newspaper editor John O'Sullivan in the July–August 1845 issue of the *United States Magazine and Democratic Review* to describe the mindset of a divine sanction for the continental and subsequent international expansion of the United States, over the years the term "manifest destiny" has taken on tones of emigration, expansionism, imperialism, and Christian mission work and conversion—as well as the moral obligation toward these efforts. See James Bradley, *The Imperial Cruise: A Secret History of Empire and War* (New York: Little, Brown, 2009), especially chap. 2, "Civilization Follows the Sun," 11–60. See also Reginald Horsman, *Race and Manifest Destiny: The Origins of American Racial Anglo-Saxonism* (Cambridge, Mass.: Harvard University Press, 1981).

Anglo-Saxon civilization westward, the four new regiments began their work, and, like those of the 1st through 6th, were authorized to include mounted bands for ceremonial and motivation work, and two field trumpeters for each company for moving and directing troops using a variety of alarm, service, drill and field, and miscellaneous calls in maneuvers.[7] So-called field trumpets in the United States by the end of the nineteenth century were related more to the bugle than to the historical field trumpet (see page 42), and in a letter dated 23 April 1867 to his wife, Jennie, from a camp near Fort Hays, Kansas, while on the Hancock Expedition (figure 4.1), 7th Cavalry troop commander Captain Albert Barnitz reveals that the terms were used interchangeably even at this early date, and that some people knew the difference. Moreover, he distinguishes between the field trumpeters and the members of the band in the same letter: "Guard mounting is just taking place. The music (of our eight buglers, or 'trumpeters' rather) is really very fine. They are improving daily. The *Band*, as I have written you, has been sent back to Fort Riley for instruction and practice—they will join us by the time the officers' wives come on."[8]

While records do not indicate how widespread European-style trumpeter corps were in the U.S. Army, this one was probably assembled simply as a substitute ensemble in the band's absence, performing for the daily guard mount as well as for whatever other engagements required their services. Performances by U.S. Army bands of the era continued to revolve around military ceremonies, parades and reviews, troop departures for individual missions, and formal and informal concerts and dances, and, like the 7th Cavalry trumpet ensemble, were well received by regimental members and the public alike.[9] Forrestine Hooker, daughter of Lieutenant Charles Cooper, voices what was probably a common sentiment when she states that the 10th Cavalry Band "entertained the soldiers, officers and their families, or visitors on special occasions, breaking the monotony of a lonely, isolated post."[10]

---

7. "An Act to Authorize the Employment of Volunteers to aid in Enforcing Laws and Protecting Public Property," Section 2, 22 July 1861, cited in *History of U.S. Army Bands*, 19.

8. Robert Utley, ed., *Life in Custer's Cavalry: Diaries and Letters of Albert and Jennie Barnitz, 1867–1868* (New Haven, Conn.: Yale University Press, 1977), 39. Departing from Fort Riley, the "Hancock Expedition to the Plains" was the brainchild of commander of the Department of the Missouri, General Winfield S. Hancock, as an expedition force of approximately two thousand men intended to "overawe" or defeat any hostile Indians. The main outcome of the expedition appears to have been to provoke full-scale war during the summer of 1867.

9. William H. Leckie, *The Buffalo Soldiers: A Narrative of the Negro Cavalry in the West* (Norman: University of Oklahoma Press, 1967), 17.

10. Forrestine C. Hooker, *Child of the Fighting Tenth: On the Frontier with the Buffalo Soldiers*, ed. Steve Wilson (New York: Oxford University Press, 2003), 12.

Many soldiers, however, were not only stationed at lonely posts but were often stationed at lonely posts in isolated areas without bands. Because regiments were typically spread over several states with the band and headquarters company often being distanced from most of the regiment, soldiers regarded themselves as fortunate when they were serving near their band, which continued to be in varied assignments across the country.[11] An example of band and headquarter company stations for U.S. Cavalry units in January 1867 was Fort Vancouver, Washington Territory, for the 1st Cavalry; Fort McPherson, Nebraska, for the 2nd; Fort Marcy, New Mexico, for the 3rd; Fort Mason, Texas, for the 4th; Sedgwick Barracks, Washington, D.C., for the 5th; Austin, Texas, for the 6th; Fort Riley, Kansas, for the 7th; Benicia Barracks, California, for the 8th; New Orleans, Louisiana, for the 9th; and Fort Leavenworth, Kansas, for the 10th.[12]

These latter two regiments—the 9th and 10th—hold unique places in history as their enlisted ranks were comprised exclusively of black soldiers raised along with the 24th and 25th Infantry Regiments in recognition of the 180,000 black soldiers who served during the Civil War.[13] Of the 10th Cavalry, E. L. N. Glass indicates that

---

11. Noting this situation in a House of Representatives hearing in 1872, Major William R. Price of the 8th Cavalry suggested that by periodically consolidating and more thoughtfully rotating regimental units, regimental pride would be built and "officers and men [would] have an opportunity of seeing their regimental colors and of hearing their regimental band." William R. Price, Major Eighth U.S. Cavalry, Brevet Colonel, U.S. Army, H.R. Rep. No. 74, 42nd Congress, 3rd sess., serial 1576, 135.

12. U.S. Army, Return of the 1st Regiment of Cavalry, Army of the United States, for the month of January 1867, Lt. Col. W[ashington] L[afayette] Elliott, Commanding, Fort Vancouver, Wash. Territory; U.S. Army, Return of the 2nd Regiment of Cavalry, Army of the United States, for the month of January 1867, Major G[eorge] W. Howland, Commanding, Fort McPherson, Neb.; U.S. Army, Return of the 3rd Regiment of Cavalry, Army of the United States, for the month of January 1867, Major W. B. Lane, Commanding, Fort Marcy, N.Mex.; U.S. Army, Return of the 4th Regiment of Cavalry, Army of the United States, for the month of January 1867, Major John P. Hatch, Commanding, Fort Mason, Tex.; U.S. Army, Return of the 5th Regiment of Cavalry, Army of the United States, for the month of January 1867, Col. W[illiam] H[emsley] Emory, Commanding, Sedgwick Barracks, Washington, D.C.; U.S. Army, Return of the 6th Regiment of Cavalry, Army of the United States, for the month of January 1867, Col. James Oakes, Commanding, Austin, Tex.; U.S. Army, Return of the 7th Regiment of Cavalry, Army of the United States, for the month of January 1867, Col. A[ndrew] J. Smith, Commanding, Fort Riley, Kans.; U.S. Army, Return of the 8th Regiment of Cavalry, Army of the United States, for the month of January 1867, Col. J[ohn] I[rvin] Gregg, Commanding, Benicia Barracks, Calif.; U.S. Army, Return of the 9th Regiment of Cavalry, Army of the United States, for the month of January 1867, Major J[ames] F. Wade, New Orleans, La.; and U.S. Army, Return of the 10th Regiment of Cavalry, Army of the United States, for the month of January 1867, Col. Benjamin Grierson, Fort Leavenworth, Kans., all in *Returns from Regular Army Cavalry Regiments, 1833–1916*, NARA, RG 391, Microfilm Publication M744.

13. Wooster, *American Military Frontiers*, 189. Dobak and Phillips indicate that more than 2,000 of these 180,000 U.S. Colored Troops joined the new black regiments. William A. Dobak and Thomas D. Phillips, *The Black Regulars, 1866–1898* (Norman: University of Oklahoma Press, 2001), 50.

very few of the recruits assigned to the regiment could read or write, many of them being plantation hands [slaves] from the South. Seldom could one be found capable of clerical duty, so that the officers were obliged to do most of their paper work. Quite a number of the recruits had served in the colored regiments during the Civil War, and these furnished the non-commissioned officers. On the whole the men were obedient, amenable to discipline and anxious to learn, besides being proud of their uniform. Even the band was organized, not from musicians, but by selecting men who could read and write and teaching them music. General Grierson, who was himself an accomplished musician, gave them his personal attention and soon succeeded in having a competent leader enlisted and assigned to the regiment.[14]

William H. Leckie adds to the picture by stating that the 10th Cavalry Band of the 1860s was Grierson's pride and joy, and echoes Hooker's words indicating that the band's music "did much to soften the rough work and loneliness at Fort Sill [Oklahoma]."[15] Moreover, Hooker recalls that, at the onset of a two-month scouting mission in July 1877 to look "for signs of wandering Indians," the regimental band led Troop A in their departure from Fort Concho, Texas: "It was customary for the band to escort a departing troop out of the garrison. Our band was our pride. At its head rode George Brenner, the band leader, on his black horse. Brenner was a white man and a fine musician. Back of him, on milk white horses, followed the rest of the band—all of them colored soldiers."[16]

Charles Kenner cites several contemporary accounts that mention the fine musicianship of bandsmen in the black regiments, suggesting that, "in the eyes of whites, their most pronounced trait was their affinity for music."[17] Kenner, probably accurately, suggests that, while black soldiers may have had a love for music, it is likely that observers were prone to exaggerate. Nonetheless, he cites several contemporary accounts describing music—including instances where it could be heard at "every permissible hour" at Fort Concho, Texas, performed by individuals with "most extraordinary talent."[18] Moreover, as playing music was one of the few occupations open to black men that required abilities beyond physical strength, enough musicians typically enlisted to supply the regiments with bandsmen. When

---

14. Major E. L. N. Glass, *History of the 10th Cavalry* (Tucson, Ariz.: Acme Printing, 1921), 17–18.

15. Leckie, *Buffalo Soldiers*, 50.

16. Hooker, *Child of the Fighting Tenth*, 129.

17. Charles L. Kenner, *Buffalo Soldiers and Officers of the Ninth Cavalry, 1867–1898: Black and White Together* (Norman: University of Oklahoma Press, 2014), 16.

18. Ibid., 17.

shortages did occur, officers took initiatives to find replacements to ensure that bands were staffed as fully as possible.[19] Many chief musicians (bandmasters) of the time were formally trained and European born, with one of their duties being to instruct the band's sixteen musicians. It would not be until after the turn of the century when black regiments were led by black bandmasters.[20]

The new "white" regiments, those of the 7th and 8th Cavalries, also boasted mounted bands but operated considerably differently from one another. While both provided music for soldiers in camp playing for retreat and guard mount, as well as for ceremonies, parades, and concerts, which were often attended by civilians, the 8th Cavalry Band operated more conventionally and kept its instruments packed in wagons during over-the-road marches.[21] Members of the 7th Cavalry Band however, kept their instruments with them—playing on expeditions and even in battle at the orders of the regiment's colorful second in command (field commander), Lieutenant Colonel George Custer.[22] Consequently, this group of soldier-musicians was one of the most historically documented bands of the era—and therefore figures heavily in this chapter.[23]

---

19. Dobak and Phillips, *Black Regulars*, 52, 158.

20. Peter M. Lefferts, "U.S. Army Black Regimental Bands and the Appointments of Their First Black Bandmasters," *Black Music Research Journal* 33, no. 1 (2013). U.S. War Department, General Orders. 1908, General Orders, No. 192, issued November 18, 1908: Transfer of colored regiments' white bandmasters to white regiments and assignment of colored bandmasters to colored regiments. CIS index to presidential executive orders and proclamations. Washington, D.C.: Congressional Information Service, 1987. Part I, 3:1436 (1908–54–27).

21. William G. Wilkinson "The Border-to-Border March of the Eighth Cavalry, 1888," *Winners of the West*, October 1938, reprinted in Jerome A. Greene, *Indian War Veterans: Memories of Army Life and Campaigns in the West, 1864–1898* (New York: Savas Beatie, 2006), 68.

22. Custer's various military ranks have generated confusion over the years, especially brevet ranks, which, rather than given to fill in for fallen officers as commonly been thought, were awarded for heroism of a specific nature as "gallant and meritorious service" in a specified battle or campaign. Just before Gettysburg in 1863, Custer was a Captain in the 5th Cavalry in the Regular Army (constituted 3 March 1855 as the 2nd Cavalry; redesignated 3 August 1861 as the 5th Cavalry) and was promoted to the rank of brigadier general of Volunteers—and took command of the Michigan Brigade at Gettysburg. Subsequently, he served in the Volunteer Army rising by 1865 as major general of Volunteers while he retained his rank of captain in the Regular Army. After the conclusion of the war, he was mustered out in 1866 and Sheridan used his influence to get Custer a brevet major general in the Regular Army—as well as the grade of lieutenant colonel of the 7th Cavalry, one of the new regiments. Signing his name "Lieutenant Colonel 7th Cavalry, Brevet Major General USA," and being referred to as "General Custer," he and most other officers with brevet grades were typically addressed by their brevet grade—despite abolition by the War Department. Robert Utley adds, "Nor is it true that brevets were purely honorary. A brevet officer in the Regular Army could be assigned to duty in his brevet grade by order of the President. This is how Lt. Col. George Crook came to command the Department of Arizona as a Major General." Utley, Georgetown, Tex., e-mail message to author, 3 January 2014. The 7th consisted of twelve troops of cavalry, not all stationed at Ft. Riley. In fact, only troops A, D, H, and M remained at Ft. Riley, with the other troops being stationed at Ft. Lyon and Ft. Morgan, Colorado—and Ft. Hays, Ft. Harker, Ft. Wallace, and Ft. Dodge, Kansas.

23. Bruce P. Gleason, "The Mounted Band and Field Musicians of the U.S. 7th Cavalry during the Time of the Plains Indian Wars," *Historic Brass Society Journal* 21 (2009): 69–92.

While the formation of the 7th Cavalry Band is typically attributed to Custer, it was probably a product of several individuals, including Major Alfred Gibbs, one of the officers of the regiment, who wrote to Captain Myles Keogh, commander of Fort Wallace, Kansas, directing him to send all soldiers with brass band experience to Fort Riley for regimental band duty. This letter was probably a result of another one of 12 April 1867 from Colonel A. J. Smith, the commander of the regiment, ordering Custer to designate fifteen soldiers as members of the band and to proceed to Fort Riley with Major Gibbs.[24] Further, Smith specified that, to ensure that the band be "organized and made efficient as rapidly as possible, the members of the same, on their arrival at Fort Riley, Ks., will not be subject to the ordinary details for garrison duty."[25]

This directive undoubtedly enabled the 7th Cavalry Band to train and rehearse unencumbered and to rise to a place of distinction as a prominent musical organization. However, as we shall soon see, lack of garrison duty did not preclude 7th Cavalry bandsmen from seeing battle firsthand. Insisting that the band of sixteen musicians be mounted on gray horses (stemming from the European tradition of trumpeters riding "greys"), Custer selected Italian-born and conservatory-trained Felix Vinatieri to be the chief musician. In addition to being a Civil War veteran musician, Vinatieri was a graduate of Naples's Conservatorio di Musica San Pietro a Majella. While this background would have given him an advantage over many U.S. military bandmasters of the time (the major influx of Italian immigration, and consequently Italian band music, had not yet occurred by this point), his situation was not unheard of—especially in British military bands—where more than one highly trained bandmaster and musician landed a job away from his home country. As well, the first five bandmasters of the 9th Cavalry Band were German or Irish born:

> William Boerner (1834–1919), German, serving 1867–72
> Charles Spiegel (1824–1905), German, serving 1872–86
> Gustav Oechsle (1839–1913), German, serving 1886
> James Watters (1839–1913), Irish, serving 1886–92
> Carl S. Gung'l (1850–1937), German, serving 1892–1907[26]

24. This suggests fifteen musicians in addition to the chief musician. Other documentation as indicated throughout this study, however, suggests seventeen musicians total.

25. Alfred Gibbs to Myles Keogh, 28 April 1867, as cited in Thomas C. Railsback and John P. Langellier, *The Drums Would Roll: A Pictorial History of U.S. Army Bands on the American Frontier, 1866–1900* (Poole, UK: Arms and Armour Press, 1987), 17; John M. Carroll, "The Seventh Cavalry's Band," *Little Big Horn Associates' Research Review* 9 (Spring 1975): 16–18.

26. Lefferts, "U.S. Army Black Regimental Bands," 171.

Along with Vinatieri, thirteen of the sixteen musicians in the 7th Cavalry Band of 1876 were foreign born with most of them listing "musician" as their previous occupation on their enlistment papers. This makeup is not surprising since foreign-born soldiers comprised over half the Regular Army enlisted ranks throughout much of the nineteenth century.[27] Moreover, foreign-born musicians were common in nineteenth-century professional bands and orchestras in the United States—so military music was simply just one more source of steady employment where scores of musicians found work across the country.

Concerning the music performed, as mentioned in chapter 1, cavalry units in Europe generally had set marches and other pieces that were permanent fixtures in their regimental repertoires. However, while U.S. Cavalry units had their individual regimental calls (played before other signals in battle to discern who the signal was for), regimental marches were unofficial and probably adapted by popular demand, as exemplified by *Garry Owen*, which, as Custer's favorite air, by default became the regimental march for the 7th Cavalry.

It was this march that became famous throughout the West and was heard not only in forts and camps but also wherever the 7th Cavalry Band traveled. Performances even extended so that the band played it while leading several battle charges, including the one on 27 November 1868 shortly before dawn at Chief Black Kettle's village in the Wichita Mountains on the Washita River in Indian Territory (near present-day Cheyenne, Oklahoma) against a war party of Cheyennes, Comanches, and Kiowas. S. L. A. Marshall, who later served in the 7th Cavalry with men who had known Custer, colorfully describes the event: "Reveille sounded for the Seventh Cavalry Regiment at 3:00 A.M. on November 23, the ungodliest of hours, an awakening that shouldn't have to happen to a dog and is absolutely forbidden in relatively sane households. . . . Loonier still, once the horse soldiers had downed their breakfast of corn-meal mush with corn syrup and hot coffee, the regiment stepped off in the dark to the tune of their regimental theme song, 'Garry Owen,' played by the regimental band."[28]

As a West Point student, Custer would have studied cavalry tactics, and, while he may have known the Saracen custom of musicians leading troops into battle (often on horseback) during the Crusades, it is difficult to know if he was

---

27. National Park Service, U.S. Department of the Interior, "Jefferson National Expansion Memorial," *Museum Gazette* (February 1996): 1.

28. Brig. Gen. S. L. A. Marshall, *Crimsoned Prairie: The Wars between the United States and the Plains Indians during the Winning of the West* (New York: Scribner's, 1972), 107.

now copying this idea or if he merely wanted to make an impact and statement. Whatever the case, this was indeed the effect. Marshall continues:

> Custer had a passion for the music. Getting with the band was no less imperative than getting up before the crack of dawn. The column moved out and with it went the bandsmen, not as musicians converted to fighters, but as a pack of tootlers.
>
> Bizarre as it now sounds, when exactly six days later the Seventh Regiment charged pell-mell and without warning, parley, or reconnaissance into an Indian village on the banks of the Washita River, the buglers sounded the charge and the band again played "Garry Owen."[29]

Most records of U.S. military bands performing in battle suggest that, rather than being a typical practice, individual occurrences were the result of the band being in the wrong place at the wrong time.[30] However, as strange as the practice of a cavalry band playing under fire may seem, as he had done during the Civil War, Custer incorporated the band-leading-the-battle practice with the 7th Cavalry during the Indian Wars and recalled the aforementioned events of the battle at the Washita River, but with a noticeably different take from Marshall's:

> Immediately in rear of my horse came the band, all mounted and each with his instrument in readiness to begin playing the moment their leader, who rode at their head and who kept his cornet to his lips, should receive the signal. I had previously told him to play Garry Owen as the opening piece. . . . I was about to turn in my saddle and direct the signal for attack to be given, still anxious as to where the other detachments were, when a single rifle shot rang sharp and clear on the far side of the village from where we were. Quickly turning to the band leader, I directed him to give us Garry Owen. At once the rollicking notes of that familiar marching and fighting air sounded through the valley and in a moment were reechoed back from the opposite sides by the loud and continued cheers of the men of the other detachments, who, true to their orders, were there and in readiness to pounce upon the Indians the moment the attack began.[31]

---

29. Ibid., 107.

30. Francis A. Lord and Arthur Wise, *Bands and Drummer Boys of the Civil War* (New York: Thomas Yoseloff, 1966), 184–204.

31. George A. Custer, *My Life on the Plains*, ed. Milo Milton Quaife (New York: Citadel Press, 1962), 334–35.

Apparently, however, after only a few notes the valves on the instruments froze, thereby ending the band's role that day.[32] Fred Dustin's assessment of the situation echoes the thoughts of many a Custer critic: "When the weather, the situation, and the fact that the use of a brass instrument for playing at such a time could only be torture to the player, the vainglory of the thing is no less apparent than its lack of sensibility."[33] Such was the practice of George Custer. While being a knowledgeable battle tactician, it appears that an appearance of gallantry and pomp were sometimes substituted for practicality and common sense.

While by the 1870s infantry bands of Britain, the European Continent, and the United States were broadening their instrumentation to include woodwinds, cavalry bands typically held to all-brass instrumentation, especially when mounted, which probably was similar to that as described in chapter 3. However, instrumentation would have varied by band, bandmaster, available musicians, and fluctuating funds. While memoirs and records of the era list the number of musicians of the 7th Cavalry Band at sixteen, a photograph of the band taken in 1874 shows twenty-eight bandsmen, including three clarinet players (see figure 4.2).

James R. Gay confirms that the official instrumentation of the bands of the 2nd Cavalry (1876) and the 6th Cavalry (1892) of the same and later periods included E♭ cornet, B♭ cornet, alto horn, trombone, baritone, E♭ tuba, snare drum, and bass drum in the brass band tradition of the Civil War. However, in his study on Vinatieri, he cites a 1982 interview with Joe Gullion, who was a member of the 4th Cavalry Band stationed at Fort Meade, South Dakota, after World War I (1925):[34] "Many cavalry musicians were proficient on several instruments and . . . the choice of instruments (i.e., slide or valve trombone, clarinet, or cornet) for a mounted performance depended more 'upon the temperament of the horse and the need to handle the reins' than the requirements of the composer."[35]

---

32. Louise Barnett, *Touched by Fire: The Life, Death and Mythic Afterlife of George Armstrong Custer* (New York: Henry Holt, 1996), 153, 448. For centuries, field musicians with their natural trumpets had not had to worry about instruments freezing, but not so for band musicians of the nineteenth century since the advent of the valve, ca. 1815. Various approaches to counter temperatures have been used over the years, including coating the pistons with grain or ethyl alcohol.

33. Fred Dustin, *The Custer Tragedy: Events Leading up to and Following the Little Big Horn Campaign of 1876* (Ann Arbor, Mich.: Edwards Brothers, 1939), 26n5.

34. "The History of the 4th U.S. Cavalry Regiment," Official Homepage of Fort Huachuca, Arizona, http://huachuca-www.army.mil/pages/btroop/history.html.

35. Joe Gullion, former musician in the U.S. Fourth Cavalry, Rapid City, S.Dak., interview by James R. Gay, March 1982, as cited in James R. Gay, "The Wind Music of Felix Vinatieri, Dakota Territory Bandmaster" (DA diss., University of Northern Colorado, 1982), 39.

FIGURE 4.2. 7th Cavalry Band, Fort Abraham Lincoln, Dakota Territory, 1874. Chief Musician Felix Villiet Vinatieri is the cornetist seated in the middle of the front row wearing darker-colored trousers. *Courtesy of the Dakota Territorial Museum, Yankton, South Dakota.*

Proficiency on several instruments was not unusual for military bands of the period, in Europe as well as the United States. From the band's inception in 1762 to the present day, musicians of the Royal Artillery Band of Woolwich, England, have been "double-handed," with expertise on a stringed instrument in addition to woodwind or brass.[36] Members of other British staff bands have seen similar service, and the U.S. Marine Band (the President's Own) was comprised likewise from around 1899 to 1955.[37] If we are to believe that musicians of the 7th Cavalry Band played the music in the Vinatieri Archives in the National Music Museum at the University of South Dakota, which we should, brass musicians were probably playing woodwind and stringed instruments as well. This archive holds 234 pieces of music, most of which were either composed or arranged by Vinatieri in various combinations for brass, woodwind, strings, and percussion, as well

36. Gleason, "History of the Royal Artillery Mounted Band," 18, 49, 59, 67; Henry George Farmer, *Memoirs of the Royal Artillery Band* (London: Boosey, 1904), 38, 73, 116, 122, 160; "The Royal Artillery Band," British Army website, http://www.army.mod.uk/music/23942.aspx.

37. Master Gunnery Sergeant D. Michael Ressler, Chief Historian, U.S. Marine Band, e-mail message to author, 3 April 2009.

as solo piano. It includes marches, polkas, quicksteps, schottisches, mazurkas, waltzes, galops, polonaises, quadrilles, overtures, opera selections, national anthems, and excerpts from several of America's earliest comic operas.[38] As Vinatieri's ensemble was a "full-service" band, playing for concerts, dances, and other social functions in addition to mounted and other military duties would have been part of the regular performance schedule. It is therefore not surprising that a military band on the plains would have been able to exhibit a "softer" side, with arrangements that included woodwinds and strings—especially since Vinatieri was proficient on both violin and cornet.[39] It is worth noting that since many of the pieces are listed simply as "instrumental ensemble," it is difficult to determine which pieces were played on horseback. Also, many of the dates of composition are unknown and are simply listed as 1891/12/05—the date of Vinatieri's death. As the archives are Vinatieri's, and not an official library of the 7th Cavalry Band, other arrangements may have stayed with the band and, like that of other libraries, disappeared over the years.[40]

TRAINING

By the time of the Indian Wars, there was no central training point for U.S. military musicians. As with field musicians during the Civil War, on-the-job training of field musicians during the 1870s seems to have been common. Consequently, it was not unusual for Phillip Schreiber of the 18th U.S. Infantry to add bugle playing to his résumé "as they [Company H] were in need of a combination bugler and barber."[41] Preservice training was also known—as Kenneth Hammer indicates that five of the twenty-two field trumpeters of the 7th Cavalry in 1876 listed "musician" or "trumpeter" as "previous occupation."[42] Moreover, conservatory-trained Chief Musician Vinatieri would have

---

38. "Vinatieri Archive," National Music Museum website, http://orgs.usd.edu/nmm/vinatieri.html; Margaret Downie Banks, Curator of Music Instruments, National Music Museum, Vermillion, S.Dak., e-mail message to author, 9 March 2009.

39. Gay, "Wind Music of Felix Vinatieri," 39.

40. CW4 Aaron Graff, commander of the 1st Cavalry Division Band (successor to the 7th Cavalry Band), Fort Hood, Okla., indicates that no printed music of this period resides in the division's library. CW4 Aaron Graff, e-mail message to author, 12 March 2009.

41. Phillip Schreiber, "Twelve Years in the Eighteenth Infantry," *Winners of the West* (30 August 1937), reprinted in Greene, *Indian War Veterans*, 42.

42. Hammer, *Biographies of the 7th Cavalry*, 12, 49, 62, 78, 94, 110, 124, 141, 158, 174, 190, 208, 225. This information means little, however, since many records for individual soldiers do not list anything for previous occupation. Moreover, these records do not report how the person was trained initially.

been responsible, along with senior bandsmen—ten of whom listed "musician" as previous occupation upon enlisting[43]—for training band members in specific ceremony, parade, and concert functions, as well as for rehearsals and individual practice. And, as with all horse-mounted musicians, learning to ride while playing was a major consideration. As tricky as the concept might be, however, 7th Cavalry musicians, along with their horses, seemed to have figured out the process of performing on horseback, as had countless soldier-musicians before them. As mentioned previously, these skills carried musicians and horses through battle and ceremony and also ensured that they would not be left behind on what would be recorded as one of the most unusual musical ventures of the nineteenth century.

THE 1874 BLACK HILLS EXPEDITION

One of the occurrences where 7th Cavalry Band members received plenty of experience in living in the saddle was during the 1874 Black Hills Expedition, in which the band accompanied ten companies of the 7th Cavalry. Under the command of Lieutenant Colonel (General)[44] George Custer, this operation also included one company each of the 20th and 17th Infantries, as well as an engineer detachment and fire support battery of three Gatling guns and one three-inch cannon on an exploratory expedition into the Black Hills of South Dakota. This amalgamation, documented in several contemporary accounts, comprised of a force of over one thousand men, including dozens of Indian scouts, guides, interpreters, and teamsters, as well as 110 wagons and hundreds of horses, mules, and cattle,[45] sent by the U.S. government to survey the area for prospective fort sites, railway beds, and invasion routes against Indian free bands, and (unofficially) to confirm the rumors of gold in the Black Hills.[46] Lieutenant James Calhoun, Custer's brother-in-law (married to the general's younger sister, Margaret ["Maggie"]), who was attached to Headquarters Company, vividly describes the column as it left Fort Abraham Lincoln (near present-day

---

43. Hammer, *Biographies of the 7th Cavalry*, 12–16.

44. See note 22, page 66.

45. James Calhoun, *With Custer in '74: James Calhoun's Diary of the Black Hills Expedition*, ed. Lawrence A. Frost (Provo, Utah: Brigham Young University Press, 1979), 16.

46. As the 1868 Treaty of Fort Laramie guaranteed the Lakota ownership of the Black Hills, along with further land and hunting rights in South Dakota, Wyoming and Montana, the Black Hills Expedition and ensuing gold rush both violated the treaty.

Bismarck, North Dakota) on 2 July 1874: "Some of the ladies of the garrison came out to give us a parting cheer. Col. Thompson also came to bid adieu. As we commenced our march westward the Band of the 7th Cavalry played the popular air 'the girl I left behind me,' music appropriate to the occasion."[47]

George Grinnell, who served as a geologist (naturalist) on the expedition wrote, "At Fort Lincoln the expedition was detained about thirty days and then started for the Black Hills. As it left the fort a band of sixteen men mounted on white horses preceded it, playing Garry Owen, Custer's favorite air." He summed up the sight with an understatement of what must have been on most of the soldiers' minds: "To start into a supposedly hostile Indian country accompanied by a brass band was a novel experience to some of those who rode with this expedition."[48]

With the band playing regularly several times daily, members of the expedition were treated to what must have been a considerable repertoire. Testifying to the frequency of performances, Captain Luther North, who commanded the expedition's "Pawnee Scout Battalion," a U.S. Army company-sized element comprised of one hundred Pawnee Indians, recollected: "We left the fort with the band of sixteen men mounted on white horses playing Garry Owen, Custer's favorite tune. This was the first and last expedition that I was ever on in an Indian country that had a band along. Every morning upon leaving camp the band would play for two or three miles, and nearly every evening after supper the general would have them come over in front of his tent and play for an hour or so."[49]

Further accounts of the band's participation in the expedition appear in Herbert Krause and Gary D. Olson's *Prelude to Glory*, the story of the adventure as told by five newspaper correspondents who accompanied the mission. As the expedition passed through the area that Custer named Floral Valley, Samuel J. Barrows of the *New York Tribune* reported that, in addition to folk tunes and marches, the mounted band played light classics and popular music, undoubtedly arranged by Vinatieri: "As we ascended the valley, our band which favors us every morning with a variety of selections played 'How so fair' and 'The

---

47. Calhoun, *With Custer in '74*, 21. Also mentioned by Calhoun is the H Company Glee Club serenading a champagne supper hosted by Major Joseph Tilford, the ranking officer in camp, under a large tarpaulin stretched under the pine trees, when Custer led a detachment toward Harney's Peak (59).

48. George Bird Grinnell, *Two Great Scouts and Their Pawnee Battalion: The Experiences of Frank J. North and Luther H. North* (1928; repr., Lincoln: University of Nebraska Press, 1973), 240.

49. Luther North, *Man of the Plains: Recollections of Luther North, 1856–1882*, ed. Donald F. Danker (Lincoln: University of Nebraska Press, 1961), 184.

Mocking Bird.' We forgot the mocking bird in listening to the mocking hills which played an echo fuge [sic] with the band. The effect was beautiful indeed. Never before had the echoes sung to Hoffmann or Flotow, but they never missed a note in their response."[50]

Writing about the expedition reaching Hart River Crossing, about twelve miles from Fort Lincoln, at noon on 30 August 1874, Barrows indicates that the march was governed by bugle calls, and that the field and band musicians were separate entities even though they rode together:

> A halt for an hour and a half was ordered. A lunch was taken, and for the last time the familiar "To horse" and the "Advance" were sounded and we moved on the fort. A new order of march was adopted. The train was turned over to the tender mercies of the infantry. The cavalry were formed into a single column of fours, preceded by the company of scouts. Behind the scouts rode the band and the buglers. Officers' call sounded, and there was a rush of shoulderstraps to the front.[51]

It is difficult to know what was going through Custer's mind when he decided that a large expedition going into a hostile environment should include a mounted band, but as the band had previously been a part of battle proceedings as well as the Hancock Expedition of 1867, taking one on an excursion like this was not much of a stretch. As described by these chroniclers, the entire entourage must have been of unusual sight and sound, and, while the expedition had been favored with a broad repertoire of music, at least by the conclusion of the expedition, *Garry Owen* had attained some sort of sacred place within the regiment.

BATTLE OF THE LITTLE BIG HORN

The era of westward expansion hit several bumps along the way, the most famous undoubtedly being the Battle of the Little Big Horn—an effort of the Yellowstone Expedition, which set out in April and May 1876 from Fort Ellis, Montana Territory, and Fort Abraham Lincoln, Dakota Territory, in an effort

---

50. Samuel J. Barrows, *New York Tribune*, 24 August 1874, 204, as cited in Herbert Krause and Gary D. Olson, *Prelude to Glory: A Newspaper Accounting of Custer's 1874 Expedition to the Black Hills* (Sioux Falls, South Dakota: Brevet Press, 1974), 210.

51. Ibid., 226.

to move Cheyenne and Sioux tribes, which had missed deadlines in moving, to reservations.[52] Comprised of elements of the 2nd and 7th Cavalry Regiments and of the 6th, 7th, 17th, and 20th Infantry Regiments, the expedition was commanded by Brigadier General Alfred Terry, commander of the Department of Dakota. While the assumption by U.S. Army officials was that they would have a surefire win, the battle did not go as planned—due to a number of circumstances and developments, not the least of which was that they were unaware of the number of Indian warriors fighting under the command of Sitting Bull.[53]

While the battle marks a significant place in U.S. political and American Indian history, it was also a significant event in military music history. Although Custer had often taken his bands into the thick of battle during the Civil War and the Indian Wars, Brigadier General Alfred Terry ordered that they stay back. As private James Wilber recalls, "Custer wanted to take the band beyond Powder River, but Terry would not consent to it,"—fortunately for Vinatieri and the band members—as this would be Custer's last battle.[54] Sergeant Charles Windolph, who fought in the Battle of the Little Big Horn as the first sergeant of Captain Frederick Benteen's battalion (companies D, H, and K), recalled in 1946:

> I remember one thing that happened as we were leaving the Tongue [River]. Our Seventh Cavalry band was mounted on white horses, and as we were short of good mounts the bandsmen were left behind, while the horses were taken over as remounts to replace horses that had been worn down. While the column was pulling out, the dismounted band stood on a little knoll near the big river and played "Garry Owen" as the regiment rode by. It was something you'd never forget.[55]

The rest is history. On a hot June Sunday in 1876 about 2,100 warriors (Cheyennes, Arapahos, Oglalas, Hunkpapas, Sans Arcs, Miniconjous, and Blackfoot

52. The U.S. Board of Geographic Names decrees the spellings "Bighorn" and "Little Bighorn" Rivers. However, "Little Big Horn" is the historic spelling and is the spelling used during Custer's time, as well as in most of the present cited sources, and is therefore what I use throughout this chapter—except when I refer to the current Little Bighorn Battlefield National Monument, Crow Agency, Montana, below in note 60.

53. For a detailed, yet clear chronicle of the battle and events and circumstances leading to the battle, see Robert Utley, *Custer Battlefield, National Monument, Montana*, Historical Handbook Series No. 1 (Washington, D.C.: National Park Service, 1969).

54. Walter Mason Camp interview with James Wilber, undated, reprinted in Kenneth Hammer, *Custer in '76* (Salt Lake City: Brigham Young University Press, 1976), 149.

55. Windolph, *I Fought with Custer*, 66.

Sioux) wiped out five companies of cavalry on the treeless Montana ridge above the Little Big Horn River. To quote Robert Utley, in less than an hour "the most spectacular triumph of the American Indian in his four-century struggle against the relentlessly advancing European civilization" had resulted in Custer's Last Stand.[56]

Mounted field trumpeters, who were part of the ancient battlefield tradition that would still be around for more than a half century afterward, continued to be separate from the bands' trumpeters, as evidenced by the list of the battle's survivors, which indicates that only ten of the 7th Cavalry's twenty-two field trumpeters survived.[57] The band musicians whose lives were spared, however, because of the decision to use their horses as remounts were pressed into service as corpsmen to help transport the wounded of Major Marcus Reno's command fifteen miles to where Captain Grant Marsh had pushed the steamer *Far West* up the previously un-navigated Big Horn River. They also provided nursing services with what few supplies were available.[58] These duties were not unlike those of other military musicians over the centuries who have found their secondary missions of guard duty and patrol and caring for the war-wounded to be of sobering importance.

Following Custer's demise, Vinatieri was discharged in December 1876 after spending three years with the 7th Cavalry, returning to Yankton, South Dakota, where he resumed teaching music, performing, composing, and traveling with circus bands to support his wife, three daughters, and five sons.[59] Several of the sixteen musicians of the 7th Cavalry Band were discharged that same year, including Jacob Huff, who was born in Bavaria and served with the 7th Cavalry Band from 1875 to 1876; Frank Lombard, Naples, Italy (1871–76); Bernard O'Neill, Kelfurborg, Ireland (1871–76); and George Rudolph Minterheim, Bavaria (1871–76). Others completing their military music careers over the next

---

56. Robert Utley uses this and similar phrases in reference to the Battle of the Little Big Horn in several of his publications. Robert Utley, Georgetown, Tex., e-mail message to author, 25 March 2004; Utley, *Custer Battlefield*, 3.

57. Hammer, *Biographies of the 7th Cavalry*, 12, 49, 62, 78, 94, 110, 124, 141, 158, 174, 190, 208, 225.

58. Gay, "Wind Music of Felix Vinatieri," 28.

59. Ibid., 29. Vinatieri composed numerous concert, march, and dance pieces, several of which have been recorded by Steve Charpié and the New Custer Brass Band, on *Custer's Last Band: The Original Music of Felix Vinatieri, Custer's Legendary Bandmaster* (America's Shrine to Music Museum, University of South Dakota, Vermillion, South Dak., 2001). Among Vinatieri's descendants is great-great-grandson Adam Vinatieri, who at the time of this writing is the place kicker for the Indianapolis Colts (formerly of the New England Patriots). See Brady, "Vinatieri Getting a Kick Out of it All," and "Link to 'Last Stand'" both in *USA Today* (7 November 2002). C. Paul Vinatieri, Rapid City, S.Dak., telephone interview by author, 10 November 2002.

several years were Otto Arndt, Bavaria, (1870–77); Edmond Burli, Klingnow, Switzerland (1871–77); Andrew Carter, Lincoln, England (1875–77); Joseph Kneubuhler, Lucerne, Switzerland (1872–77); Julius Jungesbluth, Brunswick, Germany (1876–78); Joseph Carroll, New York City (1875–80); Peter Eisenberger, Bavaria (1875–80); Julius Griesner, Neurode, Germany (1875–80); George Merritt, Stonington, Connecticut (1875–80); Benjamin Beck, Philadelphia (1876–81); Thomas Sherborne, Kingston, Hampshire, England (1873–87); and Conrad Baumbach, Berlin, Germany (1875–78).[60]

Although there were other mounted bands within the U.S. Cavalry during the plains Indian Wars, the band of the 7th Cavalry was undoubtedly the best documented because of George Custer's notoriety, as well as his use of the band in camp, expeditions, and battle. Moreover, the work of Chief Musician Felix Vinatieri brought the band to historical fame through his compositions and arrangements—strengthening the place of mounted bands within the U.S. military—setting the stage for the decades leading to the turn of the twentieth century when mounted bands, which would be basically concert bands on horseback, would be utilized across the country.

---

60. Hammer, *Biographies of the 7th Cavalry*, 12–16; John A. Doerner, chief historian, Little Bighorn Battlefield National Monument, Crow Agency, Mont., telephone interview by author, 25 March 2004.

CHAPTER 5

The 1870s to 1890s

IN ADDITION TO THAT OF THE 7TH CAVALRY, OTHER U.S. CAVALRY regiments in the 1870s were involved in the work of western expansion, with much of it being in the new expanded territories. One of the outcomes of the Treaty of Guadalupe Hidalgo of 1848 at the end of the Mexican-American War was that the United States inherited governance of the indigenous Indians in the Southwest. Perhaps not surprisingly, the country was inadequately prepared for dealing with the tribes militarily and diplomatically, resulting in relations with most of the tribes in the area taking a decidedly downhill turn. This situation, coupled with increased emigration and trade traffic over the Santa Fe Trail, created a need for a heightened military presence resulting in more forts being built in the Southwest, including Fort Union, New Mexico, in 1851. With the fort's tasks being to guard the Santa Fe Trail and to serve as the quartermaster's depot, serving as a storage facility and redistribution point for military supplies for the area, several regiments moved to Fort Union in the 1870s, including two companies and the band of the 9th Cavalry from Texas.[1]

Serving in the 9th Cavalry Band, like in other U.S. Army bands, was generally good duty in comparison with many other military roles, and, as was mentioned in the preceding chapter, was a good place for musicians to find work. Moreover, performances were well received by the public and fellow soldiers, as indicated by Monroe Billington, who writes of the 9th Cavalry Band's popularity at Fort

---

1. Military policy reflected popular belief of the time suggesting that black soldiers had a strong tolerance for heat. Thus black regiments were typically assigned to the hottest, and sometimes unhealthiest, parts of the country. In addition, efforts were made following the Civil War to keep black soldiers removed from white civilians—with funds for relocating regiments to be sparse. As Kevin Adams states, "Simply put, being black in the frontier army meant being consigned to the hottest, most isolated, most demanding posts." Kevin Adams, *Class and Race in the Frontier Army: Military Life in the West, 1870–1890* (Norman: University of Oklahoma Press, 2009), 173. See also Kenner, *Buffalo Soldiers*, 15, 85; and Dobak and Phillips, *Black Regulars*, 90–113.

Union as well as with the public in Santa Fe: "Being in the band had advantages over being a regular cavalryman: an enlisted man who could play a musical instrument enjoyed the diversions afforded by military ceremonies, Fourth of July celebrations, weddings, parties, grand openings, serenades, and political rallies. Some of these events even gave the musician an opportunity to make trips away from the post, providing an escape from some monotonous garrison life."[2] As many 9th Cavalry soldiers of this period, including band members, were ex-slaves, military service was often a welcome new life.

Diplomatic-ceremonial work was also part of the picture for all army bandsmen at the time, as illustrated by a performance of the 9th Cavalry Band for President Rutherford B. Hayes during his visit to Santa Fe in October 1880 as part of his Great Western tour. Arriving in Santa Fe as a passenger on the newly arrived Atchison, Topeka & Santa Fe Railway, the Hayes contingency was privy to a 9th Cavalry Band concert under the direction of Chief Musician Charles Spiegel at the Santa Fe Plaza pagoda. The band played "a potpourri of national melodies of different nations, arranged by Prof. Spiegel," including *Hail Columbia*, *What Is the German Fatherland*, the Russian national anthem, *La Marseillaise*, *America*, and *Yankee Doodle with Variations*. A *Santa Fe Weekly New Mexican* reporter of the time claimed that the performance was "made with taste, and rendered in a manner reflecting greatly to the credit of the Professor and all members of his band."[3]

As bands were often the main point of contact between the public and the military, musical performances helped with these military-community connections. Another newspaper account, this time in the *New Mexican*, records that in 1875, a concert by the 8th Cavalry Band from Fort Marcy was well received by the public and by the reviewer-reporter: " 'The Eighth U.S. Cavalry Band discoursed a finely cast programme last evening in the Plaza. . . . The execution was delicate and in excellent time and with fine harmony and expression; arresting the attention of the refined ear for music and holding him to the end

---

2. Monroe Lee Billington, *New Mexico's Buffalo Soldiers, 1866–1900* (Niwot: University Press of Colorado, 1991), 116–17.

3. *Santa Fe Weekly New Mexican*, 1 November 1880; James J. Garvey, "Rutherford B. Hayes: The Great Western Tour of 1880," unpublished manuscript (Chicago: Loyola University, 1966), 55–60. Charles Spiegel (1824–1905) is a good example of a European-born musician who found work as a white bandmaster of a black U.S. regimental band. A native of Berlin, Prussia, he served as a Civil War bandmaster of the Second Massachusetts Infantry beginning 25 May 1861 and was discharged 16 August 1862 when regimental bands of the volunteer forces were discharged. He served as the chief musician (bandmaster) with the 9th Cavalry Band from 1872 to 1886. Alonzo H. Quint, *The Record of the Second Massachusetts Infantry, 1861–65* (Boston: J. P. Walker, 1867), 18, 474, 513; Lefferts, "U.S. Army Black Regimental Bands," 171.

of the programme.' "[4] Similarly, William G. Wilkinson recalls that the 8th U.S.
Cavalry's march from Texas to Dakota Territory in 1888 drew a lot of attention
from people for miles around and that "the principal attraction . . . was the
band, as every night, weather permitting, the band played a concert [which]
was quite a treat to the people, as there were very few civilian bands in that
territory in those days."[5]

In the same vein, the 5th Cavalry Band was highlighted in the *Tucson Citizen*
(along with announcements for the organization of a "Young Men's Literary
Society" and J. S. Mansfeld advertising "the opening of a circulating library at
his Pioneers News Depot") when it played for a send-off hosted by the officers
of the 8th Infantry for those in the 5th Cavalry at the quarters of the post sut-
ler at Fort Lowell, Arizona, on 27 April 1875. The article mentions that the
performance was well received—observing the role that military music played
in cultivating the frontier:

> The building was tastefully decorated and . . . invitations had been issued to the
> various ladies and gentlemen and these, added to the society of the camp, made
> a "goodly company." All went merry as a marriage bell. The music by the Fifth
> Cavalry Band couldn't help but be good; the dances were happily arranged; the
> ladies were good-natured the men were more bearable than usual (several of them
> brought out new neckties, but space will not permit description of these), and in
> fact all who were present felt that it was good for them to be there. The supper
> and wines were excellent, and altogether when the party broke up, "just before
> the dawning," the officers who gave and the officers who received this compliment
> had a large addition made to the pleasant memories of their lives.[6]

As U.S. military organizational efforts developed over the years—especially
after the Civil War—bands and musicians found more consistent, stabilized,
and standardized duty within infantry and cavalry arenas. By 1873, further
delineation concerning regimental makeup was being prescribed—including
that of the chief musician, who would also serve as an instructor of music and a

---

4. William G. Huey, "Making Music: Brass Bands on the Northern Plains, 1860–1930," *North Dakota History* 54, no. 1 (1987): 3–13, citing the *New Mexican*, September 1875.

5. Wilkinson, "Border-to-Border March of the Eighth Cavalry," 68.

6. Dean Frank C. Lockwood and Capt. Donald W. Page, *Tucson—The Old Pueblo* (Phoenix: Manufacturing Stationers, 1930), 75, 81, citing *Tucson Citizen*, April 1875.

chief trumpeter with field music responsibilities: "Each regiment of cavalry shall consist of twelve troops, one colonel, one lieutenant-colonel, three majors, one surgeon, one assistant surgeon, one adjutant, one quartermaster, one veterinary surgeon, with the rank of regimental sergeant-major, one sergeant-major, one quartermaster-sergeant, one saddler-sergeant, one chief musician, who shall be instructor of music, and one chief trumpeter."[7] Band regulations continued to follow those established in the 1860s with sixteen privates serving as musicians "in a separate squad under the chief musician, with the non-commissioned Staff" with "the proportion to be subtracted from each company for a band." However, while they were dropped from company muster rolls, they were still "instructed as soldiers, and [were] liable to serve in the ranks on any occasion."[8] It is difficult to surmise the frequency of band musicians returning to serve in the ranks. This likely depended on the band and the regiment and on whether there was a war going on.

INSTRUMENTS AND INSTRUMENTATION

A helpful newspaper reporter of the *Santa Fe Weekly New Mexican* provides an indication of cavalry band instrumentation in 1880 along with names and ranks of musicians of the 9th Cavalry Band serving with Chief Musician Charles Spiegel. Notice that the number of musicians is moving above the allotted sixteen:

Sgt. Stephen Taylor, E♭ Cornet
Pvt. William Cee, E♭ Cornet
Pvt. Edward Lyons, E♭ Cornet
Pvt. John Smith, 1st B♭ Cornet
Pvt. William N. Coleman,
   2nd B♭ Cornet
Pvt. Alexander Robinson,
   3rd B♭ Cornet
Cpl. Edward Lee, Solo Alto
Pvt. Patrick Straw, 1st Alto
Pvt. Fielding Jones, 2nd Alto

Pvt. Benjamin Seals, 3rd Alto
Pvt. Richard Reed, 1st Tenor
Pvt. James H. White, 2nd Tenor
Sgt. Joseph Marshall, Baritone
Pvt. Nicholas Dunlap, B♭ Tuba
Pvt. John Butler, E♭ Tuba
Pvt. Samuel H. Asburry, E♭ Tuba
Pvt. George Camphor, Small Drum
Cpl. Elijah Mason, Bass Drum
Pvt. William T. Lee, Bells[9]

7. U.S. Army, *Revised Statues of the United States, Passed at the First Session of the Forty-Third Congress, 1873–74* (Washington, D.C.: Government Printing Office, 1875), 203, Sec. 1102.

8. U.S. Army, *Revised United States Army Regulations of 1861*, 19, article 12, nos. 81, 82, and 83.

9. Thanks to Monroe Billington for including this list in his history of black soldiers serving in post–Civil War New Mexico. Billington, *New Mexico's Buffalo Soldiers*, 226; *Santa Fe Weekly New Mexican*, 28 March 1880.

FIGURE 5.1. Tenor horn player of the 2nd Cavalry Band, Fort Wingate, New Mexico, ca. 1894. *Courtesy of U.S. Army Heritage and Education Center, Carlisle, Pennsylvania.*

FIGURE 5.2. 1st Cavalry Band, Fort Meade, South Dakota, ca. 1890s. Band members are wearing the corded, plumed U.S. Army dress helmet of the time. *Courtesy of U.S. Army Heritage and Education Center, Carlisle, Pennsylvania.*

These instruments may have been in bell-forward, bell-up, or wrap-around circular helicon-styled configurations, which developed toward the conclusion of the century (figures 5.1, 5.2, and 5.3; see also figures 6.1, 6.2, and 6.3) and were popular with cavalry bands because they were easier to hold onto and play with one hand—with the other hand holding the horse's reins.[10]

Photographs of North American mounted bands of the late nineteenth century show that percussion typically consisted of combinations of bass drums and cymbals, along with snare and/or side drums in the dragoon tradition. While kettledrums were still probably rare, the *Regulations for the United States Army, 1895,* reveal that "mounted bands may be supplied with a pair of kettledrums in lieu of the bass and tenor drums, cymbals and triangles; and also with altos, trombones, and bassos of helicon shape."[11] Presumably, with this regulation, kettledrums were used more often than they had been in the past.

10. Baines, *Brass Instruments*, 248.

11. U.S. Army, *Regulations for the United States Army, 1895* (Washington, D.C.: Government Printing Office, 1895), 168, para. 1201; also referred to in William Carter White, *A History of Military Music in America* (New York: Exposition Press, 1944), 98. "Basso(s)" was a common spelling for bass instruments, but probably even more so for bass singers, especially operatic basses.

FIGURE 5.3. 2nd Cavalry Band, Fort McKinney, Wyoming, 1892. Band members are wearing the corded, plumed U.S. Army dress helmet of the time. *Courtesy of the National Park Service, Fort Laramie National Historic Site.*

Stringed instruments appear in several accounts of cavalry bands—in one 1875 instance in Tucson at Levin's Hotel pavilion, where various celebrations and parties included concerts, fashionable private balls, and what Dean Frank C. Lockwood and Captain Donald W. Page record as "dances of a semi-public nature, for all of which [Alexander] Levin provided music of excellent quality." They also recount, "The string band of the Sixth Cavalry gave particular delight to Levin's patrons. It was said that this orchestra provided the best music to be enjoyed in the Southwest."[12] Other evident occasions for strings within cavalry bands were with the 9th Cavalry string band providing the music for a party at Fort Ellis, Kansas, in 1883[13] and with the 7th Cavalry orchestra performing under the direction of James Brockenshire of two decades later, as shown in figure 5.4. In all of these cases, musicians were probably doublehanded— playing stringed instruments on some occasions and brass or woodwind on others.

12. Lockwood and Page, *Tucson*, 83.
13. Kenner, *Buffalo Soldiers*, 28.

FIGURE 5.4. 7th Cavalry Orchestra, Camp George H. Thomas, Georgia, 1902, with bandleader James O. Brockenshire. *Courtesy of the U.S. Cavalry Association.*

TRAINING

Training of field and band musicians continued to vary during the nineteenth century. While band musicians would typically have had prior musical experience, the 1895 *Regulations* indicate that the band sergeant and musicians were supplied by individual companies, and thus it is difficult to determine general past musical experience of bandsmen: "The regimental commander will designate the company from which the sergeant is to be taken and the number of men of each company to serve with the band. Vacancies thus caused will not be filled."[14]

─────────

14. U.S. Army, *Regulations for the United States Army, 1895*, (1895), 35, para. 245.

As cavalry musicians had found in other eras, combining music with horses had drawbacks, and training of band horses was a necessity, if not always observed. In an effort to perform on horseback for a parade with the 19th Ward Republican Cavalry, members of Drum's Band in Brooklyn, New York, found that while there was concern about the musicians' equestrian skills, little thought had been given to the horses' musical tenacity and tastes:

> By this time, it appears, some misgivings had arisen as to the equestrian qualifications of the band and, in order to test them, it was required that they should mount and ride around Zindel Park, playing as they went the "Star Spangled Banner." They mounted, but on the first blast of the bassoon every horse seemed to be dancing a hornpipe on his account and the instruments were under the musicians' arms, the musicians having all they could do to keep from rolling out of the saddles.[15]

While it is possible that this band included a bassoonist, it is unlikely. It is more likely that the writer knew the word "bassoon" and assumed it was a brass instrument. Nonetheless, the point is still made that horses and musical instruments are not a natural combination.

In addition to the bands of the U.S. Army, and the aforementioned Drum's Band, which seems to have been a private enterprise, mounted and dismounted bands in the evolving National Guard system continued to develop during the post–Civil War years. Military leaders were eager to promote a positive image of their units by having them appear in high-profile military and civic events—and there was no better way of doing this than through music; and as horse units continued to evoke a heroic warrior image, mounted music was even better. One example of a performance of this nature is of a mounted band that took part in a review by New York governor John Thompson Hoffman of the 1st Division, New York National Guard on "Thursday afternoon last" (10 October 1872). Among the units were the 5th Infantry with a full brass band and drum corps, as well as the "Third Cavalry, with mounted band,"[16] which was one of the precursors to the nineteen cavalry bands allotted to the National Guard in the early twentieth century.[17]

---

15. "Drum's Band: Its Members Beat the Tattoo Upon Each Other," *Brooklyn Daily Eagle*, Monday, 12 May 1890, 6.

16. "Military Gossip," *New York Times*, 13 October 1872.

17. Bruce P. Gleason, "A Chronicle of the Pre–World War II Cavalry Bands of the U.S. National Guard—with Recollections of Those Who Rode," *Journal of the World Association for Symphonic Bands and Ensembles* 13 (2006).

Another of these state militia mounted bands was that of the 1st Battalion Massachusetts Volunteer Militia Cavalry (encompassing the National Lancers of chapter 2; see pages 28 and 36), which, according to the 1878 *Annual Report of the Adjutant-General of the Commonwealth of Massachusetts*, rode with eighteen pieces escorting "his Excellency the Governor to Harvard University, Jan. 26, at the annual commencement," along with three commissioned officers and seventy-six enlisted men.[18] Interestingly, section 12 of the *Acts and Resolves Passed by the General Court of Massachusetts* published two years earlier in 1876, maintains that "no allowance shall be made for mounted bands."[19] Thus it is not clear whether "allowance" referred to funding, support, management, or something else—or whether the unit was not supported governmentally but simply was encouraged. In 1883, on 19 June, the Massachusetts Volunteer Militia (M.V.M.) with mounted band was again involved in Harvard's commencement exercises: "Capt. Benj. W. Dean, Company A, First Battalion Cavalry, M.V.M., will report with his command and mounted Band at the State House, at 8.45 o'clock A.M., on Wednesday, 27th instant, for the purpose of escorting His Excellency the Governor to Harvard College upon the occasion of the annual commencement exercises. Permission is given the company to appear in its private uniform with lances."[20]

As with many militia units, there were several redesignations and amalgamations predating National Guard units. John Stuart Barrows, writing in 1906, states that 1876 was a critical period, as a reorganization of the militia called for a reduction of the organizations in the mounted branch. In Boston alone, there were the National Lancers, Troop A; the Boston Light Dragoons, Troop B; the Prescott Guards, Troop C; and the Roxbury Horse Guards, Troop D. Upon consolidation, the fittest survived with the National Lancers and the Roxbury Horse Guards being united in the 1st Squadron of Cavalry, M.V.M.[21]

Another appearance of a pre–National Guard militia mounted band took place in a Philadelphia Independence Day parade in 1876. Among the lineup

---

18. Commonwealth of Massachusetts, Adjutant-General's Office, *Annual Report of the Adjutant-General of the Commonwealth of Massachusetts for the Year Ending December 31, 1878* (Boston: Rand, Avery, 1879), 9. Barrows, "National Lancers," 412–13.

19. Commonwealth of Massachusetts, *Acts and Resolves Passed by the General Court of Massachusetts, in the Year 1876 . . .* , Chapter 205 (Boston: Wright and Potter, 1876), 193.

20. Commonwealth of Massachusetts, Adjutant-General's Office, *Annual Report of the Adjutant General of the Commonwealth of Massachusetts for the Year Ending December 31, 1883*, Special Orders No. 70 (Boston: Wright and Potter, 1884), 172.

21. Commonwealth of Massachusetts, Adjutant-General's Office, *Annual Report of the Adjutant-General* (1879), 9; Barrows, "National Lancers," 412–13.

were "Black Hussars— Captain, Christopher Kleinz; First Lieutenant, Wm. S. Osler; Mounted band. Thirty men."[22] As this was not a federal unit, there were no regulations concerning the size and makeup. Moreover, as often happened also with federal bands, the unit's field trumpeters may have ridden with the band, but an uninitiated observer would not have known the difference between the two groups of musicians. Thus some of the thirty may have been field trumpeters—if the unit had field trumpeters. Funding the band was probably done by the men themselves as well as by the organization of the Black Hussars in general.

These private independent companies were not unusual, and in fact traversed a tradition that had been commonplace in the United Kingdom as well as in several American cities where groups of private citizens formed independent volunteer units (militias) to reinforce undermanned police departments and to assist other authorities in times of local emergency. As Marcus Cunliffe explains,

> The history of these dazzling volunteer units is complicated to explain, not least because most of them also had militia designations. They were, however, a very different phenomenon from the "common" or "beat" militia, as the word "volunteer" suggests. Militia service was in conception universal and obligatory: the volunteer companies themselves elected to serve, prescribing their own patterns of training, dress and organizations. The origin of these organizations lay in Britain with London's Honourable Artillery Company, which was founded in 1537, with a direct imitation being Boston's Ancient and Honorable Artillery Company of 1638—the oldest of the American independent companies.[23]

With the number of these independent units multiplying in the eighteenth and nineteenth centuries, and often consisting of a city's financial and social elite, several of these units, including the First Troop Philadelphia City Cavalry (1774), the Chatham Artillery Company (Savannah, Georgia, 1786), the National Lancers (1836), the Cleveland Grays (1837), the Sacramento Hussars (1859) and the 1st City Troop of Cleveland (1877), offered their members the martial training of a military organization and the camaraderie of a social club. Cunliffe continues, "It is clear that whatever its military uses the volunteer

22. Thomas South Lanard, *One Hundred Years with the State Fencibles . . . 1813–1913* (Philadelphia: Nields Company, 1913), 243.

23. Marcus Cunliffe, *Soldiers and Civilians: The Martial Spirit in America* (Boston: Little, Brown, 1968), 215–23.

movement fulfilled a number of other purposes. The companies were clubs, conferring status and identity. Their members also acquired a kind of second identity. On parade, or dining together and applauding florid toasts, they were liberated from domestic and commercial preoccupations, and transformed by magnificent costume. They could feel patriotic, and therefore democratic, and yet elevated into a romantic-genteel realm where one might talk without embarrassment of nobility, honor, chivalry, gallantry."[24]

On a larger plain, the volunteer military units were probably part of a "joining" mentality across the country. As Cunliffe states,

> The volunteer movement . . . appealed as much to immigrants, seeking to find the community, as to native Americans seeking to preserve what they imagined the community to be. In this sense it is an early example of the American joining habit, a forerunner of the Elks, Red Men, Lions and Rotarians of a later generation. Volunteer companies, like these service clubs, developed an extensive network of relationships. The chronicles of the volunteer military abound in examples of friendly visits between company and company, striving to outdo one another in deportment and hospitality.[25]

Cunliffe maintains that prior to the Civil War, "the vast majority of volunteer companies had been incorporated within the state militias, at least on paper."[26] As indicated in this and other chapters, several of these pre–National Guard units hosted bands.

Transporting Musicians and Horses

Following the period after the Civil War and the Indian Wars, infantry, artillery, and cavalry bands continued to develop in scope, size, organization, appearance, and quality and continued to support troop efforts and to participate in civilian, community, and military events. Due to these latter tasks, bands found themselves traveling to "gigs," which, depending on the event, could be across the country. During wartime, most mounted bands would have traveled from and to performances by horseback since performances were typically near their

24. Ibid., 230.
25. Ibid., 230–31.
26. Ibid., 220.

accommodations.[27] However, when traveling to perform for larger military and civilian events—especially in the latter part of the century—transportation could include train travel, as evidenced in this 1896 account of the 6th U.S. Cavalry for the visit of Li Hung Chang [Li Hongzhang] from China to the United States:

> The ferryhouse of the Pennsylvania Railroad Company in Jersey City took on a warlike appearance yesterday afternoon upon the arrival from Fort Myer, Va., of a detachment [four troops][28] of the Sixth United States Cavalry, which is to act as escort to Li Hung Chang, the Chinese Viceroy, during his stay in the city. He is expected to arrive here to-morrow on the steamship *St. Louis*.
>
> The troops left Washington yesterday morning, the men and camp equipage occupying one train, and the horses the other. In the detachment there are 210 men and 15 officers, besides the mounted band of twenty pieces, which is said to be one of the best musical organizations in the army. The first train arrived about 3 o'clock P.M., and the other a half hour later. The annex boats transferred the men and horses to Fort Hamilton, where the troops will make their camp while on duty here.[29]

One of the largest peacetime undertakings for transporting military personnel, which included mounted bandsmen and their horses, was for the World's Fair Columbian Exposition in Chicago, 1892–93—especially for the exposition's dedication military parade on Michigan Avenue on 21 October 1892. Joining various civilian and professional organizations, including Sousa's fifty-piece band, were several military units, including the Chicago Hussars, who escorted Chicago's mayor.[30] An official program of the event indicates that traveling from

27. As history indicates, transporting horses for warfare to another country was another story and sometimes met with disaster, as the Mounted Rifles (predecessor of the 3rd Cavalry) lost most of their horses in a storm during the voyage across the Gulf of Mexico, leaving the regiment to fight as infantry during most of the Mexican War. Third Cavalry Museum, *Blood and Steel! The History, Customs, and Traditions of the 3d Armored Cavalry Regiment* (Fort Hood, Tex.: 2010–11), 2.

28. Another newspaper article distinguishes the detachment: "Orders have been issued to the four troops of cavalry, with the mounted band, stationed at Ft. Myer, opposite this city, to leave for New York Wednesday morning by train to take part in the parade in honor of Li Hung Chang." "Condensed News Gathered from all parts of the Country by Telegraph," *Marietta (Ohio) Daily Leader*, 26 August 1896.

29. "To Escort Li Hung Chang, Arrival of Four Troops of the Sixth Cavalry," *New York Times*, 27 August 1896.

30. *Columbian Exposition Dedication Ceremonies Memorial: A Graphic Description of the Ceremonies at Chicago, October, 1892, The 400th Anniversary of the Discovery of America* (Chicago: Metropolitan Art Engraving and Publishing, 1893), 118.

installations from across the country were the "Fifth Cavalry mounted band of twenty pieces from Ft. Riley, Kansas,"[31] and "Band and two troops Sixth Cavalry: Troop L. Sixth Cavalry" (the band and troops F, G, and L) from Fort Niobrara, Nebraska.[32] The same program explains, "The mounted band of the Fifth United States cavalry . . . play[ed] martial music for troops A and B, of the First Illinois cavalry, which turned out respectively thirty-six and forty sabers."[33] While the 6th Cavalry Band photograph of figure 5.5 was taken two years after the Columbian Exposition, it is likely that some or perhaps most of these soldier-musicians would have taken part. This photo is an unusual find, as all of the subjects were identified and documented by one of the subjects, trombonist August Schmidt (No. 14).

1. William H. Gordon, E♭ Tuba
2. Jules Direen, 1st Cornet
3. Jules Leichsinger (leader), Solo Cornet
4. Edward Philip, Cymbals
5. Joseph Colbright, Baritone
6. Henry Alden, 3rd Alto
7. Henry Romer, E♭ Cornet
8. William F. Daugherty, Bass Drum
9. Axel Braberg, E♭ Tuba
10. William Klerche, 1st Trombone
11. George Southerland, 2nd Cornet
12. Charles Henriechberg, Snare Drum
13. George Brassler, 2nd Alto
14. August Schmidt, 2nd Trombone
15. Anton Humm, 3rd Cornet
16. Gustav Geckler, 1st Alto
17. Fred Willer, B♭ Bass[34]

31. J. F. Martin, *Martin's World's Fair Album-Atlas and Family Souvenir* (Chicago: C. Ropp, 1892), 131.

32. "Dedication at Chicago, Arrangements for the Big Military Parade," *New York Times*, 12 October 1892; U.S. House Executive Document 1, pt. 2, 53rd Cong., 2nd sess., serial 3198, 123.

33. *Columbian Exposition Dedication*, 119.

34. As this is a rare find, I have elected to include all musicians' names here in the text along with instrumentation to aid future researchers. As names were indicated on the back of the photograph in century-old cursive handwriting, I worked diligently on deciphering. I hope I was accurate.

FIGURE 5.5. 6th Cavalry Band at Fort Niobrara, Nebraska, June 1894. Photo donated
to the Jefferson National Expansion Memorial in 1962 by Mrs. August Schmidt of
Ithaca, New York. *Courtesy of the National Park Service, Jefferson National Expansion
Memorial Archives, RU 101.*

Moreover, as Schmidt indicates exact instrumentation, this photo, along with
the 9th Cavalry personnel list above, is an excellent example of the makeup of a
sixteen-piece ensemble with an additional leader. This 6th Cavalry instrumentation was probably typical of other U.S. Cavalry bands and included instrument
names indicative of the modern era, and, differing from that of the 9th Cavalry
(see page 82), used trombones rather than tenor horns.

   This photo was probably one of the last to be taken of a cavalry band before
bands were increased in size. Paragraph 245 within the *Regulations for the United
States Army, 1895* indicates that bands were increased from sixteen to twenty-
two—twenty privates, one sergeant, and a chief musician—in 1894, with
an addition of a chief trumpeter and principal musician raising the total to
twenty-four ("the number of men in and attached to the band will not exceed

twenty-four") in 1895. Moreover, these particular regulations, which specifically included cavalry bands and their organization, also indicate that band governance was becoming more regulated with operational plans initiated for instruments, supplies, and uniforms.[35]

Plenty of cavalry activity, along with subsequent music, was taking place throughout the western territories during the last part of the century, with bands being stationed in January 1887 at Fort Custer, Montana (1st Cavalry), Fort Walla Walla, Washington (2nd Cavalry), Fort Davis, Texas (3rd Cavalry), Fort Huachuca, Arizona (4th Cavalry), Fort Riley, Kansas (5th Cavalry), Fort Bayard, New Mexico (6th Cavalry), Fort Meade, Dakota Territory (7th Cavalry), Post of San Antonio, Texas (8th Cavalry), Fort McKinney, Wyoming (9th Cavalry), and Santa Fe, New Mexico (10th Cavalry).[36]

This same year, a cavalry presence returned to eastern venues when General Philip H. Sheridan, the army's commanding general, decided that Fort Myer, Virginia, should become the nation's cavalry showplace. Originally named Fort Whipple (after Civil War Brigadier General Amiel Weeks Whipple) in 1881, the installation's name was changed to Fort Myer after Brigadier General Albert J. Myer, who established the Signal School of Instruction for Army and Navy Officers there in 1869. With this cavalry establishment, Sheridan subsequently transferred the communications unit out and assigned horsemen to the post. Sheridan's decision may very well have been a result of his trip to

---

35. U.S. Army, *Regulations for the United States Army, 1895* (Washington, D.C.: Government Printing Office, 1899), 34, 35–36, 38, 41, 42, 52, 58, 108, 109, 121, 166, 168, 250.

36. U.S. Army, Return of the 1st Regiment of Cavalry, Army of the United States, for the month of January 1887, Col. N[athan] A[ugustus] M[onroe] Dudley, Commanding, Fort Custer, Mont.; U.S. Army, Return of the 2nd Regiment of Cavalry, Army of the United States, for the month of January 1887, Col. N[elson] B[owman] Sweitzer, Commanding, Fort Walla Walla, Wash.; U.S. Army, Return of the 3rd Regiment of Cavalry, Army of the United States, for the month of January 1887, Col. Albert G[allatin] Brackett, Commanding, Fort Davis, Tex.; U.S. Army, Return of the 4th Regiment of Cavalry, Army of the United States, for the month of January 1887, Col. William B. Royall, Commanding, Fort Huachuca, Ariz.; U.S. Army, Return of the 5th Regiment of Cavalry, Army of the United States, for the month of January 1887, Col. Wesley Merritt, Commanding, Fort Riley, Kans.; U.S. Army, Return of the 6th Regiment of Cavalry, Army of the United States, for the month of January 1887, Col. Eugene A. Carr, Commanding, Fort Bayard, N.Mex.; U.S. Army, Return of the 7th Regiment of Cavalry, Army of the United States, for the month of January 1887, Col. James W. Forsyth, Commanding, Fort Meade, Dakota Territory; U.S. Army, Return of the 8th Regiment of Cavalry, Army of the United States, for the month of January 1887, Elmer Otis, Commanding, Post of San Antonio, Tex.; U.S. Army, Return of the 9th Regiment of Cavalry, Army of the United States, for the month of January 1887, Col. Edward Hatch, Commanding, Fort McKinney, Wyo.; and U.S. Army, Return of the 10th Cavalry, Army of the United States, for the month of January 1887, Col. Benjamin H. Grierson, Commanding, Santa Fe, N.Mex., all in *Returns from Regular Army Cavalry Regiments, 1833–1916*, NARA, RG391, Microfilm Publication M744.

Europe in 1870, where he observed the Franco-Prussian War as an official U.S. observer. Spending time in Prussia, England, and France, he would have seen not only cavalry showmanship but also cavalry ceremony as practiced within elements of large contingencies in European capitals. While a strong battlefield tactician, Sheridan also understood the power of pomp and ceremony—and the idea of the heroic warrior evidenced in horse units—which he may well have been eager not only to bolster in the United States but to bring to the nation's capital in European style.

Over the next two decades, Fort Myer became a center for U.S. Army horsemanship where as many as 1,500 horses were stabled. Because of its proximity to the nation's capital, the army, and the populous East Coast, as well as its proximity to Arlington National Cemetery, Fort Myer became a focal point for elite ceremonial units.[37] Within these units were the various horse-mounted cavalry bands of various regiments that were stationed there over the years. Thus, cavalry units were able to supply mounted troops and bands for official events in Washington, D.C., similar to those in Berlin, London, and Paris—with those of the Household Cavalry in London and the Garde Républicaine in Paris still performing mounted at the time of this writing as they have for centuries.

One momentous peacetime occasion that called for elite Fort Myer troops was the Grant Day parade of 27 April 1897 in New York City, commemorating the seventy-fifth anniversary of Grant's birth, and the dedication ceremony of what would later be officially called the "General Grant National Memorial" (Grant's Tomb). Among the thousands of National Guard and Regular Army troops and hundreds of Union and Confederate veterans participating in the parade were the bands of the 9th Infantry, Governors Island (presumably 13th Infantry), 2nd Artillery, 4th Artillery, 5th Artillery, and the mounted band and four troops (A, E, G, and H) of the 6th Cavalry then stationed at Fort Myer.[38]

---

37. Additionally, within the installation, Quarters One—initially designated to serve as the post commander's house—became the residence of the army's senior uniformed officer and thus Fort Myer further became an important part of the official and social life in Washington. William Gardner Bell, *Quarters One: The United States Army Chief of Staff's Residence, Fort Myer, Virginia* (Washington, D.C.: Center of Military History, United States Army, 2011), 2–11.

38. "Grant Monument Parade, Assurances of One of the Greatest Military Displays Ever Seen in This City," *New York Times*, 26 March 1897; "Federal Troops Designated, Largest Number to Parade on Grant Day Seen Together Since the War," *New York Times*, 4 April 1897; "In Memory of Gen. Grant, Probability that Many Confederate Veterans Will Be in the Parade," *New York Times*, 30 March 1897; "Federal Troops for the Parade, Special Orders from the Headquarters of the Department of the East," *New York Daily Tribune*, Monday, 19 April 1897, 7.

The question of traveling between a gig and their home fort for the troopers of this event had a simple answer. An article in the *Washington (D.C.) Morning Times* indicates that the 6th Cavalry and other troops from Fort Myer and surrounding installations bypassed the idea of troop trains and simply rode back to Fort Myer from New York: "The regular troops from Fort Myer and Washington barracks, who left about a month ago to take part in the Grant Day parade in New York, arrived at their home stations shortly after 1 o'clock yesterday afternoon, having marched overland from New York to this city, a distance of about 250 miles." The same reporter recalls that leaving New York on 1 May with "the band playing and colors flying," field dressed in campaign hats, blue flannel shirts, and regulation trousers and leggings, the cavalry and light battery proceeded on their first day's march through Hoboken, Jersey City, and Newark on their way to Elizabeth, New Jersey. Headed by Colonel Samuel Sumner and staff and followed by the mounted band and four troops of cavalry, the troops were a hit with flags flying along the route and hundreds of mill and factory workers waving handkerchiefs.[39]

Reports of occasions involving mounted bands at Fort Myer did not always indicate which mounted band it was—as illustrated by a newspaper account for the 1897 funeral of Major James F. Gregory of the Corps of Engineers. Consisting of the relatives, friends, and fellow officers of Major Gregory, the procession was met at the end of the Aqueduct Bridge "by a troop of cavalry and the mounted band from Fort Myer, and escorted to the cemetery. . . . Funeral music was played by the band along the line of march, and the casket containing the body was wound with the Stars and Stripes."[40] This band was presumably that of the 6th cavalry as per the Grant Day parade citation and because it was mentioned again a few months later as participating in Washington, D.C., in General Albert Ordway's funeral procession from St. John's Church

---

39. "The End of a Long March, Regular Troops Finish Their Overland Journey," *Washington (D.C.) Morning Times*, Tuesday, 25 May 1897, 8. Other overland treks of cavalry troops were not unheard of. As late as 1921, the 1st Squadron, including the band, along with Troop L, Training Center Squadron No. 6 of the 14th U.S. Cavalry changed station by marching overland from Fort Des Moines, Iowa, to Fort Sheridan, Illinois, 26 September to 16 October 1921. Colonel Robert A. Brown indicates, "The march was one of the most successful ever made by units of this regiment. Through arrangements previously made with the mayor or the American Legion Post at the various stops, camp sites and water for the troops were obtained at no expense to the Government. In return for these considerations, exhibition drills, baseball games, band concerts, and dances were given by the troops." Col. Robert A. Brown, "Fourteenth Cavalry—Fort Des Moines, Iowa," Regimental Notes, *Cavalry Journal* 31, no. 126 (January 1922), 107.

40. "Major Gregory Buried, Interred in Arlington Cemetery with Full Military Honors," *Washington (D.C.) Morning Times*, Thursday, 5 August 1897, 4.

to Arlington Cemetery: "At 2:10 P.M. the line moved en route to Arlington, the mounted band of the Sixth Cavalry playing the 'Dead March' from *Saul*. The line of march was down H street to Connecticut avenue, then north to K street, to Farragut Square, to M street, to Georgetown, over the Aqueduct Bridge, and then along Military road to the cemetery."[41]

While the band of the 6th Cavalry was busy performing on the East Coast, those of other regiments continued to work in the West—worlds away—with that of the 1st Cavalry at Fort Riley, Kansas; 2nd Cavalry at Fort Wingate, New Mexico; 3rd Cavalry at Jefferson Barracks, Missouri; 4th Cavalry at Fort Walla Walla, Washington; 5th Cavalry at Fort Sam Houston, Texas; 7th Cavalry at Fort Grant, Arizona Territory; 8th Cavalry at Fort Meade, South Dakota; 9th Cavalry at Fort Robinson, Nebraska; and the 10th Cavalry at Fort Assiniboine, Montana—rotating stations but serving in roles in which they had been working for decades.[42] The performances these bands rendered during this post–Civil War era and during the continued years of western expansion continued to gain in stature and quality. Tasks of supporting patriotism in official and civic functions continued to be a part of horse-mounted and foot musicians' duty across the country with the close of the century bringing a new role for the U.S. military on the world stage.

---

41. "Laid to Rest at Arlington, General Albert Ordway's Remains Borne to the Grave," *Washington (D.C.) Times*, Thursday, 25 November 1897, 4.

42. U.S. Army, Return of the 1st Regiment of Cavalry, Army of the United States, for the month of January 1897, Col. Abraham K. Arnold, Commanding, Fort Riley, Kans.; U.S. Army, Return of the 2nd Regiment of Cavalry, Army of the United States, for the month of April 1897, Col. George G. Hunt, Commanding, Fort Wingate, N.Mex.; U.S. Army, Return of the 3rd Regiment of Cavalry, Army of the United States, for the month of April 1897, Col. Anson Mills, Commanding, Jefferson Barracks, Mo; U.S. Army, Return of the 4th Regiment of Cavalry, Army of the United States, for the month of April 1897, Col. Charles E. Compton, Commanding, Fort Walla Walla, Wash.; U.S. Army, Return of the 5th Regiment of Cavalry, Army of the United States, for the month of April 1897, Col. James F. Wade, Commanding, Fort Sam Houston, Tex.; U.S. Army, Return of the 6th Regiment of Cavalry, Army of the United States, for the month of April 1897, Col. Samuel S. Sumner, Commanding, Fort Myer, Va.; U.S. Army, Return of the 7th Regiment of Cavalry, Army of the United States, for the month of April 1897, Col. E[dwin] V[ose] Sumner, Fort Grant, Ariz. Territory; U.S. Army, Return of the 8th Regiment of Cavalry, Army of the United States, for the month of April 1897, Col. Caleb H. Carlton, Commanding, Fort Meade, S.Dak.; U.S. Army, Return of the 9th Regiment of Cavalry, Army of the United States, for the month of April 1897, Col. David Perry, Commanding, Fort Robinson, Neb.; and U.S. Army, Return of the 10th Regiment of Cavalry, Army of the United States, for the month of April 1897, Col. John K. Mizner, Commanding, Fort Assiniboine, Mont., all in *Returns from Regular Army Cavalry Regiments, 1833–1916*, NARA, RG 391, Microfilm Publication M744.

CHAPTER 6

Spanish-American War Era

As the Plains Indian Wars were coming to a close in the 1890s and with expansion of the country from coast to coast further realizing the idea of manifest destiny, commerce and industrialization were not far behind—or, in fact, were leading the way. By the time President William McKinley took office in 1897, John D. Rockefeller, Andrew Carnegie, J. P. Morgan, Thomas Edison, and other industrialists had substantially shaped U.S. economics, business, industry, and sociopolitical interests to the point that protective tariffs and other initiatives to support U.S. efforts on the international front were a strong part of the country's foreign policy. Amidst this climate, U.S. initiatives in foreign countries, including that of nearby Cuba, where American sugar interests owned vast tracts of land, had grown unstable. And, as Cuba had been pushing for independence from Spain for decades, war involving the United States on the side of Cuba was seemingly inevitable.

While the Spanish-American War was one of the shortest U.S. conflicts in the nation's history, it was also one of the most pivotal—as the results of the war further propelled the country onto a new world stage. With reasons for the conflict being several, not the least of which was simple imperialism, the initial thrust of the war was to support Cuban efforts at ousting their Spanish overlords in an effort to recognize the country's independence. As the United States gained economic and industrial strength throughout the post–Civil War decades, attitudes about the country's place in the world developed as well.

With the unaccounted-for blowing up of the USS *Maine* in Havana Harbor on 15 February 1898, the U.S. government's response served as a warning to Spain—as well as a precaution for protecting U.S. citizens living in Cuba—and the war was soon on. Beginning with an entire U.S. Army of only 2,143 officers and 26,040 enlisted men, of which the cavalry claimed 6,000 (as opposed to

Spain's 150,000 regulars and 80,000 native volunteers in Cuba alone), Congress empowered the president to raise a huge fighting force of temporary volunteers. As state militia forces were able to muster only 4,800 cavalrymen, on 22 April the secretary of war was authorized to raise 3,000 "United States Volunteers," comprised of three mounted units, and on 25 April the United States declared war on Spain. On the day following, the Regular Army was enlarged to 64,719 officers and men.[1] Of the regular cavalry regiments, the 1st, 2nd, 3rd, 6th, 9th, and 10th served in Cuba along with the 1st U.S. Volunteer Cavalry—Teddy Roosevelt's Rough Riders.[2] While thousands of men had been enlisted and commissioned for service, training was minimal, and logistical planning at times appears to have been nonexistent.[3] Because of limited space on transport ships, each cavalry regiment left behind four full troops and all but the senior officers' horses. Consequently, cavalrymen fought on foot, and cavalry bandsmen performed as well.

Personal recollections indicate that cavalry bandsmen, like their counterparts in the infantry and artillery, were soldiers first as exemplified by Sergeant Tom Davis, who, serving as a tuba player for three years with the 1st Cavalry Band, participated in the Battle of San Juan and the siege and surrender of Santiago.[4] Likewise, traveling to Cuba in June 1898, the band of the 10th Cavalry served alongside headquarters and troops A, B, C, D, E, F, G, H, and I and was in action at Santiago and San Juan Hill in July.[5]

As Sargent and others had done in earlier times, field musicians periodically transferred to bands from other capacities within a regiment (as suggested with the 1895 regulation cited in chapter 5, page 86). Among these was Fred D. Culver

---

1. Urwin, *United States Cavalry*, 166.

2. Sawicki, *Cavalry Regiments*, 152, 154, 156, 163, 169, 171; Kenneth E. Hendrickson, Jr., *The Spanish-American War* (Westport, Conn.: Greenwood Press, 2003), 30.

3. While the United States had advanced to an industrial lead on several world fronts, U.S. military leaders were not accustomed to engaging in warfare offshore at this point and were hampered logistically as well as organizationally with a structure that had changed little since the War of 1812. Consequently, the army was ill-prepared for a rapid expansion of both men and material to wage war. "From Santiago to Manila: Spanish-American War Logistics," Army Logistics University, http://www.almc.army.mil/alog/issues/JulAug98/MS305.htm.

4. Tom Davis, "A Chronology of the 1st United States Cavalry: The Diary of Tom Davis," Spanish American War Centennial website, http://www.spanamwar.com/1stUScav.htm.

5. U.S. Army, Return of the 10th Regiment of Cavalry, Army of the United States for the month of June 1898, Col. Guy V. Henry, Commanding, Sevilla, Cuba; and U.S. Army, Return of the 10th Regiment of Cavalry, Army of the United States for the month of July 1898, Col. Guy V. Henry, Commanding, Camp Hamilton, Santiago, Cuba, both in *Returns from Regular Army Cavalry Regiments, 1833–1916*, NARA, RG 391, Microfilm Publication M744. By the time the return was signed by Woodward on 29 September 1898, headquarters company of the 10th Cavalry was at Camp Wikoff, Long Island.

of Milford, Nebraska, who, following in the steps of his brothers, Harry H. and Elwin E.—who had both enlisted as trumpeters at young ages (Elwin at thirteen in 1875, and Harry at thirteen in 1893) in Troop A of the Nebraska National Guard—likewise enlisted at the age of fourteen in 1896. Serving in this capacity when the Spanish-American War broke out a year later, he was mustered in with the 3rd U.S. Volunteer Cavalry and went to Camp Thomas, located on the former Civil War battlefield of Chickamauga, Georgia. Serving a short time as chief trumpeter for the regiment, he served as second cornetist with the mounted band when it was organized. However, as neither the 2nd or 3rd U.S. Volunteer Cavalry Regiments ever made it to Cuba, and were disbanded shortly afterward, Culver spent the remainder of the war in Georgia with the rest of the unit. As all three Culver brothers enlisted as trumpeters, it is probable that they had had some musical training beforehand. Moreover, their father, Jacob H. Culver, who had organized and commanded Troop A, had begun his military career at sixteen as a drummer with Co. K, 1st Wisconsin Regiment during the Civil War in 1861.[6]

After only several months, the war ended with Spain's surrender on 17 July 1898 at a ceremony attended by thousands of people, where the U.S. flag was hoisted over the governor's palace in Santiago while the Spanish flag, with the legend "Vive Alphonso XIII," was lowered. The proceedings were accompanied by the 6th Cavalry Band playing the U.S. national anthem, as recalled by James Otis in 1898:

Across the plaza was drawn up the Ninth Infantry, headed by the Sixth Cavalry band. In the street facing the palace stood a picked troop of the Second Cavalry, with drawn sabres, under command of Captain Brett.

All about, pressing against the veranda rails, crowding to windows and doors, and lining the roofs, were the people of the town, principally women and non-combatants.

As the chimes of the old cathedral rang out the hour of twelve, the infantry and cavalry presented arms. Every American uncovered, and Captain McKittrick hoisted the stars and stripes. As the brilliant folds unfurled in the gentle breeze against the

---

6. J. Sterling Morton, *Illustrated History of Nebraska*, vol. 2 (Lincoln, Neb.: Jacob North, 1907), 624. Clarence C., a fourth Culver, was also a member of Troop A and of the 3rd U.S. Volunteer Cavalry, but records do not indicate that he was a musician (621). See also Daniel M. Carr, ed., *Portrait and Biographical Album of the State Officers and the Members of the Nebraska Legislature, Twenty-Eighth Session, 1903–1904, Containing a Directory of the Legislature and Official State Directory* (Fremont Neb.: Progress Publishing, 1903), 171.

fleckless sky, the cavalry band broke into the strains of "The Star Spangled Banner," making the American pulse leap and the American heart thrill with joy.[7]

At the conclusion of the war, because of health considerations, some of which were present before troops even arrived in Cuba, twenty thousand men headed for Camp Wikoff at Montauk Point, Long Island, New York, for quarantine because of various forms of fever. Here again, mounted bands were part of the proceedings. One occasion in particular was when the transport ship, USAT *Minnewaska*, under the command of a Colonel Harris, of the 1st Regiment, District of Columbia Volunteers, arrived with 816 soldiers from Santiago, Cuba, on 29 August 1898. Aboard were "the 1st Battalion, 1st District of Columbia Volunteers, one battalion of engineers of the Fifth Army Corps, Troops A, C, D and F, of the 2d Cavalry, the squad of the Signal Corps that had charge of the military balloon in Cuba, and ninety-five men of the 33d Michigan. . . . There were also on board 297 horses belonging to the troops of the 2d Cavalry." The *New York Tribune* article goes on to report, "While the disembarkation was in progress troops M, E, L, H and K of the 2d Cavalry, who have been in Camp Wikoff some time, have come here from Tampa when the camp was first opened, rode down to the wharf to give their comrades a welcome home. Their mounted band headed the column, and the troop guidons fluttered gayly [*sic*] in the breeze as the cavalrymen trotted down the sandy road, kicking up great clouds of dust."[8] Also at Camp Wikoff was the band of the 6th Cavalry, which, along with other troops from the 3rd and 6th Cavalry Regiments, escorted President McKinley's visiting contingency on 3 September 1898: "The column of carriages wound up a hill, escorted by the cavalry troops and the mounted band of the Sixth Cavalry. The party paused a moment on the hill, and the President swept with his gaze the wide undulating cape, whitened on the levels and hill tops by the tents of 18,000 men laid out in geometric lines."[9]

Several efforts celebrating the conclusion of the Spanish-American War were held across the country, including the Philadelphia Peace Jubilee, which entailed speeches, parades, military reviews, church services, concerts, and other events honoring the country's soldiers over three days in October 1898. Among the twenty-five thousand troops taking part and reviewed by President McKinley

7. James Otis, *The Boys of '98* (Boston: Dana Estes, 1898), 300.

8. "At Montauk's Camp," and "Arrival of the Minneswask," both in *New York Tribune*, 58, no. 18,916, Tuesday, 30 August 1898, 1.

9. "Mr. M'Kinley at Montauk," *New York Times*, 4 September 1898.

were the band and two squadrons of the 10th Cavalry.[10] Another end-of-war event took place in New York when Squadron A, Cavalry, of the National Guard New York (N.G.N.Y.) under the command of Major Avery D. Andrews, was reviewed by New York City mayor Robert A. Van Wyck in commemoration of the unit's return from Puerto Rico. A *New York Times* article recounts, "The procession will be headed by the squadron's mounted band, under Bandmaster [August] Lederhaus, who will double the number of his musicians for the occasion."[11] This unit began life as the New York Hussars, which, as discussed in the previous chapter, like many other groups across the country, originated with the age-old idea of a group of wealthy young gentlemen who were interested in equestrian sport and camaraderie and who enjoyed serving as an escort for dignitaries, becoming Squadron A of the New York National Guard in 1889.[12]

Over the course of the next few years, U.S. Cavalry bands along with their regiments were stationed in various places across the United States with some returning to Cuba as part of the Army of Occupation—this time with their horses—as did that of the 2nd, 10th, and 7th Cavalry Regiments. The 10th Cavalry Band, along with the headquarters troop and troops A, C, G, H, L, and M, left Galveston, Texas, on the USAT *Logan* on 1 May 1899 and disembarked at Manzanillo, Cuba, on 7 May.[13] Several weeks later, headquarters troop and the 10th Cavalry Band served on a detachment with troops A and H in "pursuit of bandits."[14] The 7th Cavalry Band, along with headquarters and troops A, C, E, G, I, and L, left Savannah, Georgia, under the command of Lieutenant Colonel Michael Cooney on the USAT *Manitoba* for Havana on 13 January 1899, eventually making its way to Columbia Barracks.[15] Of these experiences,

---

10. Glass, *History of the Tenth Cavalry*, 38.

11. "Mayor to Review Troop A," in "Plan for Grand Review," *New York Times*, 7 September 1898; "August Lederhaus," in Obituary Notes, *New York Times*, 26 August 1919; "The Inauguration To-Day, Gov. Roosevelt Attended Church Yesterday with Other Dignitaries," *New York Times*, 2 January 1899.

12. Like most National Guard units with a militia-volunteer pedigree, the lineage of Squadron A is involved and outside the parameters of the present study. For further detail about this unit and its basis as the 101st Cavalry, see Sawicki, *Cavalry Regiments*, 199–201.

13. U.S. Army, Return of the 10th Regiment of Cavalry, Army of the United States for the month of May 1899, Col. S. M. Whitside, Commanding, Manzanillo, Cuba, in *Returns from Regular Army Cavalry Regiments, 1833–1916*, NARA, RG 391, Microfilm Publication M744.

14. U.S. Army, Return of the 10th Regiment of Cavalry, Army of the United States for the month of June 1899, Col. S. M. Whitside, Commanding, Bayanno, Cuba, in *Returns from Regular Army Cavalry Regiments, 1833–1916*, NARA, RG 391, Microfilm Publication M744.

15. Melbourne C. Chandler, *Of GarryOwen in Glory: The History of the Seventh United States Cavalry Regiment* (Annandale, Va.: Turnpike Press, Inc., 1960), 116; U.S. Army, Return of the 7th Regiment of Cavalry, Army of the United States for the month of January 1899, Col. Edwin V. Sumner, Commanding, Vedado, Havana, Cuba, in *Returns from Regular Army Cavalry Regiments, 1833–1916*, NARA, RG 391, Microfilm Publication M744.

Chief Musician James Brockenshire recalls, "We sailed from Savannah Dec. 16, arriving in Havana and disembarking on Dec. 19. Headquarters, Band and two Squadrons were directed to take station at Vedado, a suburb of Havana, about four miles up the coast. We remained at this place approximately four months, during which time the Band gave concerts at various points in the City."[16]

Among other significant memories for Brockenshire was the welcome change from the traditional wool blue uniforms that cavalrymen had been wearing for decades to khaki uniforms, which he indicated "were not the best fitting things in the world, [but] they surely were comfortable and presented a much better appearance under a tropical sun, than the blue uniforms we had paraded in on Washington's Birthday." He also indicates that the two performances that were the highlights of the 7th Cavalry Band's Cuban tour were the leading of General Máximo Gómez's army in a "triumphant entry into the City of Havana" and the day "we evacuated the island in May, 1902, and turned to [sic] whole shooting works over to the Cuban Government. The troops paraded and embarked aboard the Ward liner, Moro Castle, en route to Newport News, Va., to entrain for Chickamauga Park, Ga."[17]

With the 10 December 1898 Treaty of Paris concluding the Spanish-American War and awarding the United States temporary control of Cuba and indefinite colonial authority over Puerto Rico and Guam, the question of what to do with the Spanish-occupied Philippine Islands also arose. While Spain was not eager to give up this possession to the United States, it inevitably did, and the Philippine people, rather than finding the independence they hoped for, traded one oppressor for another.[18] So, after the Spanish ousting, war commenced between Filipino revolutionaries and the United States, which had numerous Regular Army regiments of cavalry serving in the Philippines between 1899 and 1901, employing 6,274 horses and 3,259 mules sent from the United States.[19]

With the war in Cuba concluded, volunteer units were scheduled to be disbanded in July 1901. Had this been occurring a century prior, past practice would have suggested narrowing the army down to a few basic units and depleting any semblance of a standing army. However, the United States had

---

16. James O. Brockenshire, "Seventh Cavalry Band," *Army and Navy Journal*, 68 (23 May 1931): 917.

17. Ibid.

18. The United States granted the Philippine people autonomy in 1916 and promised eventual self-government, which came in 1934. Following World War II, the United States recognized Philippine independence in 1946 through the Treaty of Manila—albeit with strings attached as outlined in the Bell Trade Act. See Bradley, *Imperial Cruise*, 22–23.

19. Livingston and Roberts, *War Horse*, 31. Prior to Philippine independence, thousands of cavalry and draft horses, and pack and draft mules were shipped there from San Francisco.

FIGURE 6.1. 6th Cavalry Band, Fort Riley, Kansas, 1900, prior to embarking for the Philippines. This photo is a good example of a mounted band with a full range of helicons. *Courtesy of the Kenneth Spencer Research Library, University of Kansas Libraries.*

changed considerably in one hundred years from a country that had worked at spurning any level of militarism to one that had now taken a leadership role as a "defender of democracy." Thus, rather than reducing forces, a comprehensive act reorganized the artillery and increased the size of the infantry and cavalry to supplant reduced volunteer forces with the addition of the 11th, 12th, 13th, 14th and 15th Cavalry Regiments for service in the Philippines. Like the other cavalry regiments, the new ones would each include a band, and each of the twelve troops would include two trumpeters for field music.[20]

20. Mary Lee Stubbs and Stanley Russell Connor, *Armor-Cavalry*, pt. 1, *Regular Army and Army Reserve* (Washington, D.C.: Office of the Chief of Military History, U.S. Army, 1969), 30; Urwin, *United States Cavalry*, 172. U.S. Secretary of War, Sec. 2, Act of February 2, 1901 (30 Stat. L., 748), in *The Military Laws of the United States, Fourth Edition* (Washington, D.C.: Government Printing Office, 1901), 533, 1049.

FIGURE 6.2. 6th Cavalry Band at Fort Riley, 1899. Sometime between 1894 and 1899 the 6th Cavalry Band had added woodwinds, including saxophones, to its instrumentation (see figure 5.5 for comparison). It is also possible that there was a mounted instrumentation and a dismounted one, with some musicians playing different instruments depending on the formation and occasion. *Author's Collection.*

By 1899, military music had earned a prominent place within the army with these field musicians and band members; thus, these new cavalry bands as well as the preexisting ones (along with infantry and artillery bands) had been augmented to twenty-eight musicians: "1424a. Each cavalry band shall consist of one chief musician; one chief trumpeter; one principal musician; one drum major, who shall have the rank, pay and allowances of a first-sergeant; four sergeants; eight corporals; one cook, and eleven privates."[21] Twenty-eight, although an official number, was probably relative—based on available enlisted soldiers and other factors. The instrumentation spread across each band would have varied somewhat as well, and for the same reasons. See variations between figures 6.1 and 6.2., as well as the variety of instruments, including strings, shown in figure 6.3.

---

21. U.S. Secretary of War, Sec. 2, Army Reorganization Act of March 2, 1899 (30 Stats., 977), in *The Military Laws of the United States, Fourth Edition, with Supplemental Showing Changes to March 4, 1907* (Washington, D.C.: Government Printing Office, 1899), 1233, para. 1424a.

FIGURE 6.3. This photo of the 1st Cavalry Band room at Fort Riley, Kansas, provides a glimpse of the instruments involved in a turn-of-the-century cavalry band. Different sizes of helicons, saxhorns, cornets, and trombones, along with several sizes of clarinets, saxophones, and stringed instruments, indicate that the repertoire must have been extensive. It is hard to say how many cavalry bands were equipped with helicons, which aided with mounted playing. *Courtesy of the Kenneth Spencer Research Library, University of Kansas Libraries.*

HORSE TRANSPORTATION

As the United States had little experience in shipping masses of horses for warfare at this point, considerable planning was undertaken to ensure smooth sailing for all—especially since the journey to the Philippines was considerable (some tactics were borrowed from the British, who had become experts at transporting horses by sea in their various colonizing ventures throughout the world).[22] Consequently, band horses, along with those of the rest of the U.S. Cavalry, were transported with care on specially designed transport ships outfitted with bilge keels to keep them as steady as possible and with interiors built specifically to keep them safe, comfortable, well fed, and watered. Loading and unloading horses was a chore all of its own and was typically done by laying gangways from a dock to a hatchway. If a hatchway could not accommodate a gangway, animals needed to be loaded or unloaded in flying stalls (large wooden open crates) or slings by crane—a tedious process at best. William Carter indicates that if transports could not get close enough to shore for any of these unloading procedures, horses were sometimes simply unloaded into the sea and coaxed to swim to shore.[23]

While accounting for all of the U.S. Cavalry bands serving in the Philippines is outside the scope of this study as they, along with their regiments, were continually being reassigned to new duty stations, the *Annual Reports of the War Department for the Fiscal Year Ended June 30, 1901*, documents that several were stationed in various Philippine locations during this period. The band of the 5th Cavalry commenced duty along with the regiment's headquarters and 1st and 3rd Squadrons in April 1901 in the sixth district of the Department of Northern Luzon.[24] The 9th Cavalry Band was stationed with headquarters and one squadron at Nueva Cáceres in August 1900. The 6th Cavalry Band with headquarters and Troops A, B, C, and D, along with the 4th Cavalry Band with headquarters and Troops B, C, D, and H, were assigned to the first district in November 1900.[25] Band, headquarters, and Troops C and F of the 11th (Volunteer) Cavalry were stationed in Manila in January 1901. The entire regiment was scheduled to leave for the United States at the end of the month.[26]

---

22. DiMarco, *War Horse*, 303–306. As the British had a preference for using its own horses in their colonial service, they were experienced in moving horses by ship. They also purchased thousands of U.S.-bred horses over the years—especially during the Boer Wars in South Africa (1880–81, 1899–1902).

23. Carter, *U.S. Cavalry Horse*, 385–401.

24. U.S. War Department, *Annual Reports of the War Department for the Fiscal Year Ended June 30, 1901, Report of the Lieutenant-General Commanding the Army, In Five Parts*, pt. 5 (Washington, D.C.: Government Printing Office, 1901), 311–12. This report details that the "sixth district, embrac[ed] all that part of the province of Manila lying north of the Pasig River, the provinces of Morong and Infanta, and all islands lying eastward of the latter province, except the Calaguas group" (311).

25. Ibid., 391. This report indicates that the "first district, embrac[ed] provinces of Bataan, Pampanga, and Bulacan" (311).

26. Ibid., 393. Major General Chaffee, the author of the reports, does not indicate that this was the 11th Volunteer Cavalry as the 11th Cavalry did not exist yet (constituted 2 February 1901), so there would have been no reason to make a distinction.

Periods at duty stations were often short, and cavalry bands, like those of the infantry and artillery, continued to move with their regiments, or partial regiments. A good example of this movement is indicated by the 6th Cavalry Band, which moved from Fort Myer, Virginia, to Fort Riley, Kansas, the home of the United States Cavalry School, in December 1898 by way of Camp George H. Thomas, Chickamauga Park, Georgia; Tampa, Florida; El Poso, Cuba; Camp Hamilton, Santiago, Cuba; Camp Wikoff, Long Island; and Camp Albert G. Forse, Huntsville, Alabama. After spending almost two years at Fort Riley, the band headed for Yang Tsun, China, in September 1900, where it spent two months as part of the China Relief Expedition on the way to the Philippine Islands, where it was stationed at numerous installations until April 1903 when it headed back to the United States—first to the Presidio, San Francisco, California, and then on to Fort Meade, South Dakota.

Of these changes in duty stations, we are fortunate to have commentary concerning the 7th Cavalry's orders to proceed to Manila in May 1905 from Chief Musician James Brockenshire, who recounts that, "after a most pleasant journey across the country [from Georgia to California], and voyage across the Pacific, we arrived in Manila and were directed to take station at Batangas, Southern Luzon." Here the men remained until 1907, when they were relieved by the 9th Cavalry. Returning to the United States, Brockenshire indicates that military life at the time had some high points, with USAT *Logan* stopping at Shanghai, China, where "the entire command was given four days leave to go ashore, which was hugely enjoyed." He conveys that, after two further days in Nagasaki, Japan, "we arrived in Frisco, and proceeded to Ft. Riley for station, the home of the old regiment."[27]

As federal and state militia units continued to develop and support the United States on a grander scale, the Spanish-American War served as a catalyst and testing ground for advancements throughout the military, including those for cavalry and artillery bandsmen. With the changes that industry and commerce, and in turn politics and the army, brought to the United States, horse units and their bandsmen found themselves doing duty in heretofore unimaginable areas of the world. As the century turned, these duties continued to expand, and with them more detailed federal regulations and support, which in turn were mirrored within state militia bands.

---

27. Brockenshire, "Seventh Cavalry Band," 917.

FIGURE 7.1. 2nd Cavalry Band, Fort Des Moines, Iowa, ca. 1908. *Courtesy of the Old Guard Museum, U.S. Army.*

CHAPTER 7

Turn of the Twentieth Century

U.S. CAVALRY, INFANTRY, AND FIELD ARTILLERY BANDS CONTINUED
to rotate duty into the twentieth century in the Philippines, Cuba, the United
States, and, after its annexation in 1898 and in conjunction with the Spanish-
American War, Hawaii. During this time, brass and woodwind instrumentation
would have continued to vary by the band and available instruments. However,
by the turn of the century army regulations were specific in listing provided
instruments:

> There will be furnished by the Quartermaster's Department to all duly authorized
> bands of the Army the following-named musical instruments, viz: D♭ piccolo, terz
> and concert flutes, E♭ and B♭ cornets, E♭ and B♭ trumpets, E♭ and B♭ clari-
> onets, E♭ altos, B♭ trombones (valve or slide), B♭ baritones, E♭, B♭, and BB♭
> bassos, bass and snare drums, cymbals, triangles, music stands, and extra parts for
> the repair of the instruments; also batons with suitable cords and tassels for use
> of drum majors of all dismounted bands. Mounted bands may be supplied with a
> pair of kettledrums in lieu of the bass and tenor drums, cymbals, and triangles,
> and also with altos, trombones, and bassos of helicon shape.[1]

Regulations of 1901 added this to the above: "A flugelhorn may be furnished in
lieu of the E♭ trumpet, a euphonium in lieu of one alto, one E♭ saxophone, and

---

1. U.S. Army, *Regulations for the Army of the United States, 1895, with Appendix Separately Indexed, Showing Changes to January 1, 1901*, General Orders, No. 92, 408, Section II, para. 1201 (Washington, D.C.:
Government Printing Office, 1901). According to Edwin H. Pierce, "The Terz flute or 'Flute in F': (should
properly be called 'Flute in E flat'): [is] a flute which transposes everything a minor third higher, consequently
the part for it is written that much below where it is to sound. Called for in orchestra on a few very rare
occasions. Sometimes used in military band, in which case it may play from the part of the E flat clarinet,
with excellent effect." Edwin H. Pierce, "What Instrument Shall I Choose?," *Etude* (March 1920): 163–64.
Notice even at this late date the old spellings of "clarinet" and "bassos."

one E♭ baritone saxophone in lieu of two cornets; but under no circumstances will more than a complete instrumentation for 28 musicians be supplied."[2]

While not all U.S. mounted bands had kettledrums, regulations provided for them, and as late as 1904 both the "Drum" and "Kettle-Drum" entries in the *Grove's Dictionary of Music*, published in New York, discuss the cavalry use of kettledrums in the present—and give this usage before indicating orchestral usage: "In the cavalry two drums are used, one on each side of the horse's neck. Two are likewise required in orchestras,"[3] and "kettle-Drums are copper or brass basins, with a skin or head that can be tuned to a true musical note. Used by the bands of cavalry regiments, and in orchestras."[4] (See figure 7.1.) The helicon had similar connotations, as the 1909 entry from *Elson's Pocket Music Dictionary* defines a helicon as "a tuba made in such a shape as to circle the body and rest on the shoulder, for marching or mounted band use."[5]

With this instrumentation, bands were able to play a variety of music, including selections for dismounted performances of formal concerts, which, like those of other eras, were often in commemoration of particular events. One of these was the transfer of the newly formed 11th Cavalry from Washington, D.C., to the Philippines in December 1901 with the regiment's band performing an impressive repertoire in a "Grand Farewell Complimentary Concert" in Gaston Hall at what was then Georgetown College on Wednesday, 11 December 1901, at 8:30 P.M. under the direction of Alexander Perwein:

PART I.

1. March—*Olivet Commandery*	Thomas
2. "Overture," *Poet and Peasant*	Suppe
3. Selection—*Elisir D'Amore*	Donizetti
4. Cornet Solo—"Inflamatus" from *Stabat Mater*,	Rossini
Mr. Ernest G. Fisher	

---

2. U.S. Army, *Regulations for the Army of the United States, 1901, with Appendix Separately Indexed, Showing Changes to June 30, 1902*, 180, para. 1326 (Washington, D.C.: Government Printing Office, 1902), 180.

3. J. A. Fuller Maitland, ed. *Grove's Dictionary of Music and Musicians* (New York: MacMillan, 1904), s.v. "Drum," by Victor de Pontigny.

4. Ibid., s.v. "Kettle-Drums," by Victor de Pontigny. Even up through the 1954 edition of *Grove's*, along with a historical chronology, Kenneth Rutherford maintains that the Renaissance instruments "closely resembled the cavalry drums of to-day, being smaller than the modern orchestral drums." Eric Blom, ed. *Grove's Dictionary of Music and Musicians*, 5th ed. (New York: St. Martin's Press, 1954), s.v. "Drum," by Kenneth Rutherford.

5. Louis C. Elson, *Elson's Pocket Music Dictionary* (Boston: Oliver Ditson, 1909), s.v. "Helicon."

5. "Air de Ballet"—*Bianca*   Hoffmann
6. Characteristic—*Jumping-Jack's Jubilee*   Wood
7. Selection—*Fiddle-Dee-Dee*   Stromberg

PART II.

1. Selection—*Rigoletto*   Verdi
2. Two New Marches—(a) *General Heywood*   Santelmann
                    (b) *Colonel Moore*   Perwien
3. Clarionet Solo—*Original Air Varié*   Dagnelies
                    Mr. Albert S. Clark
4. Mélange on Popular Melodies—*A Sure Thing*   Tobant
5. Cornet Solo—*The Holy City*   Adams
                    Mr. Alex. Perwien
6. Selection—*Robin Hood*   De Koven
7. Medley Overture—*A Night in New York*   Brooks
                    Star Spangled Banner[6]

Mounted bands continued to serve in similar capacities as they had in the late nineteenth century performing for military and civilian parades, as well as drills, concerts, reviews, guard mounts, and troop movements. This went for bands in U.S. Cavalry and U.S. Field Artillery units as well as for those of the National Guard, whose structures continued to move closer in line with that of the Regular Army.

Along these capacities, and previously mentioned in chapter 6, is the band of Squadron A, Cavalry, National Guard New York, which came to figure heavily in connection with Theodore Roosevelt. Beginning with his New York gubernatorial inauguration in January 1899, the band opened the preceding church service dismounted at All Saints Cathedral in Albany with *The Palms* (presumably Faure's). In 1901, it appeared again—this time in a world's fair

---

6. The 11th Cavalry was constituted at Fort Myer, Virginia, on 2 February 1901, and headed for the Philippines in December of that year. Sawicki, *Cavalry Regiments*, 172. *Grand Farewell Complimentary Concert by the Eleventh U.S. Cavalry Band, in Gaston Hall—Georgetown College, Wednesday Evening, December 11, 1901, at 8:30 O'Clock, Director, A. Perwein, U.S.A.*, printed program lent to author by Georgetown University Library. Alexander Perwein was an Austro-German musician who made a career in U.S. Army music serving with bands of the 11th Cavalry and U.S. Military Academy at West Point. His son Alexander Hamilton Perwein was a member of the West Point class of 1920 and served active duty in the U.S. Army for twenty-eight years. Robert Perwein and Charles Holle, "Alexander H. Perwein, 1920," West Point Association of Graduates website, http://apps.westpointaog.org/Memorials/Article/6706/.

event—the Pan-American Exposition in Buffalo, New York, with other state National Guard units:

> Early on the morning of the 9th the military pageant will be formed. It will be the grandest picture of New York's soldiery that has ever been witnessed outside of New York city [sic]. Squadron A of New York city with its mounted band, the crack cavalry organization of the State, will be one of the features of the parade. The Second battery of New York and other separate organizations will be on hand. In addition to these will be all of the Fourth brigade, national guard of the State, together with all of the military now present at the Exposition. Major General Charles F. Roe will act as grand marshall [sic] of the day.[7]

Four years later in 1905, according to Squadron commander Major Oliver B. Bridgman's report, "In accordance with the request to President Roosevelt . . . Squadron 'A' acted as his personal escort on the occasion of the inauguration ceremonies at Washington, D.C., Saturday, March 4, 1905." Traveling from New York to Washington by train and boat, Bridgman records that "the Squadron, including the band of 18 pieces, consisted of 194 horses and . . . left its armory at 8 o'clock, and preceded by the mounted band, marched down Fifth Avenue to 25th Street, then west to the 24th Street ferry house of the Pennsylvania Railroad, where boats were taken to Jersey City, where trains were waiting." Bridgman further states that upon arrival in Washington, "The Squadron formed 'platoon front' and, preceded by the band, marched at the head of the President's carriage down Pennsylvania Avenue to the Capitol."[8]

Also taking part in Roosevelt's presidential inaugural parade were the band and 1st Squadron (Troops A, B, C, D) of the 7th Cavalry, which had by this point returned to the United States from Cuba, and, according to Chief Musician James Brockenshire, were detached at Fort Myer from the rest of the regiment at Fort Oglethorpe, Georgia, "relieving the 15th Cavalry, under orders to proceed

---

7. "All Aboard for Buffalo, Wednesday, October 9, New York State Day at the Pan-American Exposition," *Rome (N.Y.) Citizen*, Tuesday, 1 October 1901, 3.

8. New York State Senate, Appendix I, "Headquarters Squadron A, National Guard, N.Y., Madison Ave. and 94th St., New York, March 10, 1905," in *Documents of the Senate of the State of New York, One Hundred and Twenty Ninth Session, 1906*, vol. 4, nos. 5–8 (Albany: Brandow Printing), 440; Chandler, *Of Garry Owen in Glory*, 121; U.S. Army, Return of the 7th Regiment of Cavalry, Army of the United States, for the month of March 1905, Col. Charles Morton, Commanding, Fort Myer, Va., in *Returns from Regular Army Cavalry Regiments, 1833–1916*, NARA, RG 391, Microfilm Publication M744. The regiment headed for the Philippines later that year, where it made it to Camp McGrath, Batangas in July; Chandler, *Of Garry Owen in Glory*, 122.

to Ft. Ethan Allen. Vt."[9] However, according to Melbourne Chandler, this day was an off day for the band—at least in terms of their dress: "The mounted dress uniform, prescribed in general orders from the War Department, was worn. The uniform consisted of dark blue dress cap and coat, olive drab breeches, khaki leggings and russet leather shoes. The press claimed that the President was disgusted with its appearance. It is admitted that it was a mongrel dress, and an order from the War Department immediately followed, prohibiting the wearing of this mixture of uniform in the future."[10] But when writing of the same event, Brockenshire took a more optimistic slant, reporting only that "we were well received by the President upon passing the reviewing stand; he remembered the organization and the tune of 'Garry Own' from a visit to the Regiment while stationed in Georgia."[11]

Other appearances by the 7th Cavalry Band during these years were the Annual Spring Carnival at Chattanooga, Tennessee, and maneuvers "from which the Band was detached and directed by orders of the War Department to proceed to Nashville, Tenn., in connection with the Annual Reunion of the Veterans of the Confederacy." In the same chronicle, Brockenshire indicates that another Civil War remembrance performance for the band had taken place in Manassas, Virginia, in 1904, and had consisted of the "Annual Maneuvers where the Armies of the Blue and the Gray were represented."[12] The regiment headed for the Philippines later in 1905, where it made it to Camp McGrath, Batangas, in July.[13]

That same month, other U.S. Cavalry bands were stationed at various installations across the country and in the Philippines, with that of the 1st Cavalry at Fort Clark, Texas; those of the 2nd and 3rd Cavalry Regiments at Camp Stotsenburg, Pampanga, Philippine Islands; 4th Cavalry at Presidio of San Francisco, California; 5th Cavalry at Fort Huachuca, Arizona Territory; 6th Cavalry at Fort Meade, South Dakota; 7th Cavalry at Manila, Philippine Islands (on its way to Camp McGrath, Batangas, where it took over the horses and equipment left by the 12th Cavalry); 8th Cavalry at Fort William McKinley, Rizal, Philippine Islands; 9th Cavalry at Fort Riley, Kansas; 10th Cavalry at Fort Robinson, Nebraska; 11th Cavalry at Fort Des Moines, Iowa; 12th Cavalry at Fort Oglethorpe, Georgia; 13th Cavalry at Fort Myer, Virginia; 14th Cavalry

9. Brockenshire, "Seventh Cavalry Band," 917.
10. Chandler, *Of GarryOwen in Glory*, 121.
11. Brockenshire, "Seventh Cavalry Band," 917.
12. Ibid.
13. Chandler, *Of GarryOwen in Glory*, 122.

at Camp Overton, Mindanao, Philippine Islands; and the 15th Cavalry at Camp Overton, Mindanao, Philippine Islands.[14]

As the decade moved on, newspaper articles and official records continued to mention mounted bands in conjunction with government and civic events. The Squadron A mounted band again appeared in the limelight when it participated in New York Day on 10 October 1907 at the Jamestown Tri-Centennial Exhibition at Sewells Point, Virginia, one of several world's fairs held in the early part of the twentieth century. Addressing Adjutant General Nelson H. Henry on 25 October 1907, Bridgman again includes the number of musicians in the band (six fewer than for the 1905 inauguration) in his report and indicates that travel arrangements were similar to those of the 1905 inauguration:

> SIR.,—I have the honor to make the following report of that portion of Squadron A, Cavalry . . . to His Excellency the Governor, at the Jamestown Exposition, October 8 to 12, 1907.
>
> The total number of officers and men was 127 and 12 in the band, making a total of 139. One hundred and four horses were taken from New York, and 25 hired

14. U.S. Army, Return of the 1st Regiment of Cavalry, Army of the United States, for the month of July 1905, Major J[oseph] A[lfred] Gaston, Commanding, Fort Clark, Tex.; U.S. Army, Return of the 2nd Regiment of Cavalry, Army of the United States, for the month of July 1905, Major Franklin A. Johnson, Commanding, Camp Stotsenburg, Pampanga, Philippine Islands; U.S. Army, Return of the 3rd Regiment of Cavalry, Army of the United States, for the month of July 1905, Col. Joseph A. Dorst, Commanding, Camp Stotsenburg, Pampanga, Philippine Islands; U.S. Army, Return of the 4th Regiment of Cavalry, Army of the United States, for the month of July 1905, Col. Edgar Z. Steever, Commanding, Presidio of San Francisco, Calif.; U.S. Army, Return of the 5th Regiment of Cavalry, Army of the United States, for the month of July 1905, Col. Clarence A. Stednian, Commanding, Fort Huachuca, Ariz. Territory; U.S. Army, Return of the 6th Regiment of Cavalry, Army of the United States, for the month of July 1905, Col. William Staunton, Commanding, Fort Meade, S.Dak.; U.S. Army, Return of the 7th Regiment of Cavalry, Army of the United States, for the month of July 1905, Col. Charles Morton, Commanding, Manila, Philippine Islands; U.S. Army, Return of the 8th Regiment of Cavalry, Army of the United States, for the month of July 1905, Col. George S. Anderson, Commanding, Fort William McKinley, Rizal, Philippine Islands; U.S. Army, Return of the 9th Regiment of Cavalry, Army of the United States, for the month of July 1905, Col. Edward S. Godfrey, Commanding, Fort Riley, Kans.; U.S. Army, Return of the 10th Regiment of Cavalry, Army of the United States, for the month of July 1905, Major Robert D. Read, Commanding, Fort Robinson, Neb.; U.S. Army, Return of the 11th Regiment of Cavalry, Army of the United States, for the month of July 1905, Col. Earl D. Thomas, Commanding, Fort Des Moines, Iowa; U.S. Army, Return of the 12th Regiment of Cavalry, Army of the United States, for the month of July 1905, Col. John B. Kerr, Commanding, Fort Oglethorpe, Ga.; U.S. Army, Return of the 13th Regiment of Cavalry, Army of the United States, for the month of July 1905, Col. Charles A. P. Hatfield, Commanding, Fort Myer, Va.; U.S. Army, Return of the 14th Regiment of Cavalry, Army of the United States, for the month of July 1905, Col. Edward A. Godwin, Commanding, Camp Overton, Mindanao, Philippine Islands; and U.S. Army, Return of the 15th Regiment of Cavalry, Army of the United States, for the month of July 1905, Col. Edward A. Godwin, Commanding, Camp Overton, Mindanao, Philippine Islands, all in *Returns from Regular Army Cavalry Regiments, 1833–1916*, NARA, RG 391, Microfilm Publication M744. Chandler, *Of GarryOwen in Glory*, 121–22.

in Jamestown. Horses were hired only for the actual number men mounted, the remainder being acquired at the camp.

On the afternoon of October 8th, the horses of the squadron were taken by the quartermaster, and a detail from each troop, from the armory to the Pennsylvania railroad yards in Jersey City, and loaded on the special cars waiting . . . arriving at Cape Charles the next morning at 5:30.

On 10 October, the squadron formed for a review on the Lee Parade Grounds, to the left of the 12th United States Cavalry: "At 11 o'clock 'Boots and Saddles' was sounded, 11:20 assembly, and 11:30 adjutant's call, when the squadron, in full dress uniform, preceded by the mounted band, marched to the New York State Building, reporting to the Adjutant-General at 11:45; at 12 o'clock, it escorted Governor Hughes and party to the Auditorium, where the exercises of the day were held."[15]

It is interesting that a state-supported National Guard band would continue to hold such a strong connection with a man in federal office, but what is probably more fascinating is that leaving public office had little apparent bearing on Roosevelt's connection with Squadron A, whose band joined in an escort for the former president in a New York parade on 18 June 1910 after he returned from an extended African safari and European tour. Frederick E. Drinker and Jay Mowbray claim that "the parade was led by a squadron of mounted police, followed by the Squadron A mounted band" and that "the Roosevelt Rough Riders, who were holding their first reunion since 1905, came next escorting their former Colonel."[16]

Similarities between National Guard and Regular Army units continued to increase, especially with the 1903 and 1908 Militia Acts, which required National Guard units, including bands, to conform to the same organization as army units.[17] These actions authorized (and standardized to an extent) bands across the country, with a few cavalry National Guard units establishing mounted bands around the time of World War I—some, as we have seen, stemming from earlier bands—but with most apparently being established

---

15. New York State, Adjutant-General, *Annual Report of the Adjutant-General of the State of New York for the Year 1907*, vol. I (Albany, N.Y.: J. B. Lyon Company, 1908), 735–36.

16. Frederick E. Drinker and Jay Henry Mowbray, *Theodore Roosevelt: His Life and Work* (Washington, D.C.: National Publishing, 1919), 405.

17. Michael D. Doubler, *Civilian in Peace, Soldier in War: The Army National Guard, 1636–2000* (Lawrence: University Press of Kansas, 2003), 141–55.

during the 1920s.[18] Following these acts, the National Defense Act of 1916, which was enacted a year before the U.S. entered World War I and during the time of the Mexican Punitive Expedition, resulted in a unified structure and "guaranteed the state militias' status as the Army's primary reserve force, and it mandated the term 'National Guard' for that force."[19] This legislation also ensured that National Guard bands across the country were treated similarly in terms of instrumentation, funding, etc.[20]

Along with these Militia Acts, beginning in 1904, the first horse-breeding program was begun by the United States Bureau of Animal Industry in cooperation with the Colorado Agricultural Experimental Station with the idea that there would be a strong supply of quality animals for all purposes within the U.S. Army. Up until this point, the army had simply purchased horses as were available from private breeders, farmers, and ranchers. This system did not, however, always result in the best mounts for army work, which could be merciless on rider and horse alike—often comprising hard service, poor forage, dilapidated stables, inexperienced riders, and a shortage of veterinary surgeons.[21] By 1908 and over the next several decades, the program developed into the U.S. Remount Service within the Quartermaster Department (the agency whose assigned mission since 1775 has been to meet the material needs of the American soldier) and purchased, processed, trained, and issued horses and mules to the cavalry, infantry, pack and field artillery, transportation corps, and National Guard. A methodical system of breeding horses and mules along strict height and weight specifications developed, resulting in strong, healthy geldings (castrated males) to be used throughout the U.S. Army and National Guard—including within each branch's mounted bands.[22]

These well-bred horses were crucial for cavalry work—including that of mounted bands, which, along with performing at concerts, official ceremonies,

---

18. Major Les' Melnyk, Army National Guard historian, National Guard Bureau, Arlington, Virginia, e-mail message to author, 20 May 2003. Colonel Leonid Kondratiuk, director of Historical Services of the Massachusetts National Guard, states, "Prior to 1917 there were a number of cavalry regiments in the Guard. I do not know, nor does anyone else, how many had mounted bands. My guess is that there were very few"; Col. Leonid Kondratiuk, e-mail message to author, 21 May 2003.

19. Renee Hylton and Robert K. Wright, Jr., *A Brief History of the Militia and National Guard* (Washington, D.C.: Departments of the Army and the Air Force, Historical Services Division, Office of Public Affairs, National Guard Bureau, August 1993), 20–21.

20. For a history of U.S. National Guard cavalry bands, see Gleason, "Chronicle of the Pre–World War II Cavalry Bands," 17–30.

21. Dobak and Phillips, *Black Regulars*, 110–11; Kenner, *Buffalo Soldiers*, 29.

22. Carter, *U.S. Cavalry Horse*, 8–58. Because of behavior problems, stallions were not used, and mixing geldings with mares resulted in geldings fighting over the mares.

military and civilian parades, and other events in camp and towns, were tak-
ing part in military maneuvers along with other regimental troops. One good
example of this was the "Fall Maneuvers" taking place from Monday, 28 Sep-
tember, to Tuesday, 13 October 1903, on a 28,000-acre tract of land in West
Point, Kentucky, twenty-eight miles west of Louisville. Gathering from Camp
George H. Thomas, Georgia; Jefferson Barracks, Missouri; Fort Sheridan,
Illinois; Fort Wayne, Michigan; Fort Porter, New York; Fort Brady, Michigan;
Fort Thomas, Kentucky; Fort Columbus Arsenal, Tennessee; Fort Columbus
Barracks, Ohio; and Washington, D.C., ten thousand soldiers from infantry,
artillery, and cavalry units took part in an umpired mock war between "Blue"
and "Brown" armies. Under the order that "regimental bands . . . accompany
the troops," foot bands of the 1st and 3rd U.S. Infantry Regiments, the 1st
Wisconsin Organized Militia, the 1st, 2nd, and 3rd Indiana Organized Militia,
the 1st, 2nd, and 3rd Michigan Organized Militia, the 2nd and 3rd Kentucky
Organized Militia, and the 8th Ohio Organized Militia participated. As part
of a unified cavalry brigade, mounted bands of the 2nd, 4th, 7th, and 8th Cavalry Regiments took part in maneuvers, concerts, and reviews.[23] Such events
could hardly have gone unnoticed by the public, and, in addition to serving as a
training arena for military personnel, these occasions would have strengthened
public opinion of the U.S. military, which had gradually earned a place in the
nation's culture during peacetime. As it had for centuries, military music was
doing its part in positively connecting military forces with the public.

Consequently, military officials were amenable to having military units,
including bands, continue taking part in civilian events. Already mentioned
are the various mounted band performances at world's fairs across the country—Chicago, 1892–93; Buffalo, 1901; and Jamestown, 1907. Along with these
performances, mounted bands took part in two centennial world's fairs—the
1904 Louisiana Purchase Exposition, held in St. Louis, Missouri; and the 1905
Lewis and Clark Centennial and American Pacific Exposition and Oriental Fair,
held in Portland, Oregon. For the 1904 performance, the 8th U.S. Cavalry
mounted band, stationed at Jefferson Barracks, Missouri, took part in what must
have been a massive Independence Day parade, along with various U.S. Army
and Marine infantry, signal, hospital, and artillery units; Missouri National
Guard; Columbus Rifles and Band; Edisto Rifles; Georgia Militia; 1st Indiana

---

23. Col. Walter Fieldhouse, *Fall Maneuvers, West Point, Kentucky, 1903: Report of Colonel Walter Fieldhouse,
Inspector General, Accredited Military Representative of the State of Illinois* (Springfield, Ill.: Phillips Brothers,
1904), 12, 39, 63.

Infantry; Yale Battalion; Weil Band; Neely Zouaves; and the Northwestern Military Academy Cadets, as well as a Philippine contingency of a battalion of Philippine Scouts, Scout Band, and a battalion of Philippine Constabulary, and Constabulary Band.[24] On hand also during the month of June was the 1st Cavalry Band.[25] For the 1905 world's fair, the 4th Cavalry mounted band was on hand for the pre-opening ceremony: "Portland, Ore., May 31—Vice-President Fairbanks and the party of Congressmen who are to participate in the formal opening of the Lewis and Clark Centennial Exposition to-morrow, arrived in this city to-day, and were met at the Union Station by President H. W. Goode [of the exposition] and a delegation of citizens. A mounted band and two hundred men of the 4th United States Cavalry headed the procession that escorted the visitors through the centre of the city to their hotel."[26]

Events like world's fairs were high-profile events and were good publicity for the army. Selection to perform was an honor, but it is not always apparent how bands were chosen. While some were perhaps invited simply because they were stationed in the proximity of the event, others, like Squadron A, Cavalry, National Guard New York, were selected because of some kind of personal connection with the event. This was true for bands of the Regular Army as well, including that of the 11th Cavalry, which served in the Philippines from 1901 to 1904, when William Howard Taft was the country's first civil governor. Consequently, its band was a logical choice to perform for his 1909 presidential inauguration parade. Additionally, as the 11th Cavalry served in Cuba from 1906 to 1909 as part of President Theodore Roosevelt's Army of Cuban Pacification, the regiment had a certain connection with the outgoing president as well. What must have been an exhausting trip for men and horses of the field, staff, and band and 2nd and 3rd Squadrons of the 11th Cavalry began with their departure from Pinar del Rio, Cuba, aboard the USAT *Meade*. Upon their arrival at Newport News, Virginia, at 5:00 P.M., 2 March 1909, they proceeded by train via Southern Railroad en route to Washington, D.C., arriving at St. Asaph's Camp, St. Elmo, Alexandria County, Virginia, at 4:30 A.M. on 3 March. Remaining on the train until 7:00 A.M., 4 March, the command proceeded mounted to Washington, D.C., to participate in the infamous

24. "Route, Formation of World's Fair Fourth of July Military Parade," *St. Louis New Republic*, Tuesday, 28 June 1904, 3.

25. "The First Regiment of Cavalry, United States Army," *Cavalry Journal* 31, no. 127 (April 1922): 179.

26. "Mr. Fairbanks Reaches Portland, Visits Grounds Where the Lewis and Clark Exposition Opens To-Day," *New-York Daily Tribune*, 1 June 1905, 6.

FIGURE 7.2. 11th Cavalry Band in the inaugural parade for President William Howard Taft, 4 March 1909. *Courtesy of the Hazen Collection of Band Photographs and Ephemera, Archives Center, National Museum of American History, Smithsonian Institution.*

1909 inaugural parade, which is known for receiving the heaviest snowstorm in inaugural history. Ten inches of snow smothered the city, requiring six thousand workmen to clear Pennsylvania Avenue for the parade, in which thirty thousand people marched (figure 7.2). Upon completing the Taft inauguration mission, the 11th Cavalry contingency headed for garrison life at its new home at Fort Oglethorpe, Georgia.[27]

A performance of this type would have been arduous for all concerned and would have been on the level of detail as other traveling gigs mentioned above. Along with this rigor, the financial support would have been considerable, and, while mounted band performances were good for troop morale, ambience, and public support, the financial question was indeed raised periodically. While the traditional reason given for the discontinuance of mounted bands later during

27. U.S. Army, Return of the 11th Regiment of U.S. Cavalry, for the month of March 1909, Col. James Parker, Commanding, Fort Oglethorpe, Ga., in *Returns from Regular Army Cavalry Regiments, 1833–1916,* NARA, RG 391, Microfilm Publication M744.

World War II was because all cavalry units were becoming dismounted with the motorization of all military forces, the financial element certainly must have been a part of the equation.

While this end was still several decades away, voices were already being raised in question before World War I. Writing in 1914 and identified only as W. C. B., a concerned individual voiced his opinions about the expense of mounted bands in "Are Army Bands Necessary?" in the October issue of *Journal of the United States Cavalry Association*. While he apparently felt that bands in general were something to be retained in the army, he had difficulty with those on horseback: "If there is one element in the cavalry in which the Government fails to get its money's worth it is the mounted band. The rendition of high class music and the performance of kitchen and stable police do not go well together, and the proper maintenance of the band is the source of more petty squabbles in a regiment than almost any one other administrative feature, and places the Regimental Adjutant between two fires." W. C. B. writes further that non-band troops were taken away from other duties to help with care of band horses and other non-musical, band-related duties so that musicians could take care of musical ones. He also suggests that if cavalry bandsmen were made responsible for all necessary non-musical duties, musicians would stop reenlisting for cavalry bands and would "go to bands where their duties are entirely musical." He continues by saying that since "it is doubtful whether their turning out mounted would average more than once a week . . . the original cost and expense of the upkeep of the mounts of the band is too much considering the real military use that is made of it."[28] Therefore, he gives an alternative solution reminiscent of eighteenth- and nineteenth-century European trumpeter corps:

> When the Ninth Cavalry was at the Division Maneuver Camp at Fort Sam Houston last summer it had a trumpet corps which was a delight to hear, and it is understood that years ago the Seventh Cavalry had a similar one.
>
> This seems to point a way to the solution of the vexed question. Let us drop our expensive cavalry bands except the Chief Trumpeter and possibly the Drum Major, a bass drummer and a snare drummer and a couple of cornetists. The Chief Trumpeter should be a warrant officer with initial pay of $65.00 per month. Let the Chief Trumpeter devote his time exclusively to the training of the trumpeters, especially

---

28. W. C. B., "Are Army Bands Necessary?," Military Notes, *Journal of the United States Cavalry Association* 25, no. 104 (October 1914): 340–41.

in working together as a trumpet corps, thus forming within the regiment, at a relatively trifling expense, field music which no regiment need be ashamed of, and which will answer all the practical purposes of a mounted band. This would not mean that our men would never hear a military band by any means for the infantry and field artillery, with which cavalry is usually stationed, have bands whose music is ample for concerts and serenades, and the rendition of high class music which all delight to hear. If we ever have a post garrisoned exclusively by a brigade of cavalry, let there be established there a post band. Even under these conditions it is doubtful whether it would pay to have it mounted.[29]

As is confirmed in preceding chapters, mounted trumpet/bugle corps were evidenced in European and U.S. Cavalry regiments of past eras—and, mentioning a 7th Cavalry trumpet corps, W. C. B. is probably referring to one during the 1880s at Fort Meade, South Dakota, headed by George Hardy, chief trumpeter of the regiment, whom Brockenshire referred to as "without doubt, the best trumpeter in the Army."[30] This corps developed a considerable reputation and often took the place of the 7th Cavalry Band, which Brockenshire indicates was dismounted for a time during these years and "remained so until after the Spanish-American War, when they were mounted at Huntsville, Ala., in October, 1898 under bandleader, Mr. [Johann] Vondraeck by direction of Col. Cooney, Lieut. Colonel Commandant."[31] Consequently, as W. C. B. indicates, it was the trumpet corps under Hardy's leadership that undertook mounted music roles: "The trumpet corps, under his direction, was proverbial throughout the service, which accounted for a dismounted band, it having been proven that the spirited marches played by the trumpet corps at mounted functions were far superior to anything that could be played by the band when the regiment was assembled for mounted maneuvers."[32]

The 7th Cavalry trumpet corps was also active when the regiment was stationed at Fort Riley, Kansas, 1907–10—now in conjunction with the band—when both participated for three years running in "the Carnival at Wichita,

---

29. Ibid., 340–43.

30. Brockenshire, "Seventh Cavalry Band," 893.

31. Ibid. Johann Vondraeck was born in what is now the Czech Republic around 1842 and enlisted at the age of fifty-four in 1896. He served as the principal musician of the 7th U.S. Cavalry Band from 1896 to 1898. U.S. Army, *Register of Enlistments in the U.S. Army, 1798–1914*, NARA, Microfilm Publication M233, 81 rolls; U.S. Army, Records of the Adjutant General's Office, 1780s–1917, NARA, RG 94, College Park, Md.

32. W. C. B., "Are Army Bands Necessary?," 340–43.

Kans., St. Joe, Mo., and Omaha, Nebr." Brockenshire adds that, along with being the only mounted band in evidence, "at each of these functions, the Regimental Trumpet Corps of 24 men, assisted greatly in making a record for the Seventh Cavalry Band by the splendid manner in which it played trumpet marches in conjunction with the Band. Many of the marches played were composed and arranged especially for such functions by the Bandleader, myself."[33] To aid with these combined trumpet corps–band performances, along with band instruments, the Quartermaster's Department furnished "each light battery two small brass B♭ bugles. To every other company two G trumpets with F slides, and, if desired, detachable F crooks."[34] While W. C. B., and presumably other critics, questioned the practice of utilizing mounted bands, they would last in the U.S. Army and National Guard for another thirty years.

In 1915, opening on 3 April, another world's fair—the Panama-Pacific International Exposition—was held in San Francisco, having the threefold purpose of celebrating the opening of the Panama Canal; commemorating the 400th anniversary of the discovery of the Pacific Ocean; and celebrating the rebuilding of San Francisco following the 1906 earthquake and fire. Again, a mounted band was on hand to help with the festivities. As Frank Morton Todd wrote of the event, "Battalions of soldiers, sailors, and marines, with artillery and cavalry, rolled through the great arches and swung around the crescent above the sunken gardens, flags fluttering, trumpets blaring, the encircling walls echoing the clatter of hoofs and the rumble of limbers." Todd states further, "A squadron of the First U. S. Cavalry was assigned to the event, and with several companies of marines and sailors from the battleship 'Oregon,' the mounted regimental band of the First Cavalry, and the 'Oregon' Band, led the march from the Baker Street entrance. William Jennings Bryan, then Secretary of State, expressed his congratulations to the club, the city, and the Exposition, over a transcontinental telephone line from the Press Club of Washington."[35]

This 1st Cavalry Band mentioned here was also probably the unnamed mounted band that Todd mentions as a welcoming escort to the guests, who included a young Franklin D. (assistant secretary of the navy) and Eleanor Roosevelt, aboard the train of U.S. vice president Thomas R. Marshall, which

---

33. Brockenshire, "Seventh Cavalry Band," 942.

34. U.S. Army, Regulations for the Army of the United States, 1901, with Appendix, 181, para. 1327.

35. Frank Morton Todd, The Story of the Exposition; Being the Official History of the International Celebration Held at San Francisco in 1915 to Commemorate the Discovery of the Pacific Ocean and the Construction of the Panama Canal, vol. 3 (New York: G. P. Putnam's Sons, 1921), 30, 42.

arrived in San Francisco on 20 March to dedicate the exposition on Wednesday, 24 March 1915, in President Woodrow Wilson's absence: "An escort of cavalry and a troop of mounted police were drawn up on the Embarcadero [eastern waterfront and roadway of the Port of San Francisco], the mounted band played the 'Banks of the Wabash,' the party was taken to some waiting automobiles, and the whole made a brilliant parade through the thronging streets to the Fairmont Hotel."[36] Erwin R. Thompson explains of the event that, "to lend an army presence, the Provisional Squadron, 1st Cavalry (12 officers and 302 men), and the 1st Cavalry Band arrived from the Presidio of Monterey."[37]

Later that year on 9 September as part of the same event, California's Admission Day was held in celebration of the state's sixty-fifth birthday. Marking the day was an enormous parade comprised of various civic, official, and private military-fraternal organizations, including the California Grays, the Nationals in their Zouave uniforms, the League of the Cross Cadets, and the Columbia Park Boys. Todd relates that "there were three whole divisions made up of United States soldiers, sailors, and marines" and makes the same mistaken assertion that other American writers have made over the years: "They had with them the only mounted band in the Army, that of the United States First Cavalry."[38]

Along with early twentieth-century mounted cavalry bands, those of some artillery units were mounted as well, following nineteenth-century practice as evidenced by General Order No. 88, of 25 June 1901, which declares that, "by direction of the Secretary of War, the Ninth Band, Artillery Corps, organized under the act of Congress approved 2 February 1901, is designated as a mounted band."[39] Further, the War Department's *Annual Report* of 1907 indicates that an

---

36. Todd, *Story of the Exposition*, 27. About Wilson's absence, Todd comments, "Owing to the difficult problems confronting the Chief Executive of a great commercial nation trying to deport itself as a neutral during the European war, and owing, perhaps, as well to problems arising out of the anarchy that had prevailed in Mexico for several years, President Wilson was unable to pay San Francisco a visit during the Exposition season" (26).

37. Erwin N. Thompson, *Defender of the Gate: The Presidio of San Francisco, A History from 1846 to 1995* (San Francisco: Golden Gate National Recreation Area, National Park Service, 1995), 394.

38. Todd, *Story of the Exposition*, 138. I have periodically run across announcements, reports, articles, reviews, etc., in which the writer identified a particular U.S. mounted cavalry band as the only one in the United States. Responding in 1938 to another reader's query or a reference in a past article to the 3rd Cavalry having the only U.S. mounted military band, B. B., Jr., writes, "The 3rd Cavalry Band is not the only mounted band in the Army. A number of Cavalry units have mounted bands, although with the advent of Motorization of Cavalry, of necessity some of these have been dismounted." B. B., Jr., "Ask the Journal," *Army and Navy Journal* 75, no. 36 (7 May 1938): 794.

39. U.S. Army, Adjutant-General's Office, "General Orders, No. 88," 25 June 1901, in *General Orders and Circulars, Adjutant General's Office, 1901* (Washington, D.C.: Government Printing Office, 1902), 1, para. 2.

FIGURE 7.3. Unidentified U.S. Artillery mounted band, ca. 1907–12, depicted on a postcard. F. Mutchler, exclusive pub., U.S. Army P.C., Highland Park, Illinois. The photo may have been taken at Fort Sheridan, which is not far from Highland Park. Fort Sheridan was a cavalry post and in 1910 became the first ROTC camp, which this band may have been supporting. *Author's Collection.*

act of Congress was approved on 25 January 1907 to permanently separate the field artillery from the coast artillery with the organization of the former being six regiments, each of which would be comprised of six batteries organized into two battalions of three batteries each. This act effectively separated the mobile field artillery from the coast artillery, which "has to do with fixed defenses of our coasts."[40] As horse batteries of artillery and other units were designed to follow the cavalry, all the soldiers were mounted, and as bands would have to be horse-mobile to keep up with an artillery brigade made up of such batteries, the "Six Regimental Bands" attached to the "Six Batteries Field Artillery (Horse)"—as designated in the "Organization of Regiments and Companies"

---

40. U.S. War Department, *Annual Reports, 1907*, vol. 2. (Washington, D.C.: Government Printing Office, 1907), 216, 217.

in the *Official Army Register for 1908* (1 December 1907)—would have been mounted (figure 7.3).[41]

Even rarer would have been an appearance of a mounted U.S. Infantry band, the mention of which appears in a record of the 250th anniversary of the founding of the city of Philadelphia in 1908. During this Founders' Week, consisting of celebratory events over six days of varied themes, the opening parade for Military Day (each day had a separate parade) on Monday, 5 October, consisted of three divisions of varied military units. The first of these, marshaled by Colonel W. H. C. Bowen, along with respective companies, included eleven Coast Artillery Corps bands from Forts Hamilton, Totten, Schuyler, and Wadsworth, New York; Fort DuPont, Delaware; Forts Hancock and Mott, New Jersey; Forts Howard, McHenry, and Washington, Maryland; and Fort Hunt, Virginia. Along with these were the 13th Cavalry Band from Fort Myer, Virginia, and representatives from the 12th Infantry, including "Mounted Band and Companies E, F, G and H, 12th Infantry from Fort Jay"—altogether aggregating 3,500 men in the first of the three divisions of this first of six parades.[42]

At the turn of the twentieth century, government regulations were identifying specific instruments, including full complements of families of wind and percussion instruments for all military bands, including kettledrums for mounted bands. Performances for concerts, ceremonies, and parades continued for National Guard and Regular Army bands with large maneuvers of thousands of soldiers and further world's fairs and other civic events, including mounted band performances, which promoted a positive relationship between military forces and the public. As the new century took shape, the international scope for which the Spanish-American War had initially prepared the U.S. military specifically and the country in general expanded further in North America and Europe.

---

41. U.S. War Department, *Official Army Register for 1908, Published by Order of the Secretary of War in Compliance with Law*, Document No. 312 (Washington, D.C.: Adjutant General's Office, War Department, 1907), 546.

42. Frederick P. Henry, ed., *Founders' Week Memorial Volume* (Philadelphia: City of Philadelphia, 1909), 77–78. Following the Military Day parade were Municipal Day; Industrial Day; Medical Day and Children's and Naval Day; Historical Day; and Athletic and Knights Templar Day parades.

FIGURE 8.1. 1st Illinois Cavalry Band at R.R. Station, Brownsville, Texas, ca. 1913. Saxophonist Giuseppe (Joe) Del Principe from Chicago stands behind the bass drum, which reads, "1st Illinois Cavalry Band, Chas Horn, Chief Musician." This unit was the basis for the 106th Cavalry of the 1920s–1940s, of which the Illinois detachment included the Chicago Black Horse Troop and Mounted Band. *Author's Collection.*

CHAPTER 8

Mexican Expedition,
World War I, and the 1920s

U.S. ARMY BANDS HAD BEEN ACTIVE SUPPORTING MILITARY AND CIVIC
endeavors after the Spanish-American War and through the turn of the century. The period covering the Mexican Expedition, World War I, and the
postwar 1920s began to see a change in military logistics as U.S. forces became
more mechanized, which in turn affected mounted band procedures and
performances.

MEXICAN EXPEDITION

With the outbreak of revolution in Mexico in late 1910, twenty thousand U.S.
soldiers were deployed along the U.S.-Mexican border to prevent incursions and
sales of contraband. Launched against the paramilitary forces of Mexican insurgent Francisco "Pancho" Villa (President Woodrow Wilson's former favored
incumbent) when he attacked Columbus, New Mexico, and a detachment of the
13th Cavalry on 9 March 1916 with 485 of his "Villistas," the Mexican "Punitive"
Expedition (14 March 1916–7 February 1917) was the last occasion of horse-
mounted troops playing a significant role in an American military expedition.[1]

While the main elements of the expedition took place in 1916 and 1917,
there were several years of buildup, with one of the initial deployments of

---

1. Urwin, *United States Cavalry*, 176. A thorough investigation of the Mexican Expedition should also
entail a study of the varied aspects of the Mexican Revolution. See Frank McLynn, *Villa and Zapata: A History of the Mexican Revolution* (New York: Carroll and Graf, 2001), and John Womack, *Zapata and the Mexican Revolution* (New York: Vintage Press, 1970). The Mexican Expedition was the U.S. conflict that saw the
advent of the use of the airplane, automobile, and motorized truck in warfare, although the horse was still
the primary means of transportation and warfare for cavalry, infantry, and artillery troops.

the conflict being a maneuver division under the command of Major General William H. Carter. As reported in the *New York Times*, the ambient atmosphere of a 12 March 1911 gathering in San Antonio to view the assembled soldiers reached festival-like proportions and included "a dozen concerts going on at the same time in different parts of the camp, the band of every regiment here being ordered to do its part in entertaining."[2] Along with the arrivals of the 28th Infantry from Fort Snelling, Minnesota, and a part of the 11th Infantry from Fort D. A. Russell, Cheyenne, Wyoming, the 11th Cavalry had just arrived by train from Fort Oglethorpe on 11 March.[3] The crowd was now turning its attention to the arrival of the 9th Cavalry, which reached San Antonio on 15 March by train also from Fort Russell—and whose band by this time was being led by its second black chief musician, Wade H. Hammond.[4] What must have been a crowd-pleasing occurrence was when the 3rd Field Artillery detrained: "Just before sundown the Third Field Artillery arrived from Fort Myer, Virginia. This crack organization immediately detrained, and, led by its splendid mounted band of fifty pieces, started for the camp on the gallop. The artillerymen astride the big artillery horses made a fine sight."[5]

While it is doubtful that all regiments rotating for border patrol over the ensuing several years received this kind of attention, records indicate that bands were well received by the public for their mounted and dismounted work in

2. "Great Crowd Visits Camp. Many Mexicans from San Antonio See Gen. Carter's Troops. Special to the New York Times," *New York Times*, 13 March 1911.

3. U.S. Army, Return of the 11th Regiment of Cavalry, Army of the United States, for the month of March 1911, Col. James Parker, Commanding, Maneuver Division, San Antonio, Tex., in *Returns from Regular Army Cavalry Regiments, 1833–1916*, NARA, RG 391, Microfilm Publication M744.

4. U.S. Army, Return of the 9th Regiment of Cavalry, Army of the United States, for the month of March 1911, Col. George S. Anderson, Commanding, Maneuver Division, San Antonio, Tex., in *Returns from Regular Army Cavalry Regiments, 1833–1916*, NARA, RG 391, Microfilm Publication M744; Lefferts, "U.S. Army Black Regimental Bands," 171.

5. As a regimental band would not have had fifty musicians at this point, but rather twenty-five to twenty-eight, the field trumpeters were probably riding with the band, and an uninitiated newspaper reporter would not have known the difference between the two groups. "Great Crowd Visits Camp," *New York Times*, 13 March 1911. The Third Field Artillery field staff and band and Companies A and B had been at Fort Sam Houston since 10 August 1908, where they had arrived from Chickamauga Park, Georgia. Company C arrived at Fort Sam Houston in October 1908 from Fort Snelling, Minnesota. Companies D, E, and F arrived at Maneuver Camp, San Antonio, on 12 March 1911 from Fort Myer. U.S. Army, Return of the 3rd Regiment of Field Artillery, Army of the United States, for the month of August 1908, Col. Lotus Miles, Commanding, Fort Sam Houston, Tex.; U.S. Army, Return of the 3rd Regiment of Field Artillery, Army of the United States, for the month of September 1908, Col. Lotus Miles, Commanding, Fort Sam Houston, Tex.; U.S. Army, Return of the 3rd Regiment of Field Artillery, Army of the United States, for the month of October 1908, Col. Lotus Miles, Commanding, Fort Sam Houston, Tex.; and U.S. Army, Return of the 3rd Regiment of Field Artillery, Army of the United States, for the month of March 1911, Col. Lotus Miles, Commanding, Maneuver Division, San Antonio, Tex., all in *Returns from Regular Army Cavalry Regiments, 1833–1916*, NARA, RG 391, Microfilm Publication M744. Fort D. A. Russell is currently Francis E. Warren Air Force Base.

ceremonies, troop motivation, celebrations, and concerts. One event attesting to this popularity was the presentation by Mayor C. O. Ellis to Chief Musician Wade Hammond and members of the 9th Cavalry Band, on behalf of the citizens of Douglas, Arizona, during a September 1914 concert, of a gold medal set with diamonds, inscribed, "Presented to the chief musician, Ninth Cavalry Band by the citizens of Douglas, Arizona. September 14, 1914. Keep step to the music of the Union."[6] Hammond's appreciation letter of two days later reveals his reciprocal feelings and evidence of some improvement in race relations for black regiments: "While it is probable that no member of my race has ever enjoyed such a rare distinction, in my line of endeavor, I am loathe to accept this kindness as a personal exaltation, being mindful of the loyalty and faithfulness of each member of the Ninth Cavalry Band, whom I am pleased to recognize as my fellow and co-laborer, and to whom is due no small share of the great measure of kindness you have shown."[7]

Duty for bandsmen on the border, however, was not all music. Relaying to a *Los Angeles Times* reporter in 1991, ninety-seven-year-old Malcolm Heuring, who had served as a cavalry cornetist for seven years during this period, recalls, "The 5th Cavalry's band and two regiments were called to Columbus, N.M. [from Fort Myer] [joining the 13th Cavalry],[8] shortly after the border town had been raided. . . . After the cavalry secured the town, the band joined the punitive expedition into Mexico led by Gen. John J. Pershing."[9] Consequently, with this initial skirmish, musicians were part of the casualties. Of the seven 13th Cavalry soldiers killed in the Columbus attack were band members Sergeant John G. Nievergelt and Sergeant Paul Simon.[10] Years later, fellow bandsman William

6. "A Bandmaster," Men of the Month, *Crisis, A Record of the Darker Races, Published Monthly by the National Association for the Advancement of Colored People* 11, no. 1 (November 1915): 13.

7. Reprinted in "Public Appreciation for the Achievements of Chief Musician Wade H. Hammond," *Metronome* (1914): 55.

8. As U.S. Army practice continued to move military units throughout the world regularly, the Mexican Expedition was no exception. Following the 5th Cavalry to New Mexico were the 11th Cavalry, arriving at Columbus on 16 March 1916 from Fort Oglethorpe, and the 12th Cavalry, arriving on 19 March 1916 from Fort Robinson, Nebraska. U.S. Army, Return of the 11th Regiment of Cavalry, March 1916, Col. James Lockett, Commanding, Casas Grande, Mex.; and U.S. Army, Return of the 12th Regiment of Cavalry, March 1916, Col. Horatio G. Sickel, Commanding, Columbus, N.Mex., both in *Returns from Regular Army Cavalry Regiments, 1833–1916*, NARA, RG 391, Microfilm Publication M744.

9. Bernice Hirabayashi, "Never Too Old to Make Music," *Los Angeles Times*, 14 July 1991; U.S. Army, Return of the 5th Regiment of Cavalry, March 1916, Col. Wilber E. Wilder, Commanding, Lake Itascate, Mex., in *Returns from Regular Army Cavalry Regiments, 1833–1916*, NARA, RG 391, Microfilm Publication M744.

10. U.S. Army, Return of Casualties in 13th Cavalry in Action at Columbus, N.Mex., March 9, 1916, Col. H. J. Slocum, Commanding, Columbus, N.Mex., in *Returns from Regular Army Cavalry Regiments, 1833–1916*, NARA, RG 391, Microfilm Publication M744.

Adkins of Denver, Colorado, recalled that during this time, "we were armed with .45 Colt automatic pistols—general issue to Headquarters and Band"—another reminder that long gone were the days of musicians being noncombatants.[11]

Musical duty during the expedition would have consisted of performances for the community as already indicated, as well as military ones—ceremonial as well as motivational. As reported by a *Sausilito News* article of the time, the band of the 5th Cavalry, which remained in Mexico until 1917, provided an element that all military bands attempt—a sense of home for soldiers—in this case during the Christmas season:

> El Valle, San Buena Ventura, Chihuahua, Mexico, December 25.—There was a Fourth of July tinge to the Christmas celebration at this camp, which is the extreme southern point of the American Army's punitive expedition line. Nearly three hundred dollars' worth of fireworks, set off Christmas eve, consoled the 4000 soldiers in camp for their inability to hang up stockings, and brought something akin to alarm to the residents of El Valle and the Mexicans inhabiting the fringe of adobe huts that surrounds the camp.
>
> Christmas day itself was full to overflowing with amusements. They varied from Christmas carols, which the Fifth Cavalry Band played at the headquarters of each organization immediately after reveille, to a bountiful spread at noon and a bullfight in the afternoon.[12]

Cornet player Malcolm Heuring recalls that, upon returning to El Paso in 1917, the 5th Cavalry Band continued to be engaged in typical duty of playing in daily concerts in the bandstand, as well as on horseback during parades.[13] Adkins, with the 13th, recalls similarly, "Our bandmaster, Officer [Chief Musician Oscar P.] Luedtke [sometimes spelled Luedeke], liked to parade us around

---

11. William Adkins, "The Story of Pancho Villa at Columbus, New Mexico," pt. 1, *Family Tree* 1, no. 1 (1969—1970): 41. Adkins also recalls, "We of the 13th Cavalry used to shoot craps with Pancho's men and sell them American cigarettes. Pancho printed his own money—una peso, cinco peso, duis peso, and viente peso—paper money. We would give them five packs of cigarettes for one of each of the bills, and send a set of the bills to our girl friends up in the States" (40). Of pistol use by bandsmen, Training Regulations, 130–15 indicates, "The band is ordinarily armed only with the pistol. Instruction in the use of this arm, mounted and dismounted, should be given according to a modified scheme of training based on the simple uses of the pistol as prescribed in Training Regulations on the subject." U.S. War Department, *The Band: Formations, Movements, Inspections, Etc., Mounted and Dismounted*, section 1, 1.f.,g.,h.,j., Training Regulations, No. 130—15, 2 (Washington, D.C.: Government Printing Office, 15 February 1926), NARA, RG 287, College Park, Md.

12. "Mexicans Scared by Fireworks," *Sausalito (Calif.) News*, December 1916.

13. Hirabayashi, "Never Too Old to Make Music."

FIGURE 8.2. 8th Cavalry Band and field trumpeters, Fort Bliss, Texas, August 1916. *Courtesy of Fort Bliss and Old Ironsides Museums, Fort Bliss, Texas.*

town, mounted, playing waltzes, two-steps, marches, etc." He also recounted that kettledrums were part of the picture: "We had a pair of kettle drums that hung over the horse's neck in front of the saddle of the musician."[14]

Along with cavalry units of the Regular Army, federalized National Guard units headed for Mexico as well, including the 1st Illinois Cavalry, which began as the 1st Illinois Volunteer Cavalry at the beginning of the Spanish-American War in 1898 when it was stationed at Chickamauga, Georgia. Resuming state status later that year, it was redesignated as 1st Illinois Cavalry, 22 June 1899. The unit was federalized again in 1916 for the Mexican Punitive Expedition and along with their band, headed south (see figures 8.1–8.3).[15]

With the official conclusion of the Mexican Expedition coming on 7 February 1917,[16] cavalry regiments with their bands were still in place and intact the preceding December with some in Mexico—including the 5th in El Valle,

14. William Adkins, "The Story of Pancho Villa at Columbus, New Mexico," pt. 2, *Family Tree* 1, no. 2 (1969—1970): 51.

15. *1940 National Guard of the U.S. Naval Militia State of Illinois*, 106th Cavalry Collection, Chicago Historical Society, 420, 427.

16. Although 7 February 1917 was the official concluding date, skirmishes along the U.S.-Mexican border occurred for several years following.

FIGURE 8.3. Mounted Band, El Paso, Texas, ca. 1917. Probably troops and band of the 8th Cavalry from Fort Bliss. *Courtesy of Fort Bliss and Old Ironsides Museums, Fort Bliss, Texas.*

and the 7th, 10th, 11th, and 13th regiments in Colonia Dublan. Others were stationed in U.S. border states, including the 1st in Douglas, Arizona, the 12th in Columbus, New Mexico, and six stationed in Texas—the 3rd in Mercedes, the 6th in Marfa, the 8th and 17th at Fort Bliss, the 14th in Del Rio, and the 16th at Fort Sam Houston.[17]

17. U.S. Army, Return of the 1st Regiment of Cavalry, December 1916, Col. Frederick F. Foltz, Commanding, Douglas, Ariz.; U.S. Army, Return of the 3rd Regiment of Cavalry, December 1916, Col. Augustus P. Blocksom, Commanding, Mercedes, Tex.; U.S. Army, Return of the 5th Regiment of Cavalry, December 1916, Col. D. L. Tate, Commanding, Lake Itascate, Mex.; U.S. Army, Return of the 6th Regiment of Cavalry, December 1916, Col. J. A. Gaston, Commanding, Marfa, Tex.; U.S. Army, Return of the 7th Regiment of Cavalry, December 1916, Col. Selah R[eeve] H[obbie] Tompkins, Commanding, Colonia Dublan, Mex.; U.S. Army, Return of the 8th Regiment of Cavalry, December 1916, Col. John W. Heard, Commanding, Fort Bliss, Tex.; U.S. Army, Return of the 10th Regiment of Cavalry, December 1916, Col. E. W. Evans, Commanding, Colonia Dublan, Mex.; U.S. Army, Return of the 11th Regiment of Cavalry, December 1916, Col. William J. Nicholson, Commanding, Colonia Dublan, Mex.; U.S. Army, Return of the 12th Regiment of Cavalry, December 1916, Col. Horatio G. Sickel, Commanding, Columbus, N.Mex.; U.S. Army, Return of the 13th Regiment of Cavalry, December 1916, Col. Henry T. Allen, Commanding, Colonia Dublan, Mex.; U.S. Army, Return of the 14th Regiment of Cavalry, December 1916, Col.

FIGURE 8.4. 4th Cavalry Band, Mid-Pacific Carnival, Honolulu, military parade, ca. 1912–18. *Courtesy of the Hazen Collection of Band Photographs and Ephemera, Archives Center, National Museum of American History, Smithsonian Institution.*

While the 2nd was stationed at Plattsburg Barracks, New York, others— like the 9th at Camp Stotsenburg in the Philippines, the 15th at Fort William McKinley in the Philippines, and the 4th at Schofield Barracks, Oahu, Hawaii (figure 8.4)—serve as a reminder that U.S. concerns in the Pacific and Asia were still evident and would be for some time to come.[18] Some of these units remained in the southwestern United States during World War I serving as

Augustus C. Macomb, Commanding, Del Rio, Tex.; U.S. Army, Return of the 16th Cavalry, December 1916, Col. William S. Scott, Commanding, Fort Sam Houston, Tex.; and U.S. Army, Return of the 17th Cavalry, December 1916, Col. Willard A. Holbrook, Commanding, Fort Bliss, Tex., all in *Returns from Regular Army Cavalry Regiments, 1833–1916.* NARA, RG 391, Microfilm Publication M744.

18. Joseph I. Lambert, *One Hundred Years with the Second Cavalry* (Fort Riley, Kans.: 1939; repr., San Antonio, Tex.: Newton Publishing, 1999), 185–86. U.S. Army, Return of the 4th Regiment of Cavalry, December 1916, Col. John F. Guilfoyle, Commanding, Schofield Barracks, Hawaii; U.S. Army, Return of the 9th Regiment of Cavalry, December 1916, Col. Thomas B. Dugan, Commanding, Camp Stotsenburg, Pampanga, Philippine Islands; and U.S. Army, Return of the 15th Regiment of Cavalry, December 1916, Col. William H. Hay, Fort William McKinley, Philippine Islands, all in *Returns from Regular Army Cavalry Regiments, 1833–1916.* NARA, RG 391, Microfilm Publication M744.

patrols but also serving as a frontline of defense in case Mexico should decide to enter the war on the side of the Central powers (Germany, Austria-Hungary, Bulgaria, the Ottoman Empire).[19]

Through all of these duties, like that of other eras, cavalry music was indeed a specialized profession, and bandsmen needed to be accomplished musicians as well as skilled horsemen who in turn relied on musically trained horses. Of his duty with the 5th Cavalry, Heuring recalls, " 'We never blew right over the horses' heads. . . . We blew to the side. Band horses were well trained. You could even let go of the reins and (play with) both hands.' "[20] However, Adkins, with the 13th, recalls that some band members were just as skittish as the horses, including Corporal George Manufella, "a very good musician. He didn't like to play his clarinet while riding his horse on parade. He was always worried about the horse throwing its head up and knocking his B-Flat clarinet down his throat."[21] It appears that civilians also were skeptical of the combination of horses and musical instruments, as conveyed by a 1934 report revealing that the 5th Cavalry's band debut at Schofield Barracks, Hawaii, in 1908 drew a crowd that "turned out in thousands expecting to see the band run away."[22]

However, horses were trained and, in fact, often reacted positively to music. While not going so far as to be able to march/walk/prance in step with a band's music, as is suggested in some references—a task that more than one horse trainer has assured me is not possible—horses did learn to react and sometimes seemed to enjoy music. Of this, W. D. Smithers writes, "Anyone who has seen a regiment of Cavalry in review with their mounted band playing those marches knows that the horses enjoyed the music, showing it by their steps and the way they held their heads and being so alert."[23]

WORLD WAR I

While the United States was focusing on Mexican border difficulties along with territorial expansions, Europe was involved in similar imperialistic issues that, in some cases, had been brewing for centuries. The assassination on 28 June

19. Friedrich Katz, *The Secret War in Mexico: Europe, the United States, and the Mexican Revolution* (Chicago: University of Chicago Press, 1981), 328–29, 350–78.

20. Hirabayashi, "Never Too Old to Make Music."

21. Adkins, "Story of Pancho Villa," pt. 2, 51.

22. *Schofield Barracks Horse Show, Official Program, 1934*, 8 and 9 June 1934, 3.

23. W. D. Smithers, "The U.S. Cavalry," *Western Horseman* 24, no. 11 (November 1960): 24; reprinted in *Cavalry Journal* 36, no. 2 (June 2011): 16.

1914 of Archduke Franz Ferdinand, the heir to the throne of Austria-Hungary, was the catalyst that finally brought the world into war on 28 July 1914, initially with Austria-Hungary declaring war on Serbia—resulting in much of Europe and its allies being involved. As the war progressed, it was evident that technological changes had altered warfare forever. After attempting gallant charges in centuries-old traditions across battlefields and meeting up with barbed wire, trenches, machine gun fire, and quick-loading artillery, commanders of the great cavalries of Europe found their mounted regiments reduced to secondary roles of reconnaissance, diversion, transportation, and filling gaps in defensive lines. Thus, World War I was primarily a trench war carried on by infantry troops, and while a European cavalry presence was minimal, mounted troops of the United States were nearly nonexistent—especially since the United States was only officially part of the war from 6 April 1917 to the armistice on 11 November 1918. Moreover, the Mexican Expedition had served as an excellent proving ground for use of the airplane, automobile, motorcycle, and motorized truck in warfare, and the Great War would now serve as the next testing ground for these technological developments. Even so, four cavalry regiments—the 2nd, 3rd, 6th, and 15th—served with the American Expeditionary Forces in Europe, mainly engaged dismounted as rear area security and remounting duty, with only the 2nd Cavalry serving mounted.[24]

The initial European entry for the 2nd Cavalry occurred when the regiment furnished for General Pershing's headquarters an increment of thirty-six men, who sailed for France on 28 May 1917 to serve as the general's bodyguard, accompanying him during the first part of the war.[25] Then on 8 January 1918, the entire 2nd Cavalry Regiment received orders to depart for Europe from Hoboken, New Jersey, aboard the USAT *Martha Washington* and two other transports, convoyed by the cruiser *Pueblo*. Major Joseph Lambert, who served with the 2nd Cavalry in the 1930s and '40s recounts that duty onboard ship consisted of "life-boat drill, assignment to boat stations, and physical exercises to keep the men fit. When the war zone was entered, the men were required to wear life preservers all the time. The submarine chasers joined the convoy on April 1 in order to protect the ships near the coast of France where the submarines were thickest." While the initial plan was to bring all horses and equipment,

24. The Third Cavalry Museum indicates, "Arriving in France in November [1917], the Regiment operated three major remount depots until the war's end." Third Cavalry Museum, *Blood and Steel!*, 17. Urwin, *United States Cavalry*, 180; Sawicki, *Cavalry Regiments*, 154, 156, 163, 180.

25. Lambert, *One Hundred Years with the Second Cavalry*, 192.

ironically and interestingly (and perhaps bizarrely, à la the planning style of the Spanish-American War), because of limited ship space, the horses were left behind. Thus, the regiment was furnished with animals in France with which they were not familiar and which they had not trained—or trained with.[26]

The initial mention of the 2nd Cavalry Band during World War I in historical accounts was two days after the regiment landed at Pauillac, France, when on 6 April 1918 a parade was formed consisting of the band, field musicians, and Troops F, G, and H in honor of the memory and Revolutionary War leadership of Marquis de La Fayette, who had embarked from this port for the American colonies 141 years before. This parade would have been on foot, as it was not until 18 April that the first horses for the regiment were secured for Troops H and I. While some troops of the regiment were allotted horses, whether the 2nd Cavalry Band served mounted in Europe is still a mystery. While Lambert indicates that horses were gradually supplied to the other troops, his account of horses supplied to the Provisional Squadron (Troops B, D, F, and H) may be an indication that the 2nd Cavalry Band serving mounted in Europe is doubtful:

> They ranged in type from the draft horse to the Spanish pony. Most of them were hardly bridle wise and unaccustomed to the use of weapons. The training was necessarily at slow gaits, marching usually being done at the walk. The horses were grazed two hours every evening, and special care was given to feeding. During the short time the squadron was at Camp Jeanne d'Arc their condition improved, but the work of the troops was later handicapped by the inability of the horses to do regular cavalry work.[27]

While this may not be an accurate description of the horses for the entire regiment, four troops is a significant number. Thus, if combat troops were not receiving horses that were accustomed to working with weapons, it is doubtful that the band received horses that were accustomed to the sounds of musical instruments.

Lambert indicates that after the armistice on 11 November 1918, Troops A, B, C, D, I, and M and the regimental headquarters and band of the 2nd Cavalry "marched with the invading army into Germany [from France] and were stationed on the Rhine River with the American Army of Occupation"

---

26. Ibid., 194.
27. Ibid., 202—203.

and then by various routes and factions traveled on to Coblenz, Germany. On 18 January 1919, the regimental headquarters and band reversed the march and headed to Dombasle-en-Argonne, France—a distance of two hundred miles. As the term "march" could refer to marching on foot, riding on horseback, or traveling by truck or by train, Lambert's use of the word is not helpful in discerning how the band traveled.[28]

While U.S. mounted bands at the front would have been rare and perhaps nonexistent—and with those of other countries including Britain, France, and Germany appearing only occasionally, and those of Austria having been dismounted by this point—military bands in general were not scarce during World War I. In fact, D. Royce Boyer indicates that U.S. forces alone included approximately 7,500 bandsmen and bandleaders serving in the conflict over the course of the war's last two years.[29]

Moreover, even though mounted bands were not part of the picture at the European front during the war, they were active at home as indicated by Carl Landrum, historian and newspaper columnist from Quincy, Illinois. Writing in 1996 about vaudeville and big band musician Nicholas L. Musolino, Landrum relates, "During World War I, he played the trombone in the old 304th Cavalry Band and liked to tell how you had to go to the stables and become a friend of the horse before you ever attempted to play trombone on the horse's back. He spent a little over two years in the Army. He later served in World War II, where he also played in the band."[30]

The 304th was one of fifteen cavalry regiments (301st–315th) constituted 18 May 1917 as part of the National Army, a combined conscript and volunteer force formed from the core of the regular U.S. Army and augmented with units of the National Guard and a large draft of men by the U.S. War Department—and a precursor to the Army Reserves. With the goal of succeeding the 15th Cavalry Division, consisting of the 1st, 5th, 6th, 7th, 8th, 14th, 15th, 16th, and 17th Cavalry Regiments patrolling the Mexican border so that the 15th Cavalry Division could head for Europe with its horses (which did not happen), some of

---

28. Ibid., 202–203, 209, 211. The 2nd Cavalry Regiment returned to the United States, arriving in Hoboken, New Jersey, on 29 June and then going to Fort Riley, Kansas, on 6 July 1919.

29. When the dualistic state of Austria-Hungary was formed, cavalry bands in Austria and Hungary, where mounted musicians had performed for four centuries, were discontinued in 1868 under the authority of Emperor Franz Joseph I. Spiridion Jovovic, "Hoch zu Roß!," *Österreichische Blasmusik* 1 (January 1995): 7; D. Royce Boyer, "The World War I Army Bandsman: A Diary Account by Philip James," *American Music* 14, no. 2 (Summer 1996): 187.

30. Carl Landrum, "Nick Musolino Played with Big Band Greats," *Quincy (Ill.) Herald-Whig*, 5 May 1996.

the National Army cavalry regiments, like the 304th, headed to the border as planned. Also on 18 May, Congress authorized the immediate implementation of the National Defense Act of 1916, which entailed the organization of the 18th through the 25th U.S. Cavalry Regiments, along with other regular units.[31]

However, both of these measures were unrealistic. A little over four months later on 1 October, Congress ordered the eight new regular cavalry regiments converted into field artillery, and in August of 1918, the fifteen National Army cavalry units were reorganized into artillery and trench mortar batteries.[32]

Another mention of a mounted band during World War I was that of the 1st Ohio Field Artillery. In giving updates about Sigma Nu Fraternity of Mount Union College, the *Delta* of October 1917 reports, "Roland Jones, '17, Alliance, Ohio, has been appointed bandmaster for the 1st Ohio Field Artillery. He is commissioned to recruit the first mounted band to leave the state of Ohio in the world war."[33] This unit saw service in several areas of the United States, including the Texas-Mexican border; Fort Sheridan, Illinois; Fort Benjamin Harrison, Indiana; and Camp Sheridan, Alabama. While it is not clear whether Jones was successful in his task of raising a mounted band, by July 1918, the regiment had been redesignated as the 134th Field Artillery and, along with the band, had been shipped to England without horses. Traveling by train to Southampton in preparation to leave for Le Havre, France, the yearbook of 134th Field Artillery's Battery B indicates that, during the wait at the docks before boarding boats to take them across the English Channel, "the band of the 134th and that of the 342nd gave concerts, each band striving to outdo the other in music and volume of noise furnished." In arriving in France the next morning, the same reporter recalls, "After disembarking they were drawn up on the pier. The men stood rigidly at attention and the officers at salute while the band played the 'Star Spangled Banner' and the 'Marseillaise.'"[34]

Before moving on to the 1920s, mention should be made of another musical aspect of the U.S. involvement in World War I—that of the implementation of a singing component in training camps through a Commission on Training Camp Activities (CTCA). To curb misconduct among troops, which officials

---

31. Sawicki, *Cavalry Regiments*, 94–95.

32. Urwin, *United States Cavalry*, 179–80.

33. Edwin W. Dunlavy, ed., "Beta Iota," in Alumni Notes, *Delta* 35, no. 1 (Indianapolis, Ind.: Sigma Nu Fraternity, October 1917): 131.

34. *Red Guidon, "Soixante Quinze," Being a Complete Illustrated History of B Battery 134th Field Arillery from 1915 to 1919* (Akron, Ohio: Red Guidon Association, 1920), 72.

felt had reached a zenith along the Mexican border, President Woodrow Wilson charged the government with the responsibility for the mental, physical, and moral well-being of personnel serving in the armed forces. One of the ways of working toward this was by establishing a rigorous military training camp activities program, which included programs in athletics, libraries, theaters, clubs, and singing. To lead this initiative, Secretary of War Newton D. Baker appointed Princeton-educated urban reformer Raymond B. Fosdick, who, prior to the war, had witnessed German regiments singing and recalled getting the impression that it "brought a relief from tension and eased the long miles under heavy packs."[35] In conjunction with the National Committee on Army and Navy Camp Music, beginning in June 1917 the CTCA's song leaders led thousands of military personnel along with surrounding community choruses in making music through the end of the war.[36]

THE 1920S

With the conclusion of World War I, the United States quickly demobilized an army, which, with federalized National Guard troops, had grown to more than three million. Over several reductions, by 1921, army manpower was at 150,000 and by 1927 was at 118,750, with the 15th, 16th, and 17th Cavalry Regiments being deactivated in 1921.[37] Along with these measures, the War Department continued to hone and consolidate military units with the 1st, 2nd, 5th, 6th, 7th, 8th, 9th, 10th, 11th, 12th, and 13th Cavalry Regiments being assigned to the 1st, 2nd, or 3rd Cavalry Divisions between 1921 and 1933. The 3rd, 4th, and 14th Cavalry Regiments stood each on their own until the 1940s.[38]

During the period from 1918 to 1922, regimental bands, including those of the cavalry, were increased to forty-eight pieces. In 1922, infantry and artillery bands were reduced to thirty-six, and those of cavalry and artillery, back to twenty-eight. In October 1927, infantry and artillery bands were also reduced to their prewar strengths.[39] While the U.S. Department of Defense worked to find its place in this postwar period, bands continued to be a part of the picture

35. Raymond B. Fosdick, *Chronicle of a Generation* (New York: Harper and Brothers, 1958), 154.

36. E. Christina Chang, "The Singing Program of World War I: The Crusade for a Singing Army," *Journal of Historical Research in Music Education* 23, no. 1 (October 2001).

37. Sawicki, *Cavalry Regiments*, 179–83.

38. Ibid., 151, 154, 160, 163, 164, 166, 169, 171, 172, 174, 176.

39. White, *History of Military Music*, 104–105; *History of U.S. Army Bands*, 31.

throughout the army, serving in their age-old roles throughout the United States and U.S.-held lands. By the 1920s, the positive aspects of military music were supported through printed training regulations as evidenced in Training Regulations (TR) No. 130–5, in *The Band: Organization, Duties, and Music Instruments*, prepared under the direction of the Army Music School, which states:

> The value of a good band lies in the power it exercises in contributing to the contentment and d'esprit of troops. It is a great factor in raising morale. Its mission is well established and should be adhered to. Specifically the purpose of the band is twofold:
>
> a. To participate in and furnish the desired music at military formations.
>
> b. To furnish musical entertainment for the command on such other occasions as may be prescribed by the commanding officer.[40]

The same regulations also address issues for all army bands, including personnel, musical instruction (tuning, "unisonal" scales, programs, theoretical instruction, and ear training), and care of instruments, with detailed instruction on how to care for each instrument. Specifically for mounted bands, the regulations address the care to be taken when performing with a mounted band—reminiscent of what mounted bandsmen had been telling themselves for centuries: "A mounted bandsman playing a wind instrument should be very careful that the horse, in tossing its head, does not strike the instrument, as the bandsman in such case might be seriously injured, besides damaging the instrument. To avoid this, the instrument should be inclined to the right, only quiet horses assigned to bandsmen, and the martingale used, if necessary."[41]

Another training manual, TR 130–15, in *The Band: Formations, Movements, Inspections, Etc., Mounted and Dismounted*, which was prepared in December of the same year of 1926, but this time under the direction of the chief of cavalry, addresses the operations of mounted bands in particular, including musical and riding instruction; horse selection (quiet, well-trained gray, or off-colored horses); "positions of instruments, mounted, when not playing" (with photographs); band formations—including the placement of the "tympanist . . .

---

40. U.S. War Department, *The Band: Organization, Duties and Music Instruments*. Training Regulations, No. 130–5. Washington, D.C.: Government Printing Office, 15 February 1926. NARA, RG 287, College Park, Md .

41. Ibid., 3.

3 yards in rear of the drum major" and four feet in front of the musician in "the right center of the first rank of the band"; distance between ranks mounted and dismounted; incorporation of buglers with the band; various maneuvers; inspections; mounting while holding instruments; storage of instruments on the march in the escort wagon ("unless the band is to play"); and instructions for instrument storage and horse picketing in camp.[42] While TR 130–5 cautions mounted bandsmen to be cautious, TR 130–15 indicates that riding instruction for them was not a major undertaking: "The duties of the band, which are largely of a ceremonial nature, require only a moderate degree of instruction in horsemanship. This instruction should be carried out according to a modified scheme of training, based on the work at slower gaits (walk and trot) as prescribed in TR 50–45."[43]

Military training was also part of the picture with mounted and dismounted instruction in the use of the pistol, as well as other various soldiering elements, including "definitions; drill signals; instruction, dismounted, without arms; the saddle pack (Cavalry); to pitch and strike shelter tents, mounted troops; ceremony of guard mounting, mounted troops; and the ceremonies and inspections of the organization and branch of the service of which the band is a part."[44] Instruction was to be given "to the members of the band by the commander of the troop or battery of which the band is a section or other subdivision" in conjunction with the band leader. Therefore, the manual indicates, "Musical and military instruction thus proceed hand in hand, and recruits are able at any moment to put forth their best efforts in any form of duty they may be called upon to perform."[45]

This postwar attention to detail would have been crucial for several major undertakings, including the initial November 1921 ceremony honoring the unknown dead of World War I—for what would become one of the most revered pieces of ground in the United States. When the remains of an unknown U.S. soldier from France were returned for burial in a tomb at the Memorial Amphitheater in Arlington National Cemetery, Kirk Simpson of the Associated Press reported that the reception of the body at the Washington Navy Yard was a somber, chilling scene—enhanced by the presence of a mounted band:

---

42. U.S. War Department, *The Band: Formations, Movements, Inspections*, Training Regulations, No. 130–15. By the 1920s, official regulations were referring to kettledrums as tympani.
43. Ibid., section 1, 1.f., 2.
44. Ibid., section 1, 1.g.,h., 2.
45. Ibid., section 1, 1.j., 2.

troopers formed in line facing toward the ship as she swung broadside to her place
and the gangway was lifted to her quarterdeck. To their right a mounted band stilled
its restless horses. On the ship, the trim files of her marine guard stood at attention. Rear Admiral Lloyd H. Chandler, to whom had fallen the duty of escorting
this private soldier over the Atlantic from France, was garbed in the full, formal
naval dress as were officers of his staff.[46]

In their *Last Salute: Civil and Military Funerals, 1921–1969*, Billy Mossman and
M. Warner Stark indicate that this mounted band was that of the 3rd Cavalry
from Fort Myer, which had returned to the post in 1919[47]—and which was
accompanied by some of the top military and civil officials in the country:

> On a rainy 9 November the *Olympia* sailed up the Potomac River, receiving and
> returning salutes from military posts along the way, and docked at the Washington
> Navy Yard about 1600. On hand to receive the body of the Unknown Soldier were
> General Bandholtz, who was the escort commander; the 3d Cavalry and its mounted
> band from Fort Myer, Virginia; and military and civil officials, including the Army
> Chief of Staff, General of the Armies John J. Pershing, Chief of Naval Operations,
> Admiral Robert E. Coontz, Commandant of the Marine Corps, Maj. Gen. John A.
> Lejeune, Secretary of War John Weeks, and Secretary of Navy Edwin Denby. When
> the *Olympia* docked, the two squadrons of the 3d Cavalry were already in line facing
> the cruiser from the far side of the dock area. To the left of these squadrons, at a
> right angle to their line, was the mounted band. After members of the ship's crew
> installed the gangplank, the ship's complement of marines and the band marched
> off and formed a line at the near edge of the pier facing the cavalry squadrons. The
> military and civil dignitaries next aligned themselves at the right of the cavalrymen
> and opposite the mounted band, thus completing a box formation.

The only piece of music that Mossman and Stark mention being played on this
occasion was *Onward Christian Soldiers*, which, with text by Sabine Baring-Gould
(written in 1865) and music by Arthur Sullivan (composed in 1871) would have
been a popular hymn of the time.[48] The martial flavor of this song would have

---

46. Kirk Simpson, "Body of 'The Unknown Soldier' Arrives Home," Associated Press Night Report,
Wednesday, 9 November 1921.

47. *The History of Fort Myer Virginia, 100th Anniversary Issue, Special Edition of the Fort Myer Post*, June 1963, 10.

48. Billy C. Mossman and M. Warner Stark, *The Last Salute: Civil and Military Funerals, 1921–1969*
(Washington, D. C.: Department of the Army, U.S. Government Printing Office, 1974), 9–11.

resonated with the military personnel present as well as with the general public and diplomats.

Reporting further about the occasion in his "Regimental Notes" for the following January, Colonel William C. Rivers of the 3rd Cavalry indicates that after "the band, mounted and the squadron" received the remains of the unknown soldier and escorted them to the Capitol on 9 November, two days later on 11 November, the third anniversary of the armistice, "all the troops at Fort Myer took part in the escort of the remains of the Unknown Soldier from the Capitol to Arlington Cemetery. Many complimentary remarks were made on the very smart appearance of the command."[49]

This last statement captures what military leaders have known for perhaps millennia—not only that the skill of operations of a military unit are crucial for getting a job done but also that the quality of the appearance of the job is just as important, as that is the piece that connects soldiers with the general populace. Music cannot help but raise the stature of the experience, and if the musicians are astride war horses, the experience is only heightened. Such was the scene at the Tomb of the Unknown Soldier.

Other band work during this period consisted of garrison duty and community events like that reported by Chandler in his account of the 7th Cavalry of 1925, which by this point was back in the southwestern United States:

> The Regimental Band began the concert season on February 15 under the direction of band leader Warrant Officer Clark B. Price. During the summer months the Band gave a series of concerts at the post and in various parks in the city of El Paso, and received much praise from civilians. In August and October the band played at a fair in Roswell, New Mexico, and gave two complimentary concerts at Tularosa and at Garrizozo, New Mexico. The band also furnished music at the convention of the Chambers of Commerce of New Mexico at Ruidoso. In November the band accompanied the good will trade excursion of the businessmen of El Paso, to Chihuahua, Mexico, where a festival was in progress.[50]

---

49. Col. William C. Rivers, "Third Cavalry—Fort Myer, Virginia," Regimental Notes, *Cavalry Journal* 31, no. 126 (January 1922): 101. Along with the 3rd Cavalry Band's participation, Staff Sergeant Frank Witchey, regimental bugler, whose bugle and tabard are displayed in the Third Cavalry Museum at Fort Hood, Texas, sounded taps at the ceremony. Until 1941, the regiment provided the Honor Guard detail at the Tomb of the Unknown Soldier. Third Cavalry Museum, *Blood and Steel!*, 18.

50. Chandler, *Of GarryOwen in Glory*, 178, 180.

This same year, the 4th Cavalry, after spending World War I at Schofield Barracks, Hawaii, and then returning to the Mexican border in 1919, returned to Fort Meade, South Dakota, where the band along with the Black Horse Drill Team of Troop F would have done similar work.[51]

Other cavalry bands were busy as well. At Fort Riley, Kansas, the 2nd Cavalry Band played for a Decoration Day ceremony and concert in 1922 along with performances at polo games, which were increasing in popularity within cavalry units,[52] and a parade at Junction City, Kansas, during the pilgrimage of the Isis Shrine.[53] As well, writing in 1922, Colonel W. D. Forsyth of the 5th Cavalry wrote of the cultural life at Fort Clark, Texas: "In the evenings we have movies on Mondays, Wednesdays, and Fridays, band concerts on Tuesdays and Thursdays, dances on Saturdays, and religious services on Sundays. The officers and ladies play bridge every Thursday night at the club, following the band concert."[54] Of the 6th Cavalry Band at Camp McClellan, Alabama, Colonel R. J. Fleming wrote in the same year: "Due to the untiring efforts of Mr. Bowen, the regimental band has undergone wonderful improvement since its arrival in camp. Its ranks are about filled up now, only three vacancies remaining; these for cornetists and trombonists."[55] This type of duty would have been typical at this point for all U.S. military bands, and while cavalry regiments were adjusting to new roles as mechanization became more prevalent, there were enough military leaders who continued to believe that there was a place for the horse in defense, and consequently, horse-mounted military music in military and civic capacities.

By 1924, the 6th Cavalry Band had moved to Fort Oglethorpe, Georgia, where Colin E. Phillips played bass horn in the mounted band and string bass in the regiment (concert) band and recalls that the duty was ideal for farm boys who loved horses. In an interview almost seventy years later, Phillips recollected that he addressed the issue of mounted playing by letting the horn lay on his

51. "The History of the 4th U.S. Cavalry Regiment," Official Homepage of Fort Huachuca, Arizona, http://huachuca-www.army.mil/pages/btroop/history.html.

52. "The Cavalry School, Fort Riley, Kansas," Cavalry School Notes, *Cavalry Journal* 31, no. 128 (July 1922): 328–29.

53. Col. John S. Winn, "Second Cavalry—Fort Riley, Kansas," Regimental Notes, *Cavalry Journal* 31, no. 128 (July 1922): 330.

54. Col. W. D. Forsyth, "Fifth Cavalry—Fort Clark, Texas," Regimental Notes, *Cavalry Journal* 31, no. 128 (July 1922): 332.

55. Col. R. J. Fleming, "Sixth Cavalry—Headquarters and First Squadron, Camp McClellan, Alabama; Second Squadron, Fort Oglethorpe, Georgia," Regimental Notes, *Cavalry Journal* 31, no. 129 (October 1922): 439.

shoulder and placing the music in front of him with reins in the left hand: "You could tie a knot in your reins and the horses would follow the drum major, who was also on a horse."[56]

Just as they had done during Custer's time, cavalry bands at this point were still accompanying their regimental troops out of—and into—camp. Reporting about a 425-mile march of the 12th Cavalry from Camp Robert E. L. Michie, Del Rio, Texas, to its new station, at Fort Brown, Brownsville, Texas, on 6 October 1921, Lieutenant Colonel Nathan C. Shiverick, who accompanied the regiment, reports that music continued to be a great troop unifier and bolsterer, and that the regiment's band, like that of the 8th Cavalry a half century prior, kept its instruments in a specially provisioned band instrument wagon (see chapter 4, page 66):

> Mention should be made of the use of the band, which always played the column out of and into camp. This was possible, without causing delay, because of the convertible trailer wagon, which had been fitted up with separate compartments for each instrument. This wagon was drawn by four horses and was always with the column. The band could either draw or return instruments in less than four minutes. In the morning, the wagon would leave camp with the light train, and then at about a mile from camp it would fall out. Later, when the column reached the wagon, the band would be fallen out to return instruments. At the last halt each day the band-wagon would come up and instruments would be drawn. The music always started every one out in the morning in good spirits, and at the close of a march it brought every one into camp in a cheerful frame of mind.

Like other chroniclers, Shiverick reports that, in addition to inspiring troops in an age-old fashion, just as ancient was the idea that military music also serves as a connector between a military unit and civilians: "The band gave much entertainment to the people of villages . . . not only by playing as the column marched through . . . but by the concerts which preceded retreat."[57]

Toward similar efforts, cavalry bands continued to be engaged in civic affairs in public relations efforts as indicated in the program of the Seventeenth Annual Convention of Rotary International, held in Denver in 1926, which included the Black Horse Troop and Mounted Band of the 13th Cavalry of Fort Russell,

---

56. "Phillips' Career Spans Cavalry Trooper to Air Force Supplyman," *Air Force Enlisted Widows Home Foundation Newsletter* 21, no. 2 (Spring 1993): 1, 4.

57. Lt. Col. Nathan C. Shiverick, "The Twelfth Cavalry on the Road," *Cavalry Journal* 31, no. 126 (January 1922): 62–63.

FIGURE 8.5. 8th Cavalry in regimental formation with band in foreground, 1923, Marfa, Texas. *Courtesy of U.S. Army, 1st Cavalry Division Museum.*

Wyoming: "The applause continued and increased as the crack Black Horse troop of the 13th Cavalry went through a musical drill, the white trappings and dark hides of the horses showing to great advantage in maneuvers executed to the strains of a mounted band."[58] Another Rotarian report of the time recalls similarly,

> The Cavalry unit, noted as the Black Horse Troop and Mounted Band, easily won the admiration of the spectators. . . . To a tune by the mounted band the troop filed down from the mountainside to the plain, where it went through various

---

58. Arthur J. Follows, "Out Where the Zest Begins: The Story of the Denver Convention," *Rotarian: The Magazine of Service* (August 1926): 62.

maneuvers. Turning, circling, prancing, intermingling, swaying back and forth on the field the troop presented a magnificent spectacle in itself. At the conclusion of its demonstration the troopers with a yell drew their sabers and rushed toward the grandstand, coming to a halt a few yards from the front row of the audience. They then galloped off the field which again was darkened.[59]

The 13th Cavalry Band of the time, like those of other cavalry, infantry, and artillery units, was also involved in larger civilian-style artistic productions as related by Colonel Roy B. Harper in his October 1922 "Regimental Notes" in referring to the "13th Cavalry Band and Minstrels": "After several weeks of preparation in training chorus and rehearsing principals, a minstrel show, consisting of the band, the orchestra, and a 'circle' of twenty-four men, several of whom possessed exceptional voices, and four 'end men' who were practiced entertainers, gave its first performance in the Princess Theater in Cheyenne. The theater was filled to capacity, and the huge audience expressed their approval by repeatedly encoring the various numbers." Harper maintains that the show was so successful that it went on to Laramie and then to Fort Collins, Boulder, Denver, and Greeley, Colorado—and carrying on with a time-honored tradition playing for the infirmed with a benefit performance for the patients at the Fitzsimons General Hospital east of Denver in Fletcher (now Aurora). Profits from the tour came to a considerable sum, which was converted into the Regimental Athletic Fund.[60]

Elsewhere across the globe, the 9th Cavalry Band was continuing its service at Camp Stotsenburg, Pampanga, in the Philippines in 1921. Commanding Officer Colonel Edward Anderson recounts that the band was doing its part to provide a glimpse of home with a Christmas celebration: "On the late afternoon of December 24 the 9th Cavalry regiment formed and, with band playing,

---

59. Rotary International, *Proceedings, Seventeenth Annual Convention of Rotary International* (Denver, Colo.: June 14–18, 1926), 28 (for the 1926 Rotary Convention). Several cavalry regiments and civilian organizations in the United States have been known as the "Black Horse" troop or regiment, including the 11th and 13th Cavalry Regiments of the Regular Army, and F Troop of the 4th Cavalry (although the nickname seems to have been known more for the 11th); Company H of the 4th Virginia Cavalry during the Civil War; the Chicago Black Horse Troop of the 106th Cavalry of the Illinois National Guard; Troop A of the 107th Cavalry, Ohio National Guard; and the Black Horse Troop of Culver Military Academy, Culver, Indiana. Sousa's *The Black Horse Troop* was written for the 107th Cavalry Regiment of the Ohio National Guard in 1924—prior to the forming of this unit's mounted band. Paul E. Bierley, *The Works of John Philip Sousa* (Columbus, Ohio: Integrity Press, 1984), 42–43.

60. Col. Roy B. Harper, "Thirteenth Cavalry—Fort D. A. Russell, Wyoming," Regimental Notes, *Cavalry Journal* 31, no. 129 (October 1922): 442.

marched to the regimental Christmas tree. Every officer, man, woman, and child received a present."[61]

While technology was advancing and warfare was changing, military operations still called for ceremony—and military personnel and civilians continued to welcome the respite provided by military musicians. This went for the services of bands of federal and National Guard units, as well as those of the 301st–315th Cavalry Regiments of the National Army—of which the band of the 304th has already been mentioned. Further change came to these National Army units on 15 October 1921 when they were reassembled, consolidated, and redesignated into cavalry regiments of the Organized Reserves (O.R.), with an additional ten new cavalry regiments (316th–324th). Steven Clay indicates that several of these regiments initiated postwar bands, including the 315th Cavalry in 1923 at Providence, Rhode Island, the 318th Cavalry in 1923 at Chicago, Illinois, the 322nd Cavalry in 1923 at Des Moines, Iowa, and the 324th Cavalry, in 1928 at Cedar City, Utah, this latter one being "the only O.R. cavalry band west of the Mississippi River."[62] Some of these O.R. regiments trained with those of the Regular Army, and all were mobilized at the beginning of World War II. Some were disbanded at the end of the war, and several lived on into the 1950s.

While a strong presence of U.S. horse units during the Mexican Expedition did not set a precedent for a like situation in Europe during World War I, mounted bands continued to support official and civic events at home. In addition, these units continued to work across the country with further advancements in instrumentation and regulations throughout the decade following the Great War but were about to see further changes in federal and National Guard units of the 1930s.

---

61. Col. Edward Anderson, "Ninth Cavalry—Camp Stotsenburg, Pampanga, P.I.," Regimental Notes, *Cavalry Journal* 31, no. 127 (April 1922): 215–16.

62. Steven E. Clay, *U.S. Army Order of Battle 1919–1941*, vol. 2 of *The Arms: Cavalry, Field Artillery, and Coast Artillery, 1919–41* (Fort Leavenworth, Kans.: Combat Studies Institute Press, U.S. Army Combined Arms Center, 2010), 648, 649, 651, 653.

CHAPTER 9

The 1930s, Federal Units

THE LESSONS LEARNED IN WORLD WAR I CONCERNING THE FUTURE
of cavalry in warfare did not lessen during peacetime. In fact, during the 1930s,
the U.S. Cavalry was down to fourteen horse-mounted regiments with four of
these found in the 1st Cavalry Division spread throughout Texas. Less than one
thousand cavalry officers remained on active duty, and while regiments continued
with horses in cavalry training, the inventions of the tank and high-powered
artillery were signaling that a mobilized, mechanized army was the wave of the
future.[1] Of these developments, General MacArthur as chief of staff stated in
1931, "Modern firearms have eliminated the horse as a weapon, and as a means of
transportation he has generally become, next to the dismounted man, the slowest
means of transportation. [However], in some special cases of difficult terrain,
the horse, properly supplemented by motor transportation, may still furnish
the best mobility, and this situation is properly borne in mind in all our plans."[2]

Therefore, accompanying the creation of cavalry divisions and other changes,
some cavalry bands were dismounted or were deactivated, including that of
the 2nd Cavalry. Of this band's demise, lamenting in 1939, Joseph Lambert
writes what was probably the sentiment of all regiments losing their historic
mounted bands:

> In the year 1930, the mounted band was made inactive and the personnel transferred
> to the bands of other organizations. The plan of the War Department at this time
> was to allow generally not more than one band for each army post, and the Ninth
> Cavalry was the regiment selected to have one at Fort Riley. By the reduction in the

---

1. Bob Seals, "In Defense of Honor: General Douglas MacArthur and the Horse Cavalry of 1934,"
Cavalry Journal 32, no. 1 (March 2008): 23.
2. "Mechanized Force Becomes Cavalry," *Cavalry Journal* 40, no. 165 (May–June 1931): 5.

number of bands, it was intended to increase the combat troops in our army, which at this time was gradually being decreased in size. The members of the regiment saw with much sadness the disappearance of this organization which had done so much to maintain the morale of the command since the beginning of the Second Dragoons.[3]

The 13th Cavalry Band, which had been organized at Fort Meade, South Dakota, on 24 May 1901 met the same fate in August 1931. After serving faithfully at various posts and camps worldwide, including Columbus, New Mexico, in the initial chaos of the Mexican Punitive Expedition, the band arrived at Fort Monmouth, New Jersey, in August of 1930, where it was formally inactivated and retired. The U.S. Army Signal Corps Band was activated the same month and received personnel and equipment from the 13th Cavalry Band, which in turn was inactivated in January 1944 when the 389th Army Band was formed and activated, likewise inheriting personnel and equipment from that of the Signal Corps.[4]

However, other federal cavalry bands continued with strong performance and service schedules. Among these was the band of the 3rd Cavalry, which had rotated duty among Virginia, Montana, the Philippines (several times), Washington state,[5] and the Mexican border[6] since the turn of the century, and had returned to Fort Myer in 1919, where it remained until 1942. Because of the close proximity of this station to Washington, D.C., and to Arlington, military funerals were a primary duty for the 3rd Cavalry Band—with most of these performances being on foot. 3rd Cavalry Band trumpeter Hubert Henderson recalls:

> We would march to the chapel at the cemetery gate, wait outside for about twenty minutes for the service to conclude, and then march off at the usual slow cadence. At this part of every funeral, the snare drums were muffled by loosening the snares and the bass drum by wrapping a cloth around the head of the drumstick. The Band played a slow funeral march, usually an arrangement of the slow movement of Chopin's Piano Sonata in B-flat Minor, Op. 35; these were always very solemn occasions; we usually played a hymn prior to the chaplain's few words, one of our trumpet players played "Taps," and then the firing squad volleys closed the service.[7]

---

3. Lambert, *One Hundred Years with the Second Cavalry*, 217.

4. "History of the United States Army Materiel Command Band," U.S. Army Materiel Command Band website, http://www.music.army.mil/organizations/pages/?unit=389AB&p=history.

5. *Oregonian* (Portland, Ore.), 12 March 1908, 1.

6. Third Cavalry Museum, *Blood and Steel!*, 17.

7. Hubert Henderson, "WW-II Bandsman and Bandleader," unpublished memoirs, 1. Hubert Henderson, personal communication, 27 February 2004. Initially, Henderson was drafted as a senior trumpet performance

Other performances like troop reviews were mounted, as recalled by Betty St. John Arnold whose husband, Col. Thomas St. John Arnold was stationed with the 16th Field Artillery Battalion in 1940 at Fort Myer: "There was a mounted Garrison review each Saturday morning. The 3rd Cavalry would pass in review, first at a walk, then at a trot, and finally at a gallop, followed by the 16th Field Artillery at a walk, trot, and a gallop while the 3rd Cavalry mounted band played appropriate music."[8]

Still other mounted performances took place on a grander scale like in parades in downtown Washington, D.C., and review parades and regiment-sponsored large horse shows at Fort Myer, in which 3rd Cavalry horsemen invariably garnered many awards.[9] Henderson recalls that trumpeters also did duty at the Tomb of the Unknown Soldier on bugles: "On one occasion when the DAR held a ceremony there, I remember a nice lady thanking me afterwards and insisting that I accept a five-dollar bill." He further recounts a sign of what was to come: "After December 7, 1941, the number of funerals increased and the band spent more time playing for them."[10]

Leading this venerable 3rd Cavalry ensemble beginning in 1926 was Louis S. Yassel—whose career development seems to have been typical of military band-masters of the time. Born in Austria and growing up in northern Pennsylvania, where he learned to play the cornet, he enlisted on 14 January 1899, in Company E, 21st Infantry as a bugler. He learned bugle calls and close-order drill at Plattsburg Barracks prior to leaving for the Philippines in May 1899. While in the Philippines, Yassel transferred to the 21st Infantry regimental band on cornet—practicing five or six hours a day. He went on to serve with the 28th Infantry Band and then the 4th Coast Artillery Band at Fort Monroe, Virginia, of which he became the bandleader in 1911—taking the warrant officer examination in 1920. Transferring to the U.S. Army Band in July 1922, in which he served as the assistant bandleader, in 1926 he assumed leadership of the 3rd Cavalry Band stationed at Fort Myer, Virginia, across the Potomac River from Washington, D.C.—succeeding Warrant Officer Kenneth Herbert, who was

major at the University of North Carolina in August 1940 but received a deferment enabling him to graduate. In September 1941, he enlisted in the 3rd U.S. Cavalry so he could continue trumpet study with Winfred Kemp, cornet soloist with the U.S. Marine Band in Washington, D.C. He retired as professor of music at the University of Kentucky.

8. Thomas St. John Arnold, *Adventures of a Country Girl and Army Wife* (Lincoln, Neb.: Writers Club Press, 2003), 36.

9. Third Cavalry Museum, *Blood and Steel!*, 18.

10. Henderson, "WW-II Bandsman and Bandleader," 1.

assigned to the Army Music School, Washington Barracks, as an instructor.[11] Upon the pending transfer, Yassel recalled years later that his riding background came into question when Major General Robert C. Davis, who was serving as the adjutant general at the time, asked him if he had ever ridden a horse, to which he replied, "Never in my life [but] I'm willing to learn."[12]

Like his bandmaster, Henderson recalls, "I had never been on a horse until enlisting—and learning to ride was challenging: taking jumps, wading a river with the horse, putting the horse through its gaits, etc." Like other cavalry musicians over the centuries, bandsmen were still cavalrymen, with Henderson recalling that each man took care of "his assigned horse—feed[ing], groom[ing], muck[ing] out the stall, etc.—as well as qualify[ing] on a carbine and a revolver and keep[ing] in good shape." Juxtaposed to this duty, Henderson recounts, "I also had a weekly trumpet lesson at the Marine Barracks and played with a dance band at the Washington Hotel on weekends."[13]

Along with routine gigs, the 3rd Cavalry's band continued to play a strong role in high-profile ceremonies throughout the area including former president William Howard Taft's funeral procession on 11 March 1930 and the Washington, D.C., 6 April 1938 Army Day parade. An article in the April 1938 issue of *Army and Navy Journal* indicates that participating in this occasion were various U.S. Army, Navy, Marine, Coast Guard, and National Guard units including the U.S. Army Band, the band of the 34th Infantry, the U.S. Marine Band, the band of the 121st Engineers, the 260th Coast Artillery and its drum and bugle corps, and "the famous mounted band of the 3rd Cavalry."[14]

For these and other more specific 3rd Cavalry events, Henderson recalls playing several marches, including *Brave Rifles*, which had been deemed the official march of the 3rd Cavalry. Composed by C. Campagna in 1937 and dedicated to the regiment during the command of Kenyon A. Joyce, the twenty-sixth colonel, staff members of the 3rd Cavalry Museum maintain that "the march is customarily played at all Regimental ceremonies and formations where the

---

11. Irene Juno, "Music Chat from Washington," *Jacobs' Band Monthly* (April 1926): 55–56. Juno also indicates that "Warrant Officer Thomas F. Darcy, band leader, Army Music School, will become assistant leader of the Army Band."

12. Chief Warrant Officer Louis S. Yassel, interview by Edward M. Coffman, 1 December 1972, Washington, D.C., 21, 28; Edward M. Coffman, *The Regulars: The American Army, 1898–1941* (Cambridge, Mass.: Harvard University Press, 2004), 17, 22, 254; David McCormick, "A History of the United States Army Band to 1946" (PhD diss., Northwestern University, 1971), 220, 221, 364.

13. Henderson, "WW-II Bandsman and Bandleader," 1.

14. "Army Day," *Army and Navy Journal* 75, no. 31 (2 April 1938): 667.

FIGURE 9.1. 3rd Cavalry Band, Summerall Field, with enlisted barracks on Sheridan Avenue in the background, Fort Myer, Virginia, 1937. *Courtesy of Old Guard Museum, U.S. Army.*

Regiment passes in review."[15] The 3rd Cavalry Band undoubtedly also played at least three of Yassel's published marches: *Waltersonia* (Carl Fischer, 1929); *Post Commander* (for band with bugle and drum corps, Carl Fischer, 1933); and *National Capitol* (Fillmore, 1935).[16]

---

15. Third Cavalry Museum, *Blood and Steel!*, 78. Earlier histories ascribe the composing of the march to Yassel. See also U.S. Army, Third Cavalry Public Affairs, *History, Customs, and Traditions of the 3d Armored Cavalry Regiment*, 33–2194-B (3d ACR), 2015, 15, available at http://www.hood.army.mil/3D_CR/files/pdfs/BloodAndSteel.pdf.

16. William H. Rehrig, *The Heritage Encyclopedia of Band Music, Composers and Their Music*, ed. Paul E. Bierley, vol. 1 (Westerville, Ohio: Integrity Press, 1991), s.v. "Yassel, Louis S."; Library of Congress, Copyright Office, *Catalog of Copyright Entries*, pt. 3, *Musical Compositions*, n.s., 29 no. 1 (Washington, D.C.: Government Printing Office, 1935), 64, entry 1812.

Cavalry bands continued to play formal concerts as well, including those for civilian functions. One of these entailed the 6th Cavalry Band sharing the stage with organist McConnell Erwin at the Memorial Auditorium in Chattanooga, Tennessee, in 1934 for a concert sponsored by "the Garden Clubs of the city and the four D.A.R. Chapters." A newspaper article of the time relates, "Members of the Sixth Cavalry Band of Fort Oglethorpe, with their director, Warrant Officer Hugh Peaslack, will assist McConnell Erwin, municipal organist, at the March civic concert to be given Sunday afternoon at 3 o'clock at the Memorial Auditorium." With the concert lineup, which, like other military concerts of the era included a march composed specifically for a U.S. Cavalry regiment, the same newspaper clipping indicates that the 6th Cavalry Band performed a variety of selections: "*Sixth Cavalry Band March* (O'Callahan), *Lamento* (Riesta), overture from *Il Guarany* (Gomez), *Grand Selections from Mefistofele* (Bolto), *Fairy Suite* (LaCombe) and *Stars and Stripes Forever* (Sousa)." And as an indication of the changing times, "Transportation for the Sixth Cavalry band is being furnished through the courtesy of the Tennessee Electric Power Company."[17]

Of the mounted aspect of the period's cavalry bands, Frank Kirby, who was a trumpet player with the 11th Cavalry from 1936 to 1940 at the Presidio of Monterey, California, recalls,

> The 11th Cav were mounted only for regimental parades and special civic and big occasions such as when we rode up to play for the opening of the Golden Gate Bridge in 1937. One feels as if one could blow the horn inside out while riding. The diaphragm sits relaxed and ready while astride a McClellan saddle. We drew our horses from the Artillery regiment; I rode Whiskey and occasionally Tiny, serial #9H62. I played Trumpet for several years before enlisting in 1936, having studied with Walter M. Smith, Boston, 1929–1934. The regiment was transferred to the Mexican border in late 1940 shortly after Germany invaded Poland.

Of this band's leadership, Kirby recalls that bandmaster Warrant Officer Crockett Baxter, with well over thirty years of service, was "smart and brainy," a "fine counselor," and a graduate of the Army Music School in Washington, D.C., "and was well respected among other bandleaders and the Officer Corps

---

17. "Assist at Organ Concert," 24 March 1934, unknown Chattanooga, Tenn., newspaper clipping in author's possession.

FIGURE 9.2. 11th U.S. Cavalry, Presidio of Monterey, California, 1930, Col. Roger S. Fitch Commanding. *Courtesy of Col. George Moseley (Ret.).*

of the Troops and Squadron."[18] Kirby recalls that the band's concert work was of equal importance with its mounted performances with Baxter programming "good literature," including *1812 Overture, Custer's Last Charge,* and *A Musician Lost in the Forest.* Kirby also recalls soloing on *Carnival of Venice* and *Grand Russian Fantasia.*[19] With this focus on high-quality music, Kirby remembers with relief that Baxter tended to promote band members based on musicianship "rather than the stupid seniority system of that era."[20]

---

18. Col. Frank Kirby (Ret.), San Francisco, Calif., e-mail messages to author, 24 September 2000 and 6 October 2000. Kirby recalls that after his service with the 11th Cavalry, "I was transferred on a cadre to form a band at March Field and was appointed a Warrant Officer Bandleader to be later commissioned and took over the massed bands at Santa Ana Army Air Force Base 1942." Kirby retired as a colonel in the U.S. Air Force.

19. *1812 Overture* by Pyotr Ilyich Tchaikovsky; *Custer's Last Charge* was probably an arrangement of the 1920s popular song and piano piece by Edward Taylor Paull, who composed several battle-picture pieces including *Napoleon's Last Charge, Burning of Rome, Battle of Gettysburg,* and *Paul Revere's Ride. A Musician Lost in the Forest* was by Ernst; *Carnival of Venice* was probably the arrangement by Herbert L. Clarke or Jean Baptiste Arban; and *Grand Russian Fantasia* was by Jules Levy.

20. Kirby, e-mail message to author, 24 September 2000.

FIGURE 9.3. 7th Cavalry buglers playing long fanfare trumpets in the Sun Carnival
Parade, 1 January 1938, Fort Bliss, El Paso, Texas. Trumpeters *(left to right)*: Chavez,
Howze, Fowler, Matthews, Irwin, Kelly. *Photo postcard and last names courtesy of
William H. Irwin IV (second from right).*

Along with the bands of the 3rd, 6th, and 11th Cavalry Regiments, that of
the 7th Cavalry also continued to be active throughout the 1930s. The regiment had been stationed at Fort Bliss, Texas, since 1917,[21] and continued to
be a favorite with troop and civilian audiences. Bandmaster Warrant Officer
James B. Allen stated in 1931, "In addition to serving as a Regimental and
Post Band, the Seventh is called on many occasions to furnish music, both of a
civic and military nature, in El Paso, and the many thousands who attend the
concerts attest the Band's popularity."[22] Bill Irwin, who was a field trumpeter
with the regiment, enlisting in 1935, recalls that, while the field buglers were
not part of the band, they often rode behind the band and played bugle parts
on one-piston bugles (changing from B♭ to G) when called for on pieces like

21. Chandler, *Of GarryOwen in Glory,* 171.
22. James B. Allen, addendum to Brockenshire, "Seventh Cavalry Band," 942.

Sousa's *Semper Fidelis, Thunderer,* and *Black Horse Troop.* Training regulations of the time addressed this time-honored tradition of bugles-to-the-rear-of-the-band arrangement along with other field music in *Specialists, Field Music —The Bugles TR 75–5.*[23] Policies, regulations, and instruction for cavalry bands were addressed separately in *Band Field Manual, The Band, FM 28–5,* containing similar information to that of TR 130–15 of 1926.[24]

About the 7th Cavalry Band itself, Irwin recalls, "The bandmaster was a warrant officer by the name of Kosheeki who rode with the band off to the side and directed." Interestingly, Irwin's recollections are rare as he indicates not only a mounted kettledrummer (by the name of Croteau), but one who rode a piebald (patched black and white) horse, which had long been the British tradition. He also indicates that his own horse was nothing to sneer at: "I rode a wonderful horse—a purebred Morgan name Lady Lancaster, which was the personal horse of one of the officers. Matthews had the same. We were able to ride them by taking care of them."[25]

As in previous years, large military and civilian contingencies continued to gather for major commemorations throughout the decade—as evidenced by three thousand soldiers who made their way to Pennsylvania to take part in the celebration of the seventy-fifth anniversary of the battle of Gettysburg and "the final Blue and Gray reunion" sponsored by the Pennsylvania State Commission, chaired by State senator John S. Rice. Along with various contingencies from Fort Howard Maryland; Fort Hovie, Maryland; Fort Meade, Maryland; Fort Monroe, Virginia; Fort Myer, Virginia; Fort Washington, Maryland; Edgewood Arsenal, Maryland; and Fort Totten, New York, were the U.S. Marine Band and U.S. Army Band and various infantry, artillery, and chemical battalions, as well as the "Regimental Headquarters and Band, 12th Infantry, 4 officers and 29 men" from Fort Howard, Maryland; "Mounted Band, 6th Field Artillery, 3 officers and 100 men," from Fort Hovie, Maryland; and "Band, 3rd Cavalry, 1 officer and 30 men," from Fort Myer, Virginia. As accommodations for this many men would have been a concern, a reporter for the *Star and Sentinel* explains, "The visiting enlisted men will camp along the north side of the Emmitsburg road, adjoining the borough limits. The large display of all forms

---

23. U.S. Army, Music School, *Specialists, Field Music—The Bugles TR 75–5,* section 1, general, 3 (Washington, D.C.: War Department, 1 November 1928), 1.

24. U.S. Army, Chief of Infantry, the Chief of Cavalry, and the Army Band, *Band Field Manual: The Band, FM 28–5* (Washington, D.C.: Government Printing Office, 1941).

25. William H. Irwin, North Chicago, telephone interview by author, 30 July 2001. Irwin was one of the last buglers to be trained for mounted duty in the 7th Cavalry, enlisting in 1935.

FIGURE 9.4. Fort Riley Bugle Corps, Frontier Days Parade, in downtown Leavenworth, Kansas, 1938. It is difficult to tell if these instruments are bugles or trumpets; regardless, they do appear to be valveless. Wearing replica uniforms of the 2nd U.S. Dragoon Regiment, ca. 1833–51, and organized and equipped for the purposes of ceremonial occasions, this group is probably composed of the collected buglers of the 2nd U.S. Cavalry Regiment. The group may have been assembled for a few years to commemorate the one hundredth anniversary of the founding of the regiment. *Courtesy of the U.S. Cavalry Association.*

of armaments will be set-up in the fields opposite the Army's camp, on the south side of the Emmitsburg road."[26]

As mentioned in chapter 7, some cavalry regiments hosted trumpet/bugle corps, which for some continued into the 1930s. Although the ensemble in figure 9.4 does not include percussion as W. C. B. suggested when he was outlining

26. "3,000 United States Soldiers to Camp Here for Maneuvers at Anniversary and Reunion," *Gettysburg Star and Sentinel*, 18 June 1938, 4.

FIGURE 9.5. Mounted trumpets, U.S. Cavalry. This unidentified unit appears to be playing cavalry trumpets, probably the so-called American Legion bugle, which had a trumpet bore with a single fold, pitched in regulation G with a slide down to F. Several companies made these, including Conn and Keystone State. *Courtesy of the U.S. Cavalry Association.*

alternatives for mounted bands, it is a corps of valveless instruments.[27] Interestingly, while all musicians are playing trumpets/bugles, only the leader is riding the traditional grey trumpeter's horse. The instruments in figure 9.5 appear to be trumpets rather than bugles.

As the U.S. military continued to mechanize itself through the 1930s, several federal horse units, including the 3rd, 6th, 7th, and 11th Cavalry Regiments, continued to remain active—with their mounted bands and a few mounted trumpet/bugle corps continuing to be popular with the public and with each respective regiment. Other regiments were dismounted or disbanded entirely, which was not necessarily the same as for National Guard units.

27. W. C. B., "Are Army Bands Necessary?," 340.

CHAPTER 10

Rise of the National Guard

As the last chapter indicates, some U.S. Army cavalry bands remained active while others were on the demise during the 1930s. Those in the National Guard however, were actually increasing in number during this interwar period with nineteen spreading across the country by 1939 from Brooklyn, New York (101st Cavalry) to Albuquerque, New Mexico (111th Cavalry). The list shown in table 10.1, taken from the *National Guard Registers* for 1936 and 1939,[1] reveals the nineteen cavalry bands of the U.S. National Guard in terms of unit, location, and date of organization, with further dates given for bands whose organizations changed. In addition, bandmaster information is given for dates of promotion, births, and college degrees. I have mainly retained the original abbreviations with designated explanations in footnotes where I thought they would be helpful. After some deliberation, to help aid band and military historians, I have also retained organizational information, even with units like the 104th Pennsylvania, which has a longer and more involved lineage than the others. As I have gathered more information about some bands than others, I have included footnoted information for the same reason.

This information indicates that all of these National Guard cavalry bands were established in the 1920s, except for the band of the 104th Cavalry in Pennsylvania, which began as an infantry band in 1903, becoming part of the 104th in 1921. Because many National Guard units were constituted from existing state militia and even private units, the actual history behind these regiments and bands is often complex. Several predecessor units hosted mounted bands,

---

1. U.S. War Department, National Guard Bureau, *Official National Guard Register for 1936* (Washington, D.C.: Government Printing Office, 1936), 9–12; U.S. War Department, National Guard Bureau, *Official National Guard Register for 1939* (Washington, D.C.: Government Printing Office, 1940), 12–16.

TABLE 10.1. NATIONAL GUARD CAVALRY BANDS

GENERAL HEADQUARTERS RESERVE TROOPS (GHQ)[a]

111th Cavalry, New Mexico (1936 and 1939 in Albuquerque). 6 May 1929.[b]

Carl L. Cramer (b. Kansas 29 Oct. 1897); WO 1 June 1936,[c] NGUS WO 7 Aug. 1936[d]

112th Cavalry, Texas (1936 and 1939 in Dallas). 13 Mar. 1930.

Lester E. Harris (b. Texas 9 Apr. 1891); WO 4 Dec. 1930, NGUS WO 4 June 1934

124th Cavalry, Texas (1936 and 1939 in Mineral Wells). 2 Apr. 1923.

David Burnswick (b. Austria 28 Nov. 1898); WO 2 Dec. 1923, NGUS WO 1 May 1934

122nd Cavalry—not organized

21ST CAVALRY DIVISION:
CONNECTICUT, MASSACHUSETTS, NEW JERSEY, NEW YORK

101st Cavalry, New York (1936 and 1939 in Brooklyn). 1 June 1921.

Harwood C. Simmons (b. Kentucky 14 Aug. 1902; BA John Fletcher College, Iowa, 1925; MA Columbia University, New York, 1932); WO 23 Mar. 1936, NGUS WO 29 Apr. 1936

121st Cavalry, New York (1936 and 1939 in Rochester). 15 Feb. 28.

Austin H. Truitt (b. India 19 Nov. 1905; BA, BM Illinois Wesleyan University 1928); WO 5 Feb. 1931, NGUS WO 4 June 1934

Royal A. Furness (b. New York 7 Apr. 1906; BS Colgate University, New York, 1928); WO 14 May 1938

102nd Cavalry (Essex Troop), New Jersey (1936 and 1939 in Newark). 17 Aug. 1921.[e]

Peter E. Rosenzweig (b. Hungary 9 June 1886); WO 8 July 1931, NGUS WO 7 May 1934

110th Cavalry, Massachusetts (1936 and 1939 in Allston).[f] 30 Nov. 1921.[g]

Chester E. Whiting[h] (b. Massachusetts 22 July 1900); WO 7 Jan. 24, NGUS WO 9 July 34

---

a. The GHQ Reserve, composed of units of the various arms and services that were not otherwise specifically assigned, were held for use as reinforcements or for separate missions under GHQ.

b. Indicates the date on which the unit met qualifications for federal recognition, determined for the army by the National Guard Bureau (NGB).

c. Indicates the date that the officer received his state warrant officer commission.

d. NGUS—National Guard United States—refers to the date when the officer received federal recognition under the 1933 amendment to the National Defense Act. Until then, National Guard officers had state but not federal commissions. From 1933 on, all National Guard officers received federal commissions.

e. Originally recognized as Band Section Supply Troop 1 Cav on 7 July 1920.

f. Allston is a neighborhood of Boston, west of Kenmore Square, south of Cambridge, and north of Brookline. The Commonwealth Armory was adjacent to the site that is now Boston University's Nickerson Field.

g. Originally recognized as Band Section Service Troop Cav on 17 November 1920.

Table 10.1. National Guard Cavalry Bands *(continued)*

22nd Cavalry Division troops:
Kentucky, Ohio, Pennsylvania

103nd Cavalry, Pennsylvania (1936 and 1939 in Northumberland). 6 June 1921.

Edward S. Calhoun (b. Pennsylvania 14 June 1893); WO 21 May 1929, NGUS WO 31 Oct. 1934

104th Cavalry, Pennsylvania (1936 in Elizabethville, 1939 in Harrisburg). 1 June 1921.[i]

Percy A. Swab[j] (b. Pennsylvania 8 Nov. 1889); WO 30 July 1926, NGUS WO 25 Apr. 1934

107th Cavalry, Ohio (1936 and 1939 in Akron). 21 July 1927.

Lawrence V. Kelley (b. Texas 12 Oct. 1896; BA Emanuel College, Michigan, 1922); WO 19 May 1936

123nd Cavalry, Kentucky (1936 and 1939 in Glasgow). 1 Apr. 1929.

Wayne E. Tyree (b. Kentucky 5 May 1894); WO 22 May 1933, NGUS WO 28 Aug. 1934

23rd Cavalry Division troops:
Alabama, Georgia, Illinois, Louisiana,
Michigan, Tennessee, Wisconsin

105th Cavalry, Wisconsin (1936 and 1939 in Watertown). 1 Apr. 1921.[k]

Edwin J. Woelffer (b. Wisconsin 31 Jan. 1890); WO 3 Apr. 1928, NGUS WO 11 May 1934

106th Cavalry,[l] Illinois (1936 and 1939 in Chicago). 12 July 1929.

Thomas J. Madden[m] (b. Illinois 5 June 1905); WO 28 Apr. 1936

---

h. After leading the 110th Cavalry Band for sixteen years from 1924 to 1940, Whiting commanded several U.S. Army bands and concluded his career as the founding commander and conductor of the U.S. Army Field Band.

i. Organized originally as Band 8 Infantry on 1 May 1903

j. Served in the 316th Infantry Band, 1917–19. Edwward Worman, "1st Battalion United States Sharpshooters Civil War," New York State Military Museum and Veterans Research Center, NYS Division of Military and Naval Affairs website, http://www.dmna.state.ny.us/historic/reghist/civil/other/1stUSSS/1stUSSSMain.htm.

k. Originally recognized as Band Section 1 Cav. on 1 Nov 1920.

l. The Chicago unit of the 106th Cavalry was known as the Chicago Black Horse Troop and Mounted Band. There have been several Black Horse Troops within the U.S. military in general and within the National Guard in particular. See chapter 8, note 59.

m. Joining the band as a charter member in 1929, Madden is an example of a guardsman-musician who rose through the ranks to become the commanding bandmaster. U.S. War Department, National Guard Bureau, *Official National Guard Register for 1936*, 255.

TABLE 10.1. NATIONAL GUARD CAVALRY BANDS *(CONTINUED)*

108th Cavalry, Georgia and Louisiana (1936 in Jennings, Louisiana). 21 Mar. 29.

John A. Liesch (b. Illinois 29 Oct. 1888); WO 6 May 29, NGUS WO 19 Sep 34 (1939 in Savannah, Georgia, and New Orleans, Louisiana).[n]

Frank J. Rosata (b. Louisiana 1 Feb. 1915); WO 4 Apr. 37, NGUS WO 19 June 1937

109th Cavalry, Tennessee (1936 and 1939 in Chattanooga). 9 May 1923.

John W. Washburn (b. Tennessee 4 Mar. 1879); WO 14 May 1925, NGUS WO 18 May 1934

24TH CAVALRY DIVISION TROOPS:
COLORADO, IDAHO, KANSAS, WASHINGTON, WYOMING

113th Cavalry, Iowa (1936 and 1939 in Oskaloosa). 5 July 1928.

Lee R. Brissey (b. Iowa 14 May 1897);[o] WO 5 Sept. 1933, NGUS WO 28 Apr. 1934

---

n. U.S. War Department, National Guard Bureau, *Official National Guard Register for 1939*, places the 108th Cavalry Band at Savannah, Georgia, in the "Stations of Organization" section (p. 15), and at New Orleans, Louisiana, in the "State" section (p. 503). Major Les' Melnyk, Army National Guard historian of the National Guard Bureau states, "As for the location of the 108th Cavalry Band, it appears that one of the two entries is in error. I would guess that the listing on p. 15 is the mistake, and the state listing showing the band in New Orleans is correct. In part, I base this on the fact that the band does not show up under the state listing for Georgia, which helps confirm the fact that it was in New Orleans. It may have been that the band was initially allotted to Georgia but subsequently the allotment was transferred to Louisiana, thus accounting for the notation under the band heading in the state listing section where it shows the band was initially federally recognized, was disbanded in 1937, then federally recognized again two months later. It must have moved to Louisiana in Feb–April 1937." Melnyk, Arlington, Va., e-mail message to author, 13 October 2005.

o. Lee Roy Brissey was the final bandmaster of the 113th Cavalry Band after several others, including Roscoe V. Heringlake and Harry Peaslee. The first was C. L. (Lloyd) Barnhouse, Jr., of C. L. Barnhouse Publishing, who served from 1928 to 1931.

including the 1st Battalion of Cavalry of the Massachusetts Volunteer Militia[2] at the turn of the twentieth century (preceding the 110th Cavalry), as discussed in chapter 5.

Although all of these bands were authorized to be mounted, due to a lack of horses in general, and because some units were not allotted sufficient numbers of horses for their bands in peacetime, it is difficult to determine how many of

---

2. A 1900 photograph of the mounted band of the 1st Battalion of Cavalry, Massachusetts Volunteer Militia is in the author's possession.

TABLE 10.1. NATIONAL GUARD CAVALRY BANDS *(CONTINUED)*

114th Cavalry, Kansas (1936 and 1939 in Kansas City). 3 July 1924.

    Harry M. Swartz (b. Illinois 20 Nov. 1882); NGUS WO 4 June 1934

    Charles M. Nixon (b. Kansas 1 Aug. 1894); WO 1 Jan. 1939, NGUS WO 29 Mar. 1939

115th Cavalry, Wyoming (1936 and 1939 in Cheyenne). 26 Mar. 1926.

    Clyde G. Ross (b. New Mexico 25 Feb. 1893); WO 1 Feb. 1932, NGUS WO 13 Aug. 1934[p]

116th Cavalry, Idaho (1936 and 1939 in Caldwell). 13 Oct. 1926.

    Earl H. Tunison (b. Idaho 28 Dec. 1912); WO 18 Sept. 1935, NGUS WO 4 Mar. 1936

    Lorn E. Christensen (b. South Dakota 21 July 1909; BS South Dakota State College, 1931; Mmus Eastman School of Music, New York, 1936); WO 15 Oct. 1937, NGUS WO 9 Feb. 1936

---

p. Clyde Ross was a violinist and is a good example of a cavalry musician who spent his life in various music circles. Providing music from their own library in 1935, Ross and his wife, Alice, who was also a musician (pianist), founded the Cheyenne Little Symphony, which was one of the predecessors of the present-day Cheyenne Symphony. Ross served as the first conductor of this group and also led and played in local dance bands. The University of Wyoming School of Music continues to award the Clyde Ross Memorial Scholarship. Frank Hoadley, grandson of Clyde G. Ross, Madison, Wis., telephone interview by author, 26 May 2006; Chloe Illoway, executive director of the Cheyenne Symphony, Cheyenne, Wyo., telephone interview by author, 9 June 2006.

WO = Warrant Officer
NGB = National Guard Bureau
NGUS = National Guard United States

them actually performed on horseback.[3] Former guardsman Bill Rankin comments, "In September 1934 I, along with another clarinet player, lied about our age[s] . . . claiming to be 18 when we were actually 16 . . . and enlisted in the Cavalry Band. The 116th Cavalry Band, Idaho National Guard was not

---

3. Major Les' Melnyk, National Guard Bureau, Arlington, Va., e-mail message to author, 24 April 2003. Photographs of bands and/or verbal accounts of musicians of the 101st, 102nd, 103rd, 104th, 106th, 107th, 110th, 113th, 121st, 123rd, and 124th cavalries of the U.S. National Guard of this period (in the possession of the author) indicate that these bands were mounted.

a mounted band. However, the tympany supplied to the band had no legs and was designed to be mounted in hampers."[4] Major Les' Melnyk, Army National Guard historian of the National Guard Bureau further clarifies, "I have no doubt that your veteran's memory is correct, and he did indeed walk, but that doesn't mean he was 'supposed' to walk. His unit may simply have suffered from a lack of horses, or it is possible that the allotment of horses for the band was not authorized in peacetime—only in wartime. Guard units sometimes provided their own, privately purchased horses, just so they could train."[5]

Guard units were chronically short of horses and mules throughout the interwar period, and many of the animals that the federal government did furnish were old or infirm castoffs from the Regular Army. On 30 June 1925, there were 10,259 horses and 23 mules in the National Guard, of which 896 (8.7 percent) were state- or privately owned.[6] Records of the time (November 1927) show that the average age of the animals was nineteen—and that units had on hand, on average, 84 percent of the horses authorized for peacetime training.[7]

DUTY

The duty of National Guard cavalry bands consisted of various rehearsals, performances, and military training. George L. Shaffer of Fairfax Station, Virginia, served with the 103rd Cavalry Band in Northumberland, Pennsylvania, as a tuba player (sousaphone when mounted) from 1940 to 1941 and recalls, "Our duties consisted of playing local concerts, parades, dedications, etc., as well as two weeks of summer training comprised of maneuvers and musical performances with the regiment at Camp Drum New York."[8] Elwood Langdon of Fort Pierce, Florida, who played trumpet with the 101st Cavalry Band of Brooklyn, New York, from 1931 to 1938, adds to the picture: "The 101st was stationed at the armory on Bedford Avenue—just up the hill from Ebbets Field, home to the Brooklyn Dodgers. On Monday nights we had seated rehearsals, and had mounted rehearsals about twice a month. We played most all the Sousa

4. Bill Rankin, Caldwell, Idaho, e-mail message to author, 14 April 2003.

5. Melnyk, e-mail message to author, 24 April 2003.

6. U.S. War Department, *Chief of the Militia Bureau, Annual Report* (Washington, D.C.: Government Printing Office, 1925), 43.

7. Memorandum, Executive Officer, Militia Bureau to Assistant Chief of Staff, G-4 (Logistics), Subj: Answers to Questionnaire for Chief of Staff, 22 November 1927, 6–7. RG168/344a/325.4–Gen.–27.

8. George L. Shaffer, Fairfax Station, Va., telephone interview by author, 25 June 2001.

THE 110th CAVALRY BAND
M. N. G.

Chester E. Whiting's excellent musicianship is a well established fact. Since 1920 when he was appointed bandmaster, this band has written a splendid record of outstanding concert programs in which the works of composers from Palestrina, Bach, Beethoven, Brahms, Wagner, Tschaikowsky, to

CHESTER E. WHITING
Conductor

Sibelius, furnish much of the substance . . . The versatility of the band is further demonstrated in its excellent marching music, mounted or afoot. The 110th Cavalry Band is one of the very few mounted bands remaining in the U. S. A.

The 110th Cavalry Band is entirely equipped with
BUESCHER BAND INSTRUMENTS
by
CARL FISCHER, ℅ of BOSTON METROPOLITAN THEATRE MUSIC and INSTRUMENTS

FIGURE 10.1. 110th Cavalry Band, Massachusetts National Guard. A 1920s advertisement for Buescher Band Instruments and Carl Fischer, Inc., of Boston, publisher and purveyor of printed music and instruments. Carl Fischer's Boston store was housed in the Metropolitan Theatre, which at the time of this writing is known as the Wang Theatre. *Courtesy of the Hazen Collection of Band Photographs and Ephemera, Archives Center, National Museum of American History, Smithsonian Institution.*

marches for polo matches—some light concert pieces and cornet solos like Clarke's *Bride of the Waves* and *A Soldier's Dream*."[9] George Ramsden of Rockport, Massachusetts, who rode with the 110th Cavalry Band of Boston (Allston), Massachusetts, from 1934 to 1940 as a saxophonist, recalls, "We weren't the dressiest band, but one of the better concert bands—*1812 Overture*, we played at Revere Beach and all over—*Poet and Peasant Overture, Tiger Rag*."[10]

Warrant Officer Chester Whiting, who served as the bandmaster of the 110th from 1924 to 1940, recounts that on many occasions the band marched great distances "into other cities and rural areas, picketed the horses, changed uniforms and then played a fine concert program, often featuring the great cornet soloist Walter M. Smith." He also recalls that for special concerts it was not unusual to have guest conductors of considerable professional stature leading

9. Elwood Langdon, Ft. Pierce, Fla., letters to author, 9 April 2003 and 5 May 2003.
10. George Ramsden, Rockport, Mass., telephone interview by author, 14 March 2004.

the band, including Serge Koussevitzky of the Boston Symphony Orchestra and Edwin Franko Goldman, founder and director of the Goldman Band.[11] The rare ad shown in figure 10.1 is a testament to the 110th's unusual duty combining horse cavalry skills and professional musicianship—compounded further with their exclusive product endorsement.

Performances combining horses with music were as smooth an endeavor as musicians could make them, but periodically, as with the nineteenth-century 7th Cavalry Band, unusual duty arose. During the height of the National Guard cavalry years, probably no performance fit this description better than the 110th Cavalry Band's performance for a combination annual dinner and horse show for the Horse Lovers Association of Boston—in the second-floor ballroom of the Statler Hotel (present-day Boston Park Plaza Hotel and Towers) in 1939 or the early '40s. Whiting recalls, "The problem of getting our horses up to the ballroom was simplified by the construction of a cleated ramp over the grand staircase. Then to prevent the horses from slipping, also to keep them from destroying the beautiful floor, heavy canvas was laid and tied to braces built in the corridors. A riding Ring, a miniature compared with Madison Square Garden, took up half the floor space, around which the dinner guests were seated." The show opened with four youngsters mounted on ponies and carrying flags, heralding the entrance of Governor Leverett Saltonstall riding in an open carriage—followed by Mayor James Curley in an "Irish Jaunting Cart" followed by the mounted band. Of the unusual setting and scenario, Whiting recounts, "It was a night I shall never forget: Crepes suzettes, blatant martial music, ornate candelabra and horses; and, each one a correct appurtenance at any dinner given by the Boston Horse Lovers Association."[12]

As the 110th was geared toward the particular populace they served, other National Guard mounted bands were as well. Some, like the 124th in Mineral Wells, Texas, and the 123rd in Glasgow, Kentucky, served small-town and rural populations. Others were established as highly visible organizations, like the 110th, in major urban centers, and served as military escorts and ceremonial troops, who, in addition to their federal khaki uniforms, were often attired in specially designed dress uniforms. Some of these were parts of units that had been established as militia units in the tradition of wealthy gentlemen's riding

---

11. Chester E. Whiting, *The Mounted Cavalry Band—A Cavalryman's Soliloquy* (N.p., n.d.), 6, 7–8.
12. Ibid., 6, 8.

FIGURE 10.2. 102nd Cavalry (Essex Troop) Mounted Band, Sea Girt, New Jersey, ca. mid-1930s. *Courtesy of Ron Da Silva from the collection of former Essex Troop bandsman Joseph Torre.*

clubs.[13] Of these, the 102nd served in Newark, New Jersey, and traced its organization to the Essex Troop of 1890, and prior to that to the Essex Club in 1880.[14] Uniforms consisted of federally regulated wear as shown in figures 10.2 and 10.3 and of a style combining British military and English riding uniforms as seen in figure 10.4.

Similarly, the Chicago Black Horse Troop and Mounted Band of the 106th Cavalry in Chicago, riding matched black horses, was comprised of one hundred men (70 troopers and thirty trooper bandsmen) attired in dress uniforms patterned after U.S. dragoons of the War of 1812. Dr. Francis Mayer of St. Paul, who rode with the 106th as a clarinet player from 1929 to 1933 recalls,

13. *1940 National Guard of the U.S. Naval Militia State of Illinois*, 431; *Black Horse Troop at War*, bulletin no. 1 (Chicago: Chicago Black Horse Troop Association, May 1945), 7. By the 1920s, the idea of a local military unit serving in these capacities was of course centuries old, but is usually associated more with European courts. However, militia units serving as horse-mounted ceremonial units were also known in North America. The governor general's Body Guard of Toronto, Ontario, maintained a similar unit with a band in the 1930s, as did the 104th Cavalry of Pennsylvania, of which the First Troop Philadelphia City Cavalry of Philadelphia (formed in 1774 and serving as an escort for George Washington) continues to host a horse-mounted ceremonial unit (sans mounted band) attired in eighteenth-century-style uniforms.

14. Like many pre–National Guard troops, the Essex Troop was created by Col. James Fleming out of the Essex Club for the purpose of serving as an honor guard for special occasions. *History of the Essex Troop, 1890–1925* (Newark, N.J.: Essex Troop Armory, 1925), 3–4.

FIGURE 10.3. 102nd Cavalry (Essex Troop) bandsmen at New Jersey National Guard summer camp, Sea Girt, New Jersey. *Courtesy of Ron Da Silva from the collection of former Essex Troop bandsman Joseph Torre.*

The whole idea was for public relations. We would ride from our headquarters at the Chicago Riding Club on East Erie Street to the LaSalle Street or Dearborn station, and escort dignitaries through the streets to their hotels, or we'd take someone through the fairgrounds through the World's Fair [Century of Progress International Exposition, 1933–34]. And remember it wasn't just the mounted band—it was also seventy additional troopers on horseback. Of course we'd create quite a sensation. It was an expensive ordeal, so subscriptions were enlisted from Chicago corporate and political leaders to add to the government funds.[15]

Reasons for musicians joining mounted bands in the 1920s and '30s were similar to those of today's military musicians. Until the late 1930s, a world at war was far from the public's mind, and men who played instruments in amateur as well as professional settings found steady work in the National Guard. Several joined because of their high school band experiences, including Mayer, who joined because Albert Cook, his band director at Chicago's De La Salle

---

15. Dr. Francis Mayer, St. Paul, Minn., telephone interview by author, 25 November 2002.

FIGURE 10.4. 102nd Cavalry (Essex Troop) Mounted Band, Washington Park, Newark, New Jersey, ca. 1930s. Revealing its social club–militia beginnings, the 102nd's dress uniforms, like those of Chicago's 106th, were based on U.S. and British uniforms of the past with that of the 102nd including riding boots, jodhpurs, and busbies. *Courtesy of Ron Da Silva from the collection of former Essex Troop bandsman Joseph Torre.*

Institute (high school), was also the director of the 106th Cavalry Band. George Ramsden recalls similarly, "Warrant Officer Bandmaster Chester Whiting of the 110th Cavalry Band, who was also the music supervisor of Everett High School where I attended, asked me to be his orderly. I walked his horse and took care of his uniform, and played saxophone in the rehearsals. He gave me the equivalent of a buck private's pay out of his own pocket, as well as candy bars and tonic. I finally joined the band myself when I was eighteen."[16]

16. Ramsden, interview by author, 14 March 2004.

FIGURE 10.5. Chicago Black Horse Troop and Mounted Band of the 106th Cavalry in its first public appearance, Memorial Day Parade, Michigan Avenue, Chicago, 30 May 1930. This photo appears in several publications and papers by various authors, and is typically misdated by five years (later). I dated it by finding it in section 2, page 3 of the Friday, 30 May 1930, issue of the *Chicago Daily News*, where it appears with the caption "Black Horse Troop in First Public Appearance in Memorial Day Parade." *Courtesy of the U.S. Cavalry Association.*

Others joined to supplement their income, or to avoid other military duty. John Dittmer of Menlo Park, California, who rode with the 101st Cavalry Band in Brooklyn from 1936 to 1940 as a trombone and euphonium player and from 1940 to 1942 as the bandmaster, relates several memories about joining and recruiting:

> I had just finished my bachelor's degree in music education at Morningside College in Iowa and had come east to Columbia University for graduate work. Since the band was located in New York, we recruited at universities and the musicians' union, and we would tell the musicians, "You guys are going to get drafted if you don't do something about it. You're going to be firing a machine gun, driving a truck, etc. You'd be better off in one of the bands. Come to rehearsals on Monday nights and talk with our recruiter." Musicians who played every possible instrument from mandolin to Jew's harp would show up.[17]

And, as Elwood Langdon, also of the 101st recalls, one of the oldest reasons for joining any kind of military organization is because friends are joining: "I played with the drum and bugle corps—and later, the band of Boy Scout Troop 159 in Brooklyn. I played in a brass quartet within this band, comprised of my brother, Art and me on trumpet, Jack Wyrtzen on trombone, and George Schilling on euphonium. We all later joined the 101st band, which Art ended up leading for a while."[18]

Like their enlisted counterparts, cavalry bandleaders within this period of the National Guard probably joined to supplement their incomes, as well as to gain further leadership and conducting experience. Apart from their work in the Guard, some had non-musical civilian professions like Lee Roy Brissey of the 113th Cavalry, who worked in a factory in Oskaloosa, Iowa.[19] Others were professional musicians in civilian life, like Carl L. Cramer of the 111th Cavalry, who was the principal trumpeter of the New Mexico Symphony Orchestra, and Albert Cook of the 106th Cavalry, who, in addition to being the band director at De La Salle Institute, was the leader of the Chicago Police Band, the Elks Prize Band, and the Kilties Band and taught private lessons at his studio in

17. Col. John S. Dittmer (Ret.), Menlo Park, Calif., telephone interview by author, 25 June 2003.

18. Langdon, letter to author, 9 April 2003. Jack Wyrtzen went on to found Word of Life International, a worldwide evangelical ministerial association.

19. C. Arthur Fear, Evanston, Ill., telephone interviews by author, 1 November 2001 and 29 March 2003.

the Chicago Auditorium Building. Cook's successor, A. Boyd Pixley—who had been a baritone player in the band and who had served as vice president in the family business of Pixley and Ehlers Restaurants in Chicago and New York—composed several marches: *Chicago Black Horse Troop*, *Troopers Courageous*, *106th Cavalry*, *The Mounted Band*, and *Boots and Saddles*.[20] Others taught in public schools, like the aforementioned Chester Whiting[21] of the 110th Cavalry, who was a school band director in Malden and Everett, Massachusetts; Austin Truitt[22] of the 121st Cavalry, who was the head of the music department at Brighton High School in Rochester, New York; and Harwood C. Simmons of the 101st Cavalry, who was the conductor of the Columbia University Orchestra and the founder of the Columbia University Concert Band. Table 10.1 shows that the educational level of the bandmasters varied as well, with several having undergraduate degrees, and others, such as Simmons and Lorn E. Christensen of the 116th Cavalry in Idaho, holding graduate degrees in music by the time they were cavalry bandmasters.

Perhaps the cavalry musician of this era who attained the highest level of fame musically after his enlistment was Richard Smith "Billy" Vaughn, a member of the 123rd Cavalry Band of the Kentucky National Guard, which by 1941 had been federalized and was stationed in Mississippi. Vaughn probably played saxophone with the 123rd, but as a multi-instrumentalist and vocalist he more

---

20. Kenneth Berger, ed., *Band Encyclopedia* (Evansville, Ind.: Band Associates, 1960), s.v. "Pixley, A. Boyd." *Pixley and Ehlers* matchbook is in the author's possession. A. Boyd Pixley was the brother of Albert J. Pixley, the president and co-founder with William J. Ehlers of Pixley and Ehlers Lunch Rooms, later Restaurants, which had several slogans over the years, including "Boston Baked Beans," "A Better Place to Eat," "Serving 15 Million People Quality Food 24 Hours a Day," and "Serving a Few Things and Serving Them Well." Born December 12, 1885, in Portage, Wisconsin, A. Boyd Pixley was a baritone player in Weldon's 2nd Regiment Band (1903–1909), Manlius School Band (1906–1909), and University of Chicago Band (1908–1909). In 1909, he entered the family restaurant business and retired in 1947. He was also a member of the Chicago Elks Band and Medinah Temple Band. He received a bachelor of music degree from DePaul University in 1938. He and his wife, Ruth (who graduated from Illinois College in 1918), were the composer and author, respectively, of the "Illinois College Alma Mater." *Illinois College Catalog 2011–2012* (Jacksonville: Illinois College, 2011), 181. He died on 22 August 1974 in LaJolla, California. "Alumni News," *University of Chicago Magazine* 67, no. 3 (Spring 1975): 36; Albert Nelson Marquis, *Who's Who in Chicago and Vicinity: A Biographical Dictionary of Leading Living Men and Women of the City of Chicago and Environs Comprising Cook and Du Page Counties* (Chicago: A. N. Marquis, 1936), s.v. "Pixley, A. Boyd."

21. Chester Whiting went on to be the founding bandmaster of the First Combat Infantry Band, which was comprised entirely of soldier-musicians (including several who had served with the 110th) who had served in combat in World War II. Following the war this unit was renamed the Army Ground Forces Band and in 1950 became the United States Army Field Band. Several musicians of the 110th continued to serve with Whiting in each of these bands. Whiting, *Mounted Cavalry Band*, 1.

22. Truitt went on to earn a PhD in music education at the University of Rochester in 1953.

than likely played other instruments with the band as well. Developing his arranging and composing skills during his four-year enlistment, Vaughn went on to eventual stardom as the musical director of Dot Records—arranging for Pat Boone, Johnny Maddox, Gale Storm, and the Mills Brothers. With his own group, Billy Vaughn and His Orchestra, he recorded dozens of cover charts and continued to work with major names, including Johnny Mercer.[23]

In addition to these musical elements of National Guard work, several veteran musicians recall their summer training experiences, including George Shaffer of the 103rd, as already mentioned, who recalls that summer guard training was a prevalent part of the picture with annual two-week camps consisting of mounted and concert rehearsals and performances, as well as military training, drills, and ceremonies. Dittmer (101st New York) recounts as well, "In summer camp and active duty we did ceremonies called guard mounts, which took place every day—three out of seven days mounted in which the band would play. We took the horse cavalry regiment to North Carolina in 1941, with the horse vans carrying the horses over the road."[24]

George Ish (106th Illinois) recalls that, while the bandmaster conducted rehearsals and concerts throughout the year and during summer training, a commissioned officer from the line troop "performed administrative duties and bandsmen field and weapons training. I can remember in the field maneuvers of 1936, I was designated as the Lieutenant's horse holder and aide."[25] C. Arthur Fear of Evanston, Illinois, rode with the 113th Cavalry Band in Oskaloosa, Iowa, as a trombonist from 1926 to 1930, and recalls summer training reviews:

> We rode out on to the field at a walk while playing, and made three left-hand turns, and we would end up in the front of the reviewing stand facing the general. The rest of the troops rode out and rode around the field three times, first at a walk, then at a trot and then at a gallop. We played marches for the first two rounds, and then for the gallop we played *The Campbells are Coming*. At the conclusion of the review, we did a counter-march and marched off the field.[26]

---

23. Kenneth T. Jackson, Karen Markoe, and Arnold Markoe, *The Scribner Encyclopedia of American Lives* (New York: Scribner's, 1998), s.v. "Vaughn, Richard Smith ('Billy')," by Di Su; Gary Timlin, "Bunnellite Mounted Up: Here Comes the Kentucky Cavalry!," *News-Tribune* (Flagler Co., Fla.), ca. 1983.

24. Dittmer, interview with author, 25 June 2003.

25. Lt. Col. George Ish (Ret.), Yuma, Ariz., e-mail message to author, 26 June 2001.

26. Fear, interviews by author, 1 November 2001 and 29 March 2003.

Horse handling continued to be a primary consideration for members of mounted bands during the 1930s as Mayer remembers, "The horses were typically trained well enough to follow the horse in front of them. It was the front rank that had to worry about maneuvering, and I think that the outriders did more guiding than playing. To train the horses to get used to the sound, we played in the balcony at the Chicago Riding Club, while the hostler [horse handler] worked with the horses. The horses went crazy but learned to be eventually impervious to the sounds."[27] Chester Whiting recalls that members of the 110th Cavalry Band in Massachusetts were fairly well drilled in equitation through a lot of cross-country riding—jumping hurdles and ditches, scrambling down hills thick with underbrush, guiding their horses down sand slides, and even riding into rivers, dismounting and swimming across with their horses. He recalls further, however, that when forming a mounted band within the 110th in 1921, combining equitation with the playing of instruments was a different story. The bandsmen worked for several days in auditioning horses—finding the ones who did not react adversely to the trombone glissando on *Lassus Trombone* and other favorites.[28] Kettledrummer and trumpeter Walter Morris of the 123rd Cavalry Band of Kentucky, relates similarly, "We would pick up the most gentle horses . . . and start real slow by playing the instruments next to them. The next day we would get on the horse with our instrument, without playing, and after awhile we would start playing them."[29]

While some National Guard cavalry bands worked regularly with their horses, the men of the 123rd apparently only saw theirs during their annual two-week field training. In his account of the 123rd's initial foray into mounting their band on 20 July 1937 in preparation for a formal guard mount and parade ceremony three days later, Captain Gaylord S. Gilbert offers further comment for introducing horses and band to one another—as outlined by Warrant Officer Wayne Tyree:

1. Have the selected horses held in a circle around the dismounted band.
2. Have the band start playing dismounted.
3. Discard those horses, if any, which upset too easily.
4. Mount the band without instruments and ride in formation.

27. Mayer, interview by author, 25 November 2002.
28. Whiting, *Mounted Cavalry Band*, 2–4.
29. Morris quotes in Timlin, "Bunnellite Mounted Up."

5. Tie reins over pommel of the saddle and continue riding and practice the change of direction without the use of the reins.
6. Have attendant hand the instruments to the mounted men.
7. Change mounts that show timidity when the smaller instruments were played.
8. Ride in formation carrying instruments without playing and without touching reins as far as possible. Execute column right and column left.
9. At the halt, start playing mounted.
10. Play mounted, at the march and discard horses, if any, which are unsatisfactory.

Gaylord explains that by rotating horses in the front rank, after awhile it was apparent which ones had appropriate gaits for leading a band, and that by the day of the parade, while "one or two horses wheeled and danced . . . they soon quieted down and were under complete control when they passed the Commanding Officer." The training must have done the trick, as the commanding general ordered the 123rd Cavalry mounted band to perform for the Governor's Day 54th Cavalry Brigade Review the next week.[30]

Of course, working regularly with the same horse helped, but this did not always happen. Joining the 124th Cavalry Band of Mineral Wells, Texas, at the age of fifteen in 1931 under someone else's name and the next year under his own—but lying about his age (his father, W. W. Woodward was the bandmaster)—trumpeter and snare drum player, Roy Woodward recalls, "We didn't have the same horse each time. 'Here's your horse.' We would get our horses from the stable sergeants. Sometimes they would like to play tricks on us by giving us horses that were ringers—that were excitable, and they would prance and buck when we started playing. We looked for the meekest, docile horses that weren't afraid of trumpets and cymbals and the other instruments."[31]

While some cavalry musicians enjoyed mounted duty, others felt otherwise. Mayer (106th Illinois) recalls, "I never particularly enjoyed riding a horse. I endured it though. . . . You couldn't put a rein over your wrist because the horse would jerk its head and you'd get the clarinet bumped into your teeth." Langdon (101st New York) recalls, "For mounted-band use, our harness included

---

30. Gaylord S. Gilbert, "The Mounted Band of the 123rd Cavalry, Kentucky National Guard" *Cavalry Journal* 46, no. 5 (September–October 1937): 453.
31. Roy Woodward, Ft. Worth Tex., telephone interview by author, 8 July 1998.

a 'martingale'—an extra strap that restricted the horse from throwing his head to prevent injury to the musician rider." Shaffer (103rd Pennsylvania), who had not ridden before joining the guard, recalls that training consisted of " 'Here's your horse, get on it.' . . . I still don't like the thought of a McClellan saddle—like sitting on the top rail of a fence."[32]

While the official number of musicians for each National Guard mounted band, like those in the army, was twenty-eight, most bands supplemented this—sometimes numbering up to forty for special occasions. Depending on the band, a full complement of instruments consisted of various combinations of woodwinds, brass, and percussion. Serving in the 106th (Illinois) from 1936 to 1941, George Ish recounts,

> We had complete instrumentation of a 28-piece army band, which was the same for the 106th Cavalry Band when mounted or dismounted: 1 piccolo, 2 clarinets, 3 alto saxophones, 2 tenor saxophones, 6 trumpets, 5 trombones, and 1 tuba. The percussion consisted of 2 snare drums, 1 bass drum, 1 pair of cymbals, 1 glockenspiel, and 1 pair of kettledrums at the front of the band. In addition, the table of organization called for 1 Warrant Officer (bandmaster), and 1 drum major for a total of 28.[33]

Showing the variety of instrumentation of the time, Hubert Henderson describes how the 3rd Cavalry Band handled their twenty-eight players (twenty-nine with the warrant officer bandleader) in 1941: "The instruments included six clarinets, one flute, three saxes, six trumpets, two baritones, three alto horns, three trombones, two tubas and two percussion. . . . An enterprising bandleader could manage to substitute a pianist and/or oboist and/or a bassoonist for one of the authorized slots and in many cases these three musicians could simply be added to the authorized strength."[34]

Official standard instrumentation as outlined in the War Department's 1941 *Band Field Manual: The Band, FM 28–5* for a band of twenty-eight musicians varied from both of these, however:

---

32. Mayer, interview by author, 25 November 2002; Langdon, letter to author, 9 April 2003; Shaffer, interview by author, 25 June 2001.

33. Ish, e-mail message to author, 26 June 2001.

34. Henderson, "WW-II Bandsman and Bandleader," 1.

1 piccolo, D♭ ⎫
1 flute, D♭   ⎬ for 1 man.
1 flute, C   ⎭
1 clarinet, E♭
6 clarinets, B♭
4 cornets, B♭
2 trumpets, B♭
3 French horns (altos for mounted bands)
1 euphonium or baritone
3 trombones, B♭
1 saxophone, E♭ alto
1 saxophone, B♭ tenor
1 saxophone, E♭ baritone
1 bass, E♭, sousaphone (or BB♭ in lieu thereof)
1 bass, BB♭, sousaphone
1 drum, snare   ⎫
  Traps, as prescribed in AR 30–3000 ⎬ for 1 man.
1 drum, bass   ⎫
1 cymbals, pair ⎬ for 1 man.

The manual delineates further by indicating that this instrumentation allowed for flexibility, as mounted bands typically still had a tendency to be brass heavy and allowed for mounted kettledrums (tympani): "Modifications—In case the standard instrumentation has to be modified, it is well to remember that in marching and especially in mounted bands a preponderance of brass is desirable; while for concert work the proportion of wood-wind instruments is increased. In mounted bands, a pair of tympani may be used instead of the bass drum."[35]

---

35. U.S. Army, Chief of Infantry, Chief of Cavalry, and Army Band, *Band Field Manual*, 58–59. While past eras saw the band leader/chief musician often doing double duty as an instrumentalist and conductor, *Field Manual (FM)* 28–5 was careful to note, "The foregoing instrumentation does not include the band leader." This standard instrumentation was similar to that indicated in Training Regulations 130–5 of 1926 except that the older edition called for two cornets and four trumpets, allowed for B♭ flugelhorns "in lieu of cornets," called for three basses (one E♭ and two BB♭) rather than two, and specified helicons rather than sousaphones for mounted bands. U.S. War Department, *Band: Organization, Duties*, Training Regulations, No. 130–5, 22.

FIGURE 10.6. 123rd Cavalry Band, Kentucky, 1930s, with kettledrummer Walter Morris. *Courtesy of Kentucky Military History Museum.*

From New York to New Mexico, mounted bands of U.S. National Guard cavalry units actively performed mounted and dismounted in the late 1920s and throughout the 1930s. In rural and urban areas, performing standard patriotic fare including old and new marches, as well as current popular tunes, these bands—like their counterparts in federal units—were comprised of a variety of soldier-musicians performing for military events as well as minor and major civic engagements. Their reality, however, like that of the rest of the nation and the world was about to change dramatically.

CHAPTER 11

The 1940s,
Demise of the Tradition

THE CHANGES WITHIN THE U.S. MILITARY INITIATED IN THE 1920S
and '30s—especially in terms of motorization—were enhanced in the early
1940s with the country and much of the rest of the world on the brink of war.
As the years following World War I had brought a gradual phasing out of the
horse in the U.S. Army, the norm became motorized tanks, trucks, automobiles, and motorcycles, as well as aircraft and vehicle-drawn artillery.[1]

While a number of cavalry and pack artillery units were "dehorsed" prior
to the outbreak of World War II, with the United States declaring war on
Germany and Japan in December 1941, most of the remaining ones followed
suit—leaving a minor mounted contingency in the U.S. Army for battle duty.
Of the approximately forty thousand horses purchased and prepared for issue
prior to the war, a mere forty-nine were transported overseas, in addition to
those assigned to packtrains.[2]

This dismounting decision, however, did not go uncontested, as several
high-ranking U.S. military officials continued to argue for the continuation
of the horse cavalry within the U.S. Army, including chief of U.S. Cavalry,
Major General Leon Kromer. Recognizing the importance of strategic and road
mobility as well as the "crushing power" of mechanized cavalry, Kromer suggested that coupling these elements with the maneuverability in reconnaissance

---

1. While horse use within cavalry units continued to come into question, ironically, one of the inventions of this period was the horse portee, a four-and-a-half-ton truck tractor with a semitrailer for
transporting a squad of eight horses, as well as their riders and equipment, to areas called for in their new
roles. Thomas R. Buecker, "The Dismounting of the Fourth Cavalry at Fort Robinson 1942," *Rural Electric
Nebraskan* 43 (February 1989).

2. Livingston and Roberts, *War Horse*, 147.

and liaison work of the horse cavalry was optimal in "maintaining the great-est application of force."[3] Other pleas for cavalry retention came during and after the war from several additional generals—including Dwight Eisenhower, Omar Bradley, John Lucas, Jonathan Wainwright, George Patton, and Lucian Truscott.[4] Specifically, Eisenhower and Patton made a case for cavalry and pack artillery in Tunisia, feeling that their use would have brought an end to the African campaign sooner. Similarly, concerning the Allied invasion of Sicily, Truscott is recorded to have said, "I am firmly convinced that if one squadron of horse cavalry and one pack troop of 200 mules had been available to me at San Stefano on August 1 [1943], they would have enabled me to cut off and capture the entire German force opposing me along the north coast road and would have permitted my entry into Messina at least 48 hours earlier."[5] How-ever, these concerns fell mainly on deaf leadership who were convinced that machines were how future wars would be won.

Of the Axis powers, while numerous nations, including Japan, Italy, Roma-nia, and Hungary, had small contingents of cavalry, only the Germans fielded large horse-mounted forces during World War II, including the 1st Cavalry Division's (4,500 cavalry troops and 17,000 horses) participation in the invasion of France in 1940 and in the initial stages of Operation Barbarossa in 1941. Consequently, their cavalry units were the only ones who had an impact on major operations (of the Allied powers, only the Russians equaled the Germans in cavalry numbers).[6] While the bulk of the 1,100,000 horses that Germany maintained in military services throughout the war were utilized in the supply

---

3. "Necessity for Horsed Cavalry under Modern Conditions, Extract from Recent Hearings before the Subcommittee of the Committee on Appropriations, House of Representatives, on the War Depart-ment Appropriation Bill, 1938," reprinted from *Cavalry Journal*, May–June 1937, in *Cavalry Journal* 37, no. 3 (September 2012): 13, 16.

4. Mel Bradley, *Missouri Mule* (Columbia: University of Missouri Press, 1991), 433; Livingston and Roberts, *War Horse*, 158–59.

5. U.S. Army. Quartermaster Corps, *Horses and Mules and National Defense*, comp. Anna Waller (U.S. Army Office of the Quartermaster General, XVIII-3–009, 1958), 22.

6. DiMarco, *War Horse*, 334–36. Livingston and Roberts point out that "the Russian cavalry played an important part in the defeat of the German army, a highly mechanized and science-minded army that was considered one of the finest in the world. The hit-and-run tactics utilized by the irregular cavalry units provided disruption of German supply and communications"; Livingston and Roberts, *War Horse*, 170–71. Interestingly, even after hundreds of years of breeding, development, and training of cavalry horses the world over, in 1947 U.S. officials still felt that Hungarian horses, descendants of those used by the original Hussars, were the best military type in the world, and thus were hesitant to return animals obtained as war booty back to the Soviet-controlled Hungarian government. Helen Addison Howard, "Germany's Captured Superhorses," *Western Horseman* 42 (May 1977): 148.

and transport service or in the field artillery, unlike the United States' remount system, the well-organized German remount system continued to produce quality horses for Germany's army until the last year of the war.[7]

In contradistinction to this strong German cavalry, with the U.S. emphasis on mechanization, the era of utilizing horse units in the U.S. Army was quickly coming to a close. On 1 January 1942, the final mounted charge in U.S. history took place when Lieutenant Edwin Price Ramsey commanded a twenty-seven-man platoon of the 26th Cavalry Regiment as an advance guard for the 1st Regular Division of the Philippine Army attached to the U.S. Army—attacking and routing Japanese forces at the village of Morong, Bataan, on the Luzon Coast of the Philippine Islands.[8]

During the same year, the 3rd and 14th Cavalry Regiments were inactivated, and the 4th Cavalry went through several redesignations beginning with the 4th Cavalry, Mechanized Regiment.[9] Moreover, seven federalized National Guard horse-mechanized units were directed to turn in their horses—along with those of the 6th Cavalry. In April and May of 1943, the historic 1st Cavalry Regiment was de-horsed, and finally, in March 1944, the 2nd Cavalry Division and the 56th Brigade of the Texas National Guard—the last mounted units in the U.S. Army—received orders to do the same.[10]

Along with this U.S. Army dismounting and deactivating, so went mounted bands. However, we are fortunate to have records of two early 1940s mounted bands—one federalized National Guard band and the other in the Regular Army. Lieutenant John Eberhardt recalls a 1941 Memorial Day post horse show performance at Fort Bragg, North Carolina, by the mounted band of the 112th Field Artillery, a regiment that traces its roots to the Revolutionary War: "What a spectacle we presented as we proceeded to the site of the event! We would certainly let them know that the 112th was coming! First came our famous mounted band, blaring away as they could do so well. The horses and people that would be competing followed them." Eberhardt also recounts that, while the band members were mounted for most of their performances, "still they were one of the

7. DiMarco, *War Horse*, 343.

8. Kristine Withers, "American Mounted Cavalry Operations in World War II," *Cavalry Journal* 32, no. 2 (June 2008): 3–7; Livingston and Roberts, *War Horse*, 34, 151; Mark Schlachtenhaufen, "Hero Led Last U.S. Army Cavalry Charge," *Edmond (Okla.) Sun*, 4 October 2010, http://www.edmondsun.com/local/x537487919/Hero-led-last-U-S-Army-cavalry-charge; "Ramsey, Edwin Price, May 9, 1917–March 7, 2013," *Crossed Sabers: A Newsletter of the U.S. Cavalry Association* 13, no. 1 (Summer 2013): 3.

9. Sawicki, *Cavalry Regiments*, 156–58, 178–79.

10. Livingston and Roberts, *War Horse*, 152–53; U.S. Army. Quartermaster Corps, *Horses and Mules*, 16, 31.

best military bands that I have ever heard." Of the bandmaster and music, Eber-
hardt recalls that Mel Chamber was a well-known Broadway musical arranger
and conductor and that "his arrangements of our three favorites, the 'Artillery
March,' the 'Beer Barrel Polka,' and the 'Old Gray Mare' were outstanding."[11]
As Eberhardt states, even at this late date, the "112th Field Artillery Regiment,
Horse Drawn" was still known as one of the two "so-called 'socialite' National
Guard units in New Jersey," with the other one being the 102nd Cavalry (see
chapter 10).[12] While full-fledged war may have been the last thing on the unit's
originators' minds, like those of many other militia and social units, members
of the 112th found themselves federalized as the country went to war.

Representative of mounted bands of the Regular Army was that of the 3rd
Cavalry, which, with the declaration of war, was transferred from Fort Myer
where it had been stationed since 1919, to Fort Oglethorpe, Georgia, in February 1942 and then to Fort Benning, Georgia. Of the 3rd Cavalry move, Hubert
Henderson recalls:

> In February, 1942, the Regiment was transferred to Ft. Oglethorpe, GA. Being
> eligible for retirement, the Warrant Officer Bandleader [Louis Yassel] did not go to
> Oglethorpe; before he left he promoted me to sergeant. I was unofficially made the
> band's music director, conducting rehearsals and performances; as the tallest man
> in the Band, I also served as drum major. The Regimental Commander appointed
> a captain to serve as Commanding Officer. Adjacent to Chickamauga State Park,
> the scene of furious Civil War battles, Ft. Oglethorpe was strictly a show place
> and a cavalry regiment was apparently considered ideal for that location. We did
> enjoy Sunday afternoons, riding through the Park, and the occasional ride up the
> cog railroad to Lookout Mountain. But most of the time there was pretty boring;
> we played only a single parade in the nearby city of Chattanooga, a few concerts
> but many dances.[13]

The move was an indication of larger changes, however, and these idyllic and
sometimes placid cavalry experiences did not last long. Representative of these

---

11. John S. Eberhardt, *The Old Gray Mare* (New York: iUniverse, 2005), 82, 40–41. Eberhardt recollects
that, like other cavalrymen over the centuries, many men entering the 112th Field Artillery knew little
about horsemanship: "I, along with nearly everyone else, was unaware of how completely unfamiliar these
new men were about horses" (66).

12. Ibid., 10.

13. Henderson, "WW-II Bandsman and Bandleader," 2–3.

larger alterations, and setting the stage for other cavalry modifications that were part of a large dismounting plan for the entire U.S. Department of Defense, the 3rd Cavalry was soon reorganized and redesignated as the 3rd Armored Regiment and was assigned to the 10th Armored Division on 15 July 1942 at Fort Benning.[14] Along with the famed cavalry unit, its equally famous mounted band was no more. Other cavalry and artillery regiments and their bands followed suit. While the void in Washington, D.C., left by the 3rd Cavalry was filled partially and eventually by the 3rd U.S. Infantry and the U.S. Army Band, the heroic pageantry of mounted bands in the nation's capital was finally concluded.[15]

By the end of World War II, the U.S. Army had no mounted units remaining within the cavalry or artillery where they had faithfully served since the days before the Revolutionary War. Logically, accompanying these developments, there were no mounted bands remaining either. Thus, after more than a century of an unbroken tradition in the United States and an even longer one dating back over eight hundred plus years in Europe and the Middle East to the Crusades, mounted U.S. bands were no longer. As serving as a lead military player on the world front along with protecting the United States' national and international interests was paramount for the War Department, pageantry and tradition took a backseat, while advances in armament and mechanization stood center stage.

As the Spanish-American War had launched the United States onto a new international platform, World Wars I and II solidified the nation's place as a world leader in terms of military, economy, and industry. One indication of this comes from observing the federalization of National Guard units, when, between September 1940 and October 1941, over 300,000 Guardsmen in eighteen divisions, twenty-eight separate regiments, and twenty-nine observation squadrons were inducted into federal service, doubling the size of the army. Along with the newly formed federalized guard units were scores of others that had begun as social clubs in the previous century, and which were now part of the army, where little reflection was done on their beginnings. In addition to these dismounted guard units were those of the Regular Army, which also gave up their horses and consequently their mounted bands—two of which had been around since the days of Seminole Indian conflicts of the 1830s.

---

14. Third Cavalry Museum, *Blood and Steel!*, 19; Sawicki, *Cavalry Regiments*, 156.

15. This move led to the eventual reactivation of the 3rd Infantry to serve as a standing ceremonial unit and defender of the capital, and for the U.S. Army Band, the top band of the U.S. Army, to move to Fort Myer from Fort McNair. John Michael, *Images of America, Fort Myer* (Charleston, S.C.: Arcadia Publishing, 2011), 106, 111.

Speculation and conjecture can perhaps lead us to some kind of answer about the demise of the tradition of mounted bands in the United States. As mounted bands followed horse unit practice, questions that may be worth pursuing, and which I will mention here but leave to future historians to tackle in full, include (1) what would have become of U.S. horse units had World War II not happened, or (2) had the U.S. not participated, or (3) if the war had been fought in North America, or (4) if neither world war had happened? Had any of these scenarios happened, perhaps at least the 3rd Cavalry would have remained in its ceremonial role near the nation's capital. Perhaps the urgency of new technologies in armament and warfare would not have dictated mechanization, and perhaps cavalry and artillery units would have remained stationed around the United States as peacekeeping forces with their mounted bands. And perhaps the privately initiated militia units would have remained just that—serving as honorary escort units with their mounted bands.

Concerning fighting World War II on the United States' own turf, perhaps continued use of horse units would not have been the question it was with the war taking place in Europe, Africa, and the Pacific. Had the element of transportation been removed from the equation, perhaps horses would have found continued use in guard, reconnaissance, and harassing roles—and to support these units, perhaps mounted bands would have found continued service.

Another element that may lead to further query concerns the United States' role as a world military power, which was well in place by World War II after having moved in this direction since the close of the nineteenth century. While France and Britain were both strong militarily at this point, their individual and collective states as major imperialistic powers were winding down. Consequently, whatever they had to prove had already been set, and perhaps some kind of statement can be made for the argument of resting on laurels and honoring their traditions and letting the new players to the stage take the military lead. Accordingly, while both France and Britain, each of whom maintained hundreds of bands within their various military branches during World War II (as did the United States), lost mounted bands at the onset of the war, neither country lost all of theirs as the United States did.

On the reverse side, within the Axis powers, as Hitler continued to rebuild what had been lost with the Treaty of Versailles after World War I and the diminished Reichswehr, he seized control of the German military in 1934. With this gesture, military bands rose to become a significant part of Hitler's war machine, and those within mounted units were reintroduced to kettledrums around 1936—after little use over the past century.[16] Cameron Dall indicates that the number of German military bands serving during the Third Reich was well over 1,000, "with 27 to 37 in each band, except in the case of the special bands of the S.S., Heer, Luftwaffe, and Kriegsmarine where the bands were larger," resulting in 27,000 to 37,000 men serving in these units.[17] How many of these were mounted is difficult to determine, but as Hitler was a master at rebuilding from the past, there were probably quite a few (figure 11.1). He would have been mindful of the at least 18 cavalry bands within the 138 serving in the Reichswehr from 1920 to 1935 and the numerous horse-unit bands among the 541 in the Old Army (pre-1914).[18] Consequently, during most of the war, as the United States was drawing down mounted bands, Germany was bolstering theirs. However, as the war progressed, Dall indicates that, by 1944, "most, if not all, [German] military bands were disbanded because the soldiers were needed to fight the war. Only the military headquarters in large cities had bands in 1945."[19]

Caldwell Titcomb maintains that it was Germany's 1936 reintroduction of army kettledrums that was the basis of a 2 February 1942 French ministerial directive—complete with the publication of an official *Méthode pour timbales de cavalerie* the following year—ordering the addition of kettledrums to the brass bands of all cavalry regiments.[20] As Britain had never discontinued using kettledrums with its mounted bands, there was not the same push to strengthen them during World War II—and in fact, as in the U.S. military, mobilization and mechanization of the British military was a priority, and thus its mounted bands were reduced. Among the affected staff bands was the Royal Artillery Mounted Band, which had seen service beginning in 1878, stemming back even further to 1830 with its basis in the Royal Horse Artillery Band.[21] A major

16. Titcomb, "Kettledrums in Western Europe," 350.

17. Cameron M. Dall, "German Military Band Music during the Third Reich, 1933–1945" (master's thesis, Ball State University, 1990), 9; Panoff, *Militärmusik*, 175.

18. These included 28 dragoon regiments, 21 hussar regiments, 10 cuirassier regiments, 26 lancer regiments, 4 heavy cavalry regiments, 8 cheveauleger regiments (Bavaria), 6 horse rifle regiments, and 101 horse artillery regiments. Dall, "German Military Band Music," 7–8, citing Wilhelm Stephan, *Der Grosser Zapfenstreich* (Bonn, Ger.: Stephan, n.d.), 18.

19. Dall, "German Military Band Music," 9. Much of Dall's work is based on communication with Joachim Toeche-Mittler, German military musician during the Nazi era and author of *Armeemarsch*, vols. 1–3 (Neckargemünd, Ger.: Kurt Vowinckel Verlag, 1966, 1971, 1975).

20. Titcomb, "Kettledrums in Western Europe," 350; Robert Tourte, *Méthode pour timbales de cavalerie* (Paris: Éditions P. Naudin 1943), i.

21. Farmer, "Royal Artillery Mounted Band," 77; Gleason, "History of the Royal Artillery Mounted Band," 38–39.

musical institution—with the bulk of its musicians being doublehanded, playing stringed instruments in addition to woodwind and brass—the Royal Artillery Mounted Band was dismounted in 1939. This transition also brought a reduction in personnel with several musicians being transferred to other units and sometimes to other assignments—including that of glider pilot. Among these were B. Dury, H. Wood, and R. West, all of whom were killed at the Battle of Arnhem, and B. Black, who was taken prisoner by the Germans and later released by the Russians—reminders that the prime work of armies is not to serve as an arena for military music, but to fight wars.[22]

Another unanswerable question concerns the behavior and decision making of a people: does the age of a nation affect its retention of traditions? The British and French retained at least some horse-mounted military units and in the case of France, a mounted national police force, and in turn, mounted bands during and after the war. Similarly, Germany retained mounted bands for most of the war's duration, but the United States dismounted and disbanded all of its at the beginning of the war. Consequently, an additional question for social historians may be: how long do a people have to be a nation before traditions are so engrained that discontinuing them is unthinkable? Since the United States disbanded its mounted band tradition after it was in place a little over a century, perhaps one hundred plus years is not long enough.[23] At the time of this writing, while most mounted horse units and their accompanying mounted bands of Allied powers in Europe have met their demise, others live on—undertaking various tasks of concert and mounted work. The United Kingdom continues to maintain the Band of the Household Cavalry, which formed in 2014 after an amalgamation of the Band of the Lifeguards and the Band of the Blues and Royals (Royal Horse Guards and 1st Dragoons) in London and at Windsor. France maintains La Fanfare de Cavalerie de la Garde Républicaine in Paris; Belgium has its Kliek van de Federale Politie (Corps des trompettes de la Police fédérale) in Brussels; Sweden has its Livgardets Dragontrumpetarkår in Stockholm; and Denmark has its Gardehusarregimentets Hesteskadron Trompeterkorps

---

22. "R.A. Mounted Band," unpublished paper (Woolwich: Royal Artillery Band Archives, Royal Artillery Band Building, Royal Artillery Barracks, n.d.), Box 14, n.p. The Royal Artillery Mounted Band continued to boast a concert band and orchestra until deactivation in 1985.

23. While documenting all British mounted bands in terms of origination, dismounting, and deactivation would be a considerable study in itself, noted British mounted bands that remained active during World War II included the Life Guards, the Royal Horse Guards (the Blues), the Royal Dragoons (1st Dragoons), and the Royal Scots Greys (2nd Dragoons). Turner and Turner, *Cavalry and Corps*, 21, 25, 27, 38.

FIGURE 11.1. 12th (Sächs.) Reiter-Regiment, Dresden, 1931. *Trompeterkorps* of trumpets and drums. *Courtesy of Hasso Krappe, Deutsche Gesellschaft für Militärmusik, Leverkusen, Germany.*

in Slagelse.[24] Perhaps Germany would have a mounted ceremonial unit with mounted band within this lineup if its recent history had been different, either by avoiding World War I or by being the victors—resulting in maintaining its monarchy—or by being the victors in World War II and remaining militarily strong and retaining its traditions. However, if the latter had been the case, the other aforementioned nations probably would not have their own militaries, let alone mounted bands.

---

24. Present-day European mounted bands have varied sets of instrumentation. The British bands are full concert bands—from piccolo to tuba—on horseback. The French La Fanfare is comprised of valveless trumpets and horns with valved helicons for the basses. The Belgian Kliek is comprised of cavalry trumpets, straight horns and tenor horns. The Swedish Livgardets Dragontrumpetarkår is comprised of valved brass instruments, and the Danish Garde unit is comprised of valveless trumpets. All incorporate mounted kettledrums. The closest the United States has come to a monarchical guard would be the U.S. Marine Corps' service as a guard for the president with the U.S. Marine Band serving as the "President's Own"—albeit in dismounted capacities.

Along with longevity of tradition, another related question might concern the size of landmass of a nation. Perhaps Washington, D.C., does not hold the same center for the American people as European capitals do simply because of the geographic size of the country and because the city is not the nation's commercial-financial capital. Consequently, visitors are typically drawn to the American capital city for governmental practices and history rather than to observe traditions. As it stands, Washington, does not draw U.S. citizens and visitors the way European capitals do—especially since there is no historic guard-changing ceremony—outside that of Arlington National Cemetery. If the United States were smaller in area and more strongly connected to European roots, perhaps at least one ceremonial unit and mounted band would have continued in the nation's capital.

How governments decided which bands to discontinue or dismount is also a matter of conjecture. While the Lifeguards and Blues and Royals as staff bands were a prominent fixture in British musical and military communities, so were the bands of the Royal Artillery, of which the aforementioned Royal Artillery Mounted Band was a prominent fixture.[25] However, unlike the remaining

---

25. Farmer, "Royal Artillery Mounted Band," 77; Gleason, "History of the Royal Artillery Mounted Band," 38–39.

FIGURE 11.2. Royal Artillery Mounted Band leading the coronation parade of George VI, 1937. *Courtesy of tenor horn player Edward Roberts of Aldershot, England, who appears in this photograph.*

British mounted bands, the Royal Artillery Band and Royal Artillery Mounted Band were separate entities. While both did concert band and orchestral work, only the Royal Artillery Mounted Band performed on horseback. Had there been only one Royal Artillery Band doing double duty, perhaps its members would still have their horses.

As mounted musical units have had strong connections to nobility for centuries, a case could be made for ensembles who continue with this type of service—including the aforementioned units of Belgium, Sweden, and the United Kingdom, whose work includes serving as royal escorts. Therefore, as the United States lacks a monarchy, perhaps this was the social piece that would have been necessary to continue a mounted band tradition. By comparison, while the French revolted against their monarchy shortly after the American colonies did theirs, the French were not completely through with autocrats, thus members of France's La Fanfare trace their beginnings to 1802 to the time of Napoleon[26]—and currently serve a people who in some respects are more anti-monarchical than those in the United States.[27] As a personal reflection,

---

26. Although these traditions in turn stem from earlier ones cultivated in monarchical times.

27. Jean Loup Mayol, ed. *150 ans de Musique à la Garde Républicaine, Mémoires d'un Orchestre* (Paris: Nouvelle Arche de Noé Editions, 1998), 17.

after observing a recent La Fanfare Armistice Day performance that included several hundred horsemen in addition to forty plus mounted musicians riding along Champs-Elysées, I can verify that whatever divisions there have been between the French and a monarchy—the Bourbons and the Bonapartes—the pageantry of neither regime has disappeared. A similar statement can probably be said for mounted ceremonial units that contain mounted bands in other European countries that no longer have monarchies in place but that continue to maintain mounted ceremonial units with mounted bands—including Italy's Fanfara del 4° Reggimento dei Carabinieri, Spain's Banda Musical de la Guardia Urbana de Barcelona, and Portugal's Guarda Nacional Republicana Charanga a Cavalo. While these units, like that of the French Garde Républicaine are gendarmerie (national police force) units, separating their work and history respectively from the military of each country is impossible.

With this discussion as a guide, the demise of the mounted cavalry, and subsequently the mounted band tradition in the United States, was probably a combination of the aforementioned ideas: (1) World War II happening when and where it did; (2) the United States' trajectory of becoming a world military power at the same time most of the world's militaries were becoming motorized; and (3) the idea that the relatively short-lived tradition was not strong enough to keep at least one mounted ceremonial unit and mounted band in place in the nation's capital—perhaps compounded by the idea that the United States had never completely dispelled the notion of cavalry as an aristocratic rich man's game that does not fit within a country composed of "your tired, your poor, [and] your huddled masses."[28]

While outside the parameters of the present work, an interesting study would be to compare the duration of specific mounted-band traditions in former European colonies—none of which has a monarchy. These include Argentina (Fanfarria Alto Perú and Banda Militar "El Hinojal" del Regimiento de Caballería de Montaña 4 "Coraceros General Lavalle"), Brazil (Regimento de Polícia Montada—9 de Julho and 1° Regimento de Cavalaria de Guardas (1° RCG)—"Dragões da Independência"), Chile (Escuadrón Escolta Presidencial del Regimiento de Caballería Blindada N° 1 "Granaderos,"), and Peru (Banda y Caballería de los Húsares de Junín). But other South American countries have developed mounted ceremonial band traditions as well, including Ecuador and

---

28. Emma Lazarus, "The New Colossus" (1883)—poem engraved on a bronze plaque inside the lower level of the pedestal of the Statue of Liberty in New York Harbor.

Uruguay. Moreover, future research could take into account mounted musical traditions that have developed in Thailand, Oman, India, and Senegal.[29]

There were also mounted band traditions in Australia including those of the Anzac Mounted Division,[30] the 8th Light Horse Regiment,[31] the Queensland Mounted Infantry,[32] and the New South Wales Lancers[33]—and in Canada including those of the Queen's Own Canadian Hussars,[34] the Durham Light Cavalry,[35] the 2nd Dragoon Guards,[36] the 1st Canadian Mounted Rifles,[37] the Governor General's Body Guard,[38] and the North-West Mounted Police (precursor of the Royal Canadian Mounted Police/Gendarmerie royale du Canada).[39] South Africa also had traditions with the Cape Light Horse and the Durban Mounted Rifles.[40] It appears that none of these traditions were as strong as those in the United States, however. Therefore, how is it that the traditions have continued in some instances and have died out in others—especially when the tradition remains in some parent nations—Britain for Australia and South Africa, and Britain and France for Canada? Also, the element of tying a nation's longevity to tradition comes into question when adding the aforementioned South American countries into the mix, as several of them continue to host mounted military ceremonial units with mounted bands—some of which were inaugurated as

---

29. While I typically hesitate to mention countries where mounted bands exist at the time I am writing, I will acquiesce here and mention these simply to show that the tradition is by far from dead around the world. However, there is always the chance that I have missed a location where a mounted band has recently been formed—as well as the equal chance of naming a country whose mounted bands have been discontinued by the time of publication.

30. Photo of the Anzac Mounted Division in possession of author.

31. Photo of the 8th Light Horse Regiment in possession of author.

32. "Mounted Infantry Inspection," *Brisbane Courier,* 21 March 1898.

33. Philip V. Vernon, ed., *Royal New South Wales Lancers, 1885 to 1985* (Sydney: Royal New South Wales Lancers Centenary Committee, 1986), 15–16.

34. Dominion of Canada, *Sessional Papers,* vol. 9, *Fourth Session of the Sixth Parliament of the Dominion of Canada, Session 1890,* vol. 23 (Ottawa: Brown Chamberlin, 1890), 49.

35. *Ottawa Volunteer Review,* 18 July 1870.

36. John K. Marteinson, Brereton Greenhous, Stephen J. Harris, Norman Hillmer, William Johnston, and William Rawlings, *We Stand on Guard: An Illustrated History of the Canadian Army* (Montreal: Ovale Productions, 1992), 92.

37. Bruce P. Gleason, "Pipe Band of the 1st Canadian Mounted Rifles," *Military Collector and Historian, Journal of the Company of Military Historians* 56, no. 4 (Winter 2004): 279–82.

38. Photos of the Governor General's Body Guard in possession of author; John Marteinson with Scott Duncan, *The Governor General's Horse Guards, Second to None* (Toronto: Published for Governor General's Horse Guards Foundation by Robin Brass Studio, 2002), 140.

39. Bruce P. Gleason, "The Mounted Bands of the North-West Mounted Police," *Band International, Journal of the International Military Music Society* 27, no. 3 (December 2005): 99–103, 120.

40. G. Tylden, *The Armed Forces of South Africa,* Frank Connock Publication, no. 2 (Johannesburg: City of Johannesburg Africana Museum, 1954), 56, 77.

recently as the end of the last century. Therefore, while I lean toward the idea that it was a combination of reasons for the tradition to conclude in the United States, I am choosing to close this book with these questions mentioned and addressed, but mainly unanswered. I look forward to reading what future historians have to say about the topic—and encourage future doctoral students in music, history, sociology, military science, and cultural studies to consider these questions in their dissertations.

Another piece of the examination revolves around the horse in general and the fact that because of the status of the horse (or, more accurately, horse ownership), horse units—cavalry especially—were socially elevated above infantry units, and hence, cavalry music was as well. There was probably a dual reason for this. Horses, either by their nature or because humans have been encultured to think as such, add an appearance of nobility. Additionally, because it took money to purchase and maintain horses, wealthier men were drawn to horse units over infantry units.

I indicate in chapter 1 that full-fledged cavalry units were typically comprised of gentlemen, which by definition meant that they were men of a high social class who were entitled to a coat of arms—and could provide their own horses.[41] In fact, writing in 1670 and '71, James Turner states, "It is not above fourscore and ten years since in the raign [sic] of Maximilian the Second, all that were Enrolled in the German Cavalry were by birth Gentlemen."[42] As the pervading attitude in Europe of the sixteenth century (but which lasted for centuries) was that a nobleman's place was to fight on horseback above the common soldier, Turner's statement should not be a surprise. The point is furthered by a representative of Maximilian's German men-at-arms when it was suggested that they dismount to help storm a breach during a sixteenth-century battle: "They were not such as went on foot, nor to go into a breach, their true estate being to fight like gentlemen on horseback"[43]—not unlike the attitude of the Connecticut Light Horse troopers General Washington dispelled for the same reasons during the Revolutionary War. The insult of the suggestion to dismount and fight like infantrymen was not taken lightly, and while social historians may be better able to analyze the various aspects of this, I wonder if gentlemen-cavalrymen regarded themselves as warriors rather than simply as

41. Turner, *Pallas Armata*, 231.

42. Ibid., 163.

43. John Ellis, *Cavalry: The History of Mounted Warfare* (New York: G. P. Putnam's Sons, 1978), 104.

soldiers—someone noble, historic, and triumphant, rather than simply a fighter. General Winfield Scott's statement "A warrior on horseback looks upon foot-soldiers, beyond musket-shot, without any danger" suggests that mobility may not have been the only consideration when elevating horse units.[44]

Drawing on what I mentioned in the first chapter about dragoons, for centuries, the dual nature of riding to battle on horseback and then dismounting to engage the enemy was the holdup to regarding them as cavalry. The prevailing attitude was that gentlemen have the means to own and ride horses and that because dragoon regiments had lowered themselves to fighting on foot like infantrymen (who could not afford horses), they should not be regarded as full-fledged cavalry—and thus did not deserve kettledrums, thus elevating cavalry music along with cavalry troopers.

In coupling this stature of cavalry with the general stature of trumpets and kettledrums as identified by the trumpeters' and kettledrummers' guild, which helped maintain an exclusive "clubiness" for the instruments and their playing, cavalry music was bound to carry some kind of status of privilege: trumpets and kettledrums along with horses were for the advantaged. Thus, cavalry music could not help but take on a regal air. Although the trumpeters' and kettledrummers' guild did not make it to the United States, horsemanship—especially within the upper class as indicated in chapter 2—was taken seriously in the colonies and in some circles to the present day. This attitude continued into the twentieth century in the U.S. Cavalry, to the point that many cavalry posts had regularly scheduled polo matches—with teams often playing in civilian matches.[45] Thus, cavalry retained its elevated position of warrior versus soldier—with cavalry music doing so as well.

This part of the discussion leads us back to the primary focus of this book, which is that of horse-mounted bands. Consequently, I have barely touched on

44. *Congressional Globe*, 28th Congress, 1st session, 347, cited in Wooster, *American Military Frontiers*, 107.

45. "Great International Polo Tourney in Sight, Four Crack Teams Entered and Play Starts March 24"; and John D. Bromfield, "Canadians, Hawaiians, First Cavalry and San Mateo Stars to Swing Mallets," both in *San Francisco Call*, 16 March 1913, 4. This article and accompanying photo of Lieutenants Claude Rhinehardt, David L. Roscoe, Charles Haverkamp, and Frank Keller reports on the 1st U.S. Cavalry polo team's participation in "the opening of the international tournament on the Hillsborough fields Monday, March 24 [1913]." Many officers of cavalry units, including those of the Chicago Black Horse Troop, were also avid polo players. Several of the officers of the Chicago unit, as members of some of Chicago's wealthiest families, regarded the troop primarily as a show troop along with their polo clubs, although it was an official arm of the 106th Cavalry of the National Guard. Bruce P. Gleason, "Military Music in the 106th Cavalry: The Mounted Band of the Chicago Black Horse Troop, 1929–1940," *Journal of the Illinois State Historical Society* 104, no. 4 (Winter 2011): 319.

music within infantry and other foot units—an arena rich in the tradition of military music. While separating military music in horse units from that of foot units is not particularly fair to the cavalry, artillery, or infantry, as developments within each influenced the other, incorporating the complexities of all of these traditions in one book would have been a difficult, not to mention monumental, task. However, as several books and articles have been written about U.S. military music in general, including my article on U.S. military bands in Kurt Piehler's *Encyclopedia of Military Science*, I chose to focus on the mounted element for the present work. However, I encourage readers to study other works on various aspects of U.S. military music, many of which I have cited throughout this book: Raoul Camus's *Military Music of the American Revolution*; Fairfax Downey's *Fife, Drum and Bugle*; William Carter White's *A History of Military Music in America*; Kenneth Olson's *Music and Musket: Bands and Bandsmen of the American Civil War*; Francis Lord and Arthur Wise's *Bands and Drummer Boys of the Civil War*; Bruce Kelley and Mark Snell's *Bugle Resounding: Music and Musicians of the Civil War*; James Davis's *"Bully for the Band!" The Civil War Letters and Diary of Four Brothers in the 10th Vermont Infantry Band*; two editions of William Bircher's diary: Newell Chester's *A Drummer-Boy's Diary*, and Shelley Swanson Sateren's *A Civil War Drummer Boy: The Diary of William Bircher 1861–1865*; Margaret Hindle Hazen and Robert Hazen's *The Music Men: An Illustrated History of Brass Bands in America, 1800–1920*; Thomas C. Railsback and John P. Langellier's *The Drums Would Roll: A Pictorial History of U.S. Army Bands on the American Frontier, 1866–1900*; Richard Franko Goldman's *The Concert Band* and *The Wind Band: Its Literature and Technique*; Otto Helbig's *A History of Music in the U.S. Armed Forces during World War II*; and Chester Whiting's *The Baton and the Pendulum*, the only one of these that goes into detail about a mounted band—that of the 110th Cavalry of the Massachusetts National Guard. And to get a glimpse of a heretofore un-researched area of U.S. military music, I heartily recommend Jill Sullivan's *Bands of Sisters: U.S. Women's Military Bands during World War II*. All of these works cover in detail varying elements of the non-mounted aspect of American military music.

Several of these authors delve into pre-American military music history and thus examine the French Revolution—a major period of military and political history that influenced infantry music especially, when it was used to accompany the country's newfound national spirit. Taking part in the resulting grand fêtes were large wind bands performing pieces by the finest composers in the

country, with that of the Garde Républicaine setting the pattern for the following century. While the task of frightening the enemy had been long surpassed by
this point, the work of encouraging and motivating troops with music became
a fully entrenched mainstay of military bands. Documenting the connections
between infantry and cavalry music, however, would be a large undertaking
and, now with the present work in publication, is a task that the next historian,
I hope, will find easier.

    With this said, there are still general elements of all military music that
appear to be continuous over millennia, resulting in the constants of (1) encouraging and motivating warriors to battle; (2) organizing these same warriors
logistically and on the march; (3) providing comfort and senses of consolation
and home; (4) providing direction in battle; (5) adding solemnity, nobility, pas-
sion, and joy to ceremonies; (6) providing entertainment in concerts, dances,
and other informal civic and military performances; and (7) positively repre-
senting military institutions with the general populace. With these constants in
mind, Alan Merriam's venerable functions of music serve well as a template in
assessing military music and reveal that this is one of the few types of music that
serves all ten functions: emotional expression, aesthetic enjoyment, entertainment, communication, symbolic representation, physical response, enforcing
conformity to social norms, validation of social institutions and religious ritu-
als, contribution to the conformity and stability of culture, and contribution
to the integration of society.[46] These traits, while certainly exhibited within
the context and traditions investigated in this book, are not limited to horse-
mounted bands and could provide a basis for further research. Along these lines,
Trevor Herbert and Helen Barlow have recently published *Music and the British
Military in the Long Nineteenth Century* with Oxford University Press, addressing several philosophical and broad-based issues concerning military music's
influence on other music cultures—and, à la Merriam, how military music
has been used for imposing state authority through cultural means through its
effect on crowds and individuals. While I touch on some of these areas, as the
intent of this book was to single out the tradition of horse-mounted bands, I
leave broad-based conversations to others.

    In closing, while the United States no longer maintains mounted bands within
its military branches, there have been several general mounted detachments

---

46. Alan Merriam, *The Anthropology of Music* (Evanston, Ill: Northwestern University Press, 1964),
220–27.

activated and maintained primarily for historical, show, and ceremonial purposes within the U.S. Army in recent years, including the present-day Horse
Cavalry Detachment of the 1st Cavalry Division organized in 1972 and stationed
at Fort Hood, Texas. Perhaps a mounted musical unit will be organized and
activated at some point as well. In the meantime, descendants of some of those
bands that were disbanded at various points during World War II continue to
live on in other manifestations at the time of this writing. While untangling the
web of official activations, inactivations, assignments, reassignments, conver-
sions, redesignations, reliefs, and reorganizations of U.S. Cavalry regiments is
outside the purposes and parameters of the present study, it can be said with a
reasonable amount of certainty that the present-day 1st Cavalry Division band
can be traced to beginnings within the 1st, 5th, 7th, and 8th Cavalry Regiments, which appears to have happened over a number of years.[47]

<hr />

47. Jim Marks explains, "In 1943, the 7th Cav. Regimental Band was disbanded in Australia and the
1st Cav. Div. Band was formed bringing to a close a long and distinguished history." Jim Marks, "A Tribute
to the First Cavalry Division Band," in "Our Musical Heritage," *Saber* (November/December, 1993): 16.
Chandler explains, "The 7th Cavalry Band was established as a section in the Service Troop in 1921 and
as a separate component of the regiment under command of the Regimental Adjutant on June 22, 1927. It
was inactivated and the personnel and equipment utilized in the reorganized First Cavalry Division Band at
Luzon, Philippine Islands, on June 3, 1945." Chandler, *Of GarryOwen in Glory*, 412. Several sources appear
to be citing a 1953 memo from Erwin M. Greger, chief warrant officer of the band, who claims, "The 1st
Cavalry Division Band was organized from the battle-scared [*sic*] remnants of the three former Regimental
Bands: the 5th Cavalry Regimental Band, 7th Cavalry Regimental Band, and the 1st Cavalry Division Band,
one (1) Warrent [*sic*] Officer and twelve (12) Enlisted Men of the 1st Cavalry Division Artillery Band were
relieved from assignment thereto and reassigned to the 5th Cavalry Regimental Band on May 27, 1945.
On the same date, twelve (12) Enlisted Men of the 1st Cavalry Division Artillery Band were relieved from
assignment thereto and reassigned to the 7th Cavalry Regimental Band. Upon activation of the 1st Cavalry
Division Artillery Band, 5th Cavalry Regimental Band, and 7th Cavalry Regimental Band, were assigned
to the 1st Cavalry Division Band." Chief Warrant Officer Erwin M. Greger, bandleader, commander, Band
1st Cavalry Division, memo to Commanding General, 1st Cavalry Division, APO 201, 28 July 1953; memo
in possession of the author. As the 8th Cavalry was also assigned to the 1st Cavalry Division (13 September
1921), it would have a connection with the 1st Cavalry Division Band as well. Sawicki, *Cavalry Regiments*, 166.

APPENDIX

Veteran U.S. Cavalry Musicians

I AM PROFOUNDLY FORTUNATE TO HAVE UNDERTAKEN THE RESEARCH for this book when I did, and to have caught the stories of a handful of veteran U.S. Cavalry musicians. I am ever grateful that our life paths crossed and am humbled that, for whatever reason, I was the one chosen to chronicle these accounts.

GEORGE L. SHAFFER (1923–), tuba player with the 103rd Cavalry Band, Northumberland, Pennsylvania, 1940–41. Shaffer retired from the U.S. Army Band at Fort Meade, Maryland, in 1965. He then spent ten years as an engineer and another decade as a high school band and choir director in Maine, Pennsylvania, and New Hampshire.

DR. FRANCIS N. MAYER (1912–2007), clarinet player with the 106th Cavalry Band in Chicago, 1929–34. He went on to study conducting with Glenn Cliffe Bainum at Northwestern University and was the band director at Cretin High School in St. Paul while completing a PhD in music at the University of Minnesota in 1957. He retired in 1982 as the director of bands and chairman of the Department of Music at the University of St. Thomas in St. Paul, Minnesota.

GEORGE A. RAMSDEN (1915–2011), saxophone player with the 110th Cavalry Band in Boston, 1934–40. He retired in 1988 from a career spanning oil refining, cold storage, and restaurant hosting.

ELWOOD F. LANGDON (1913–2007), trumpet player with the 101st Cavalry Band in Brooklyn, New York, 1931–38. Langdon retired in 1977 from a career in research and development with Pratt and Whitney Aircraft.

Lt. Col. George D. Ish (1919–2003), trumpet player with the 106th Cavalry in Chicago, 1936–41. Ish served for twenty-five years with the U.S. Army military police corps, concluding his military career by serving as an assistant professor of military science at UCLA from 1957 to 1961 and as provost marshal with the 1st Cavalry Division in Korea from 1960 to 1961. He retired as an executive with the Oasis Oil Company of Libya Inc. in 1969 and as a private oil consultant in 1986.

Col. John S. Dittmer (1908–2004), trombone and euphonium player in the 101st Cavalry Band in Brooklyn, New York, 1936–40. He retired from the U.S. Army in 1968 at the Presidio in San Francisco after a thirty-year career as a U.S. Army cavalry officer (seeing combat in the Philippines, Japan, and Korea), after which he returned to a part-time career as a municipal band and orchestra conductor.

C. Arthur Fear (1910–2004), trombone player with the 113th Cavalry Band in Oskaloosa, Iowa, 1926–30. Fear served with the federalized 113th Cavalry Band, which was redesignated as the 66th Army Ground Forces Band in World War II, serving primarily in Holland and Belgium. Returning to civilian life, he made his living as a sign painter, decalcomania and silkscreen artist, and leather embosser in Chicago, retiring in 1987.

Roy F. Woodward (1915–2007), snare drum and trumpet player with the 124th Cavalry Band in Mineral Wells, Texas, 1932–38. He retired in 1976 as a full-time repair technician for the Texas National Guard. As a life member of Musicians Union Local 72, Fort Worth, Woodward played drums in his own band and in other dance bands.

Bill Rankin (1918–2012), clarinet player with the 116th Cavalry Band in Caldwell, Idaho, 1934–40. Rankin retired as a life insurance agent while continuing to work as a professional saxophone and clarinet player.

Dr. Hubert Henderson (1918–), trumpet player with the 3rd Cavalry Band, 1941–43, at Fort Myer, Virginia, and Fort Oglethorpe, Georgia, where he served as the enlisted bandleader. After serving two tours of duty with the U.S. Army Air Forces as a warrant officer bandleader and upon completing graduate work at the University of North Carolina, in 1954 he became the director of bands at Montana State University and in 1955 became director of bands at the University of Maryland. From 1965 to 1989, he served in various capacities at the University of Kentucky—as chairman of the department of music, professor of music history, and dean of the College of Fine Arts—retiring in 1989.

Bibliography

BOOKS, ARTICLES, AND OTHER PRINTED SOURCES

Adams, Kevin. *Class and Race in the Frontier Army: Military Live in the West, 1870–1890.* Norman: University of Oklahoma Press, 2009.

Adkins, William. "The Story of Pancho Villa at Columbus, New Mexico." Pt. 1. *Family Tree* 1, no. 1 (1969–70): 38–44.

———. "The Story of Pancho Villa at Columbus, New Mexico." Pt. 2. *Family Tree* 1, no. 2 (1969–70): 24, 49–55.

Ahrens, Christian. *Valved Brass: The History of an Invention.* Translated by Steven Plank. Bucina: Historical Brass Society Press, no. 7. Hillsdale, N.Y.: Pendragon Press, 2008.

Allen, James B. Addendum to "Seventh Cavalry Band," by James Brockenshire. *Army and Navy Journal* 68 (30 May 1931): 942.

Altenburg, Johann Ernst. *Versuch einer Anleitung zur heroisch-musikalischen Trompeter-und Pauker-Kunst (Essay on an Introduction to the Heroic and Musical Trumpeters' and Kettledrummers' Art).* Translated by Edward Tarr. 1795. Reprint, Nashville: Brass Press, 1974.

"Alumni News." *University of Chicago Magazine* 67, no. 3 (Spring 1975): 36.

Anderson, Col. Edward. "Ninth Cavalry—Camp Stotsenburg, Pampanga, P.I." Regimental Notes. *Cavalry Journal* 31, no. 127 (April 1922): 215–16.

"Army Day." *Army and Navy Journal* 75, no. 31 (2 April 1938): 667.

Arnold, Thomas St. John. *Adventures of a Country Girl and Army Wife.* Lincoln, Neb.: Writers Club Press, 2003.

Baines, Anthony. *Brass Instruments: Their History and Development.* New York: Dover, 1993.

Ballantine, James, ed. *Chronicle of the Hundredth Birthday of Robert Burns.* Edinburgh: A. Fullarton, 1859.

"A Bandmaster." Men of the Month. *Crisis, A Record of the Darker Races, Published Monthly by the National Association for the Advancement of Colored People* 11, no. 1 (November 1915): 13.

The Band of the Life Guards. Military brochure. London: The Band of the Life Guards, 2005.

Barclay and Co. *The Terrible Tragedy at Washington: The Assassination of President Lincoln.* Philadelphia: Barclay, 1865.

Barnett, Louise. *Touched by Fire: The Life, Death and Mythic Afterlife of George Armstrong Custer.* New York: Henry Holt, 1996.

Barrows, John Stuart. "The National Lancers." *New England Magazine, An Illustrated Monthly*, n.s., 34 (March 1906–August 1906): 401–16.

Bauer, Frederic. "Notes on the Use of Cavalry in the American Revolution." *Cavalry Journal* 47 (March–April 1938): 136–43.

B. B., Jr. "Ask the Journal." *Army and Navy Journal* 75, no. 36 (7 May 1938): 794.

Bell, William Gardner. *Quarters One: The United States Army Chief of Staff's Residence, Fort Myer, Virginia*. Washington, D.C.: Center of Military History, United States Army, 2011.

Berger, Kenneth, ed. *Band Encyclopedia*. Evansville, Ind.: Band Associates, 1960.

Bevan, Clifford. "The (P)Russian Trumpet." *Galpin Society Journal* 41 (October 1988): 112–14.

Bierley, Paul E. *The Works of John Philip Sousa*. Columbus, Ohio: Integrity Press, 1984.

Billington, Monroe Lee. *New Mexico's Buffalo Soldiers, 1866–1900*. Boulder: University Press of Colorado, 1991.

Bircher, William. *A Civil War Drummer Boy: The Diary of William Bircher, 1861–1865*. Edited by Shelley Swanson Sateren. Mankato, Minn.: Blue Earth Books, 2000.

———. *A Drummer-Boy's Diary: Comprising Four Years of Service with the Second Regiment Minnesota Veteran Volunteers, 1861 to 1865*. Edited by Newell L. Chester. 1889. Reprint, St. Cloud, Minn.: North Star Press, 1995.

Blom, Eric, ed. *Grove's Dictionary of Music and Musicians*. 5th ed. New York: St. Martin's Press, 1954.

Bowles, Edmund A. *The Timpani, A History in Pictures and Documents*. Pendragon Press, 2002.

Boyer, D. Royce. "The World War I Army Bandsman: A Diary Account by Philip James." *American Music* 14, no. 2 (Summer 1996): 185–204.

Bradley, James. *The Imperial Cruise: A Secret History of Empire and War*. New York: Little, Brown, 2009.

Bradley, Mel. *The Missouri Mule*. Columbia: University of Missouri Press, 1991.

Brixel, Eugen, Gunther Martin, and Gottfried Pils. *Das ist Österreiches Militärmusik*. Graz, Aus.: Kaleidoskop, 1982.

Brockenshire, James O. "Seventh Cavalry Band." *Army and Navy Journal* 68 (23 May 1931): 917.

Brown, Col. Robert A. "Fourteenth Cavalry—Fort Des Moines, Iowa." Regimental Notes. *Cavalry Journal* 31, no. 126 (January 1922), 107.

Buecker, Thomas R. "The Dismounting of the Fourth Cavalry at Fort Robinson 1942." *Rural Electric Nebraskan* 43 (February 1989).

Bukhari, Emir. *Napoleon's Dragoons and Lancers*. London: Osprey, 1976.

———. *Napoleon's Guard Cavalry*. London: Osprey, 1978.

———. *Napoleon's Hussars*. London: Osprey, 1978.

———. *Napoleon's Line Chasseurs*. London: Osprey, 1977.

Calhoun, James. *With Custer in '74: James Calhoun's Diary of the Black Hills Expedition*. Edited by Lawrence A. Frost. Provo, Utah: Brigham Young University Press, 1979.

Camus, Raoul. "The Military Band in the United States Army Prior to 1834." PhD diss., New York University, 1969.

————. *Military Music of the American Revolution*. Chapel Hill: University of North Carolina Press, 1976.

Carmichael, Orton H. *Lincoln's Gettysburg Address*. New York: Abingdon Press, 1917.

Carpenter, Nan Cooke. *Music in the Medieval and Renaissance Universities*. Norman: University of Oklahoma, 1958.

Carr, Daniel M., ed. *Portrait and Biographical Album of the State Officers and the Members of the Nebraska Legislature, Twenty-Eighth Session, 1903–1904, Containing a Directory of the Legislature and Official State Directory*. Fremont Neb.: Progress Publishing, 1903.

Carroll, John M. "The Seventh Cavalry's Band." *Little Big Horn Associates' Research Review* 9 (Spring 1975): 16–18.

Carter, William H. *The U.S. Cavalry Horse*. 1895. Reprint, Guildford, Conn.: Lyon's Press, 2003.

Catton, Bruce. *A Stillness at Appomattox*. Garden City, N.Y.: Doubleday, 1954.

"The Cavalry School, Fort Riley, Kansas." Cavalry School Notes. *Cavalry Journal* 31, no. 128 (July 1922): 328–29.

Celebration, at Danvers, Mass. June 16, 1852. Boston: Dutton and Wentworth, 1852.

Chalfant, William Y. *Cheyennes and Horse Soldiers: The 1857 Expedition and the Battle of Solomon's Fork*. Norman: University of Oklahoma Press, 1989.

Chamberlain, Samuel E. *My Confession*. New York: Harper and Brothers, 1956.

Chambers. Robert W. *Lorraine*. New York: Harper and Brothers, 1898.

————. *Special Messenger*. 1904. Reprint, New York: D. Appleton, 1909.

Chandler, Melbourne C. *Of GarryOwen in Glory: The History of the Seventh United States Cavalry Regiment*. Annandale, Va.: Turnpike Press, 1960.

Chang, E. Christina. "The Singing Program of World War I: The Crusade for a Singing Army." *Journal of Historical Research in Music Education* 23, no. 1 (October 2001): 19–45.

Chartrand, René. *A Scarlet Coat: Uniforms, Flags and Equipment of the British in the War of 1812*. Ottawa: Service Publications, 2011.

Clay, Steven E. *U.S. Army Order of Battle 1919–1941*. Vol. 2 of *The Arms: Cavalry, Field Artillery, and Coast Artillery, 1919–41*. Fort Leavenworth, Kans.: Combat Studies Institute Press, U.S. Army Combined Arms Center, 2010.

Coffman, Edward M. *The Old Army: A Portrait of the American Army in Peacetime, 1784–1898*. New York: Oxford University Press, 1986.

————. *The Regulars: The American Army, 1898–1941*. Cambridge, Mass.: Harvard University Press, 2004.

Columbian Exposition Dedication Ceremonies Memorial: A Graphic Description of the Ceremonies at Chicago, October 1892, the 400th Anniversary of the Discovery of America. Chicago: Metropolitan Art Engraving and Publishing, 1893.

Cunliffe, Marcus. *Soldiers and Civilians: The Martial Spirit in America*. Boston: Little, Brown, 1968.

Custer, Elizabeth B. *Following the Guidon*. New York: Harper Brothers, 1890.

Custer, George A. *My Life on the Plains*. Edited by Milo Milton Quaife. New York: Citadel Press, 1962.

————. Report No. 4, Mine Run, Virginia, 26 November 1863. In *Custer in the Civil War: His Unfinished Memoirs*. Compiled and edited by John M. Carroll. San Rafael, Calif.: Presidio Press, 1977.

Dall, Cameron M. "German Military Band Music during the Third Reich, 1933–1945." Master's thesis, Ball State University, 1990.

Degele, Ludwig. *Die Militärmusik, ihr Werden und Wesen, ihre kulturelle und nationale Bedeutung*. Wolfenbüttel, Ger.: Verlag für musikalische Kultur und Wissenschaft, 1937.

Delbrück, Hans. *The Dawn of Modern Warfare*. Vol. 4 of *History of the Art of War*. Translated by Walter J. Renfroe, Jr. Lincoln: University of Nebraska Press, 1990.

Digges, Leonard, and Thomas Digges. *An Arithmetical Warlike Treatise. . . .* London: Richard Field, 1590.

DiMarco, Louis A. *War Horse: A History of the Military Horse and Rider*. Yardley, Pa.: Westholme Publishing, 2008.

Dishman, Christopher D. *A Perfect Gibralter: The Battle for Monterrey, Mexico, 1846*. University of Oklahoma Press, 2010.

Dobak, William A., and Thomas D. Phillips. *The Black Regulars, 1866–1898*. Norman: University of Oklahoma Press, 2001.

Dodworth, Allen. *Brass Band School*. New York: H. B. Dodworth, 1853.

Doubler, Michael D. *Civilian in Peace, Soldier in War: The Army National Guard, 1636–2000*. Lawrence: University Press of Kansas, 2003.

Downey, Fairfax. *Fife, Drum and Bugle*. Fort Collins, Colo.: Old Army Press, 1971.

Drinker, Frederick E., and Jay Henry Mowbray. *Theodore Roosevelt: His Life and Work*. Washington, D.C.: National Publishing, 1919.

Dustin, Fred. *The Custer Tragedy: Events Leading up to and Following the Little Big Horn Campaign of 1876*. Ann Arbor, Mich.: Edwards Brothers, 1939.

Eberhardt, John S. *The Old Gray Mare*. New York: iUniverse, 2005.

Ellis, John. *Cavalry: The History of Mounted Warfare*. New York: G. P. Putnam's Sons, 1978.

E. L. N. "Some Interesting Incidents of Kossuth's Career." In "Louis Kossuth: The Hungarian Patriot in the United States." *Kate Field's Washington* 9, no. 14 (Washington, D.C., 4 April 1894): 214–15.

Elson, Louis C. *Elson's Pocket Music Dictionary*. Boston: Oliver Ditson, 1909.

Ewen, David. *All the Years of American Popular Music*. New York: Prentice Hall, 1977.

Farmer, Henry George. "The Great Kettledrums of the Artillery." In *Handel's Kettledrums*.

————. *Handel's Kettledrums and Other Papers on Military Music*. London: Hinrichsen, 1950.

————. *Memoirs of the Royal Artillery Band*. London: Boosey, 1904.

————. *Military Music*. New York: Chanticleer Press, 1950.

————. *The Rise and Development of Military Music*. London: W. Reeves, 1912.

————. "The Royal Artillery Mounted Band." In *Handel's Kettledrums*.

————. "Turkish Influence in Military Music." In *Handel's Kettledrums*.

Fieldhouse, Col. Walter. *Fall Maneuvers, West Point, Kentucky, 1903: Report of Colonel Walter Fieldhouse, Inspector General, Accredited Military Representative of the State of Illinois*. Springfield, Ill.: Phillips Brothers, 1904.

"The First Regiment of Cavalry, United States Army." *Cavalry Journal* 31, no. 127 (April 1922): 173–83.

Fleming, Col. R. J. "Sixth Cavalry—Headquarters and First Squadron, Camp McClellan, Alabama; Second Squadron, Fort Oglethorpe, Georgia." Regimental Notes. *Cavalry Journal* 31, no. 129 (October 1922): 439.

Follows, Arthur J. "Out Where the Zest Begins: The Story of the Denver Convention." *Rotarian: The Magazine of Service* (August 1926): 62.

Forsyth, Col. W. D. "Fifth Cavalry—Fort Clark, Texas." Regimental Notes. *Cavalry Journal* 31, no. 128 (July 1922): 332.

"Fort Des Moines." *Midwestern* 2, no. 9 (May 1908): 34–38.

Fortescue, John William. *A History of the British Army,* Vol. I. MacMillan and Co., London, 1899/1910.

Fosdick, Raymond B. *Chronicle of a Generation.* New York: Harper and Brothers, 1958.

Fox, Lilla. *Instruments of Processional Music.* London: Lutterworth Press, 1967.

Friederich, G. W. E. *The Brass Band Journal.* New York: Firth, Pond, 1853.

Fronsperger, Leonhard. *Baron of Mindelheim, Von kayserlichem Kriegsrechten Malefitz und Schuldhändlen.* Frankfurt-am-Main, 1564–65, fol. 130a.

Garofalo, Robert, and Mark Elrod. *A Pictorial History of Civil War Era Musical Instruments and Military Bands.* Charleston, W.Va.: Pictorial Histories Publishing, 1985.

Garvey, James J. "Rutherford B. Hayes: The Great Western Tour of 1880." Unpublished manuscript. Chicago: Loyola University, 1966.

Gay, James R. "The Wind Music of Felix Vinatieri, Dakota Territory Bandmaster." DA diss., University of Northern Colorado, 1982.

George, Charles, Herbert George, Jere George, and Osman George. *"Bully for the Band!" The Civil War Letters and Diary of Four Brothers in the 10th Vermont Infantry Band.* Edited by James A. Davis. Jefferson, N.C.: McFarland, 2012.

Gilbert, Gaylord S. "The Mounted Band of the 123rd Cavalry, Kentucky National Guard." *Cavalry Journal* 46, no. 5 (September–October 1937): 453.

Glass, Major E. L. N. *History of the 10th Cavalry.* Tucson, Ariz.: Acme Printing, 1921.

Gleason, Bruce P. "Cavalry and Court Trumpeters and Kettledrummers from the Renaissance to the Nineteenth Century." *Galpin Society Journal* 62 (2009): 31–54.

———. "Cavalry Trumpet and Kettledrum Practice from the Time of the Celts and Romans to the Renaissance." *Galpin Society Journal* 61 (2008): 231–39, 251.

———. "A Chronicle of the Pre–World War II Cavalry Bands of the U.S. National Guard—with Recollections of Those Who Rode." *Journal of the World Association for Symphonic Bands and Ensembles* 13 (2006), 17–30.

———. "A History of the Royal Artillery Mounted Band, 1878–1939." Master's thesis, University of Minnesota, Minneapolis, 1985.

———. "Military Music in the 106th Cavalry: The Mounted Band of the Chicago Black Horse Troop, 1929–1940." *Journal of the Illinois State Historical Society* 104, no. 4 (Winter 2011): 301–35.

————. "The Mounted Band and Field Musicians of the U.S. 7th Cavalry During the Time of the Plains Indian Wars." *Historic Brass Society Journal* 21 (2009): 69–92.

————. "The Mounted Bands of the North-West Mounted Police." *Band International: Journal of the International Military Music Society* 27, no. 3 (December 2005): 99–103, 120.

————. "Pipe Band of the 1st Canadian Mounted Rifles." *Military Collector and Historian: Journal of the Company of Military Historians* 56, no. 4 (Winter 2004): 279–82.

————. "U.S. Mounted Bands and Cavalry Field Musicians in the Union Army during the Civil War—Background, Duties, and Training," *Journal of Historical Research in Music Education* 27, no. 2 (April 2006), 107–108.

Goldman, Richard Franko. *The Concert Band*. New York: Rinehart, 1946.

————. *The Wind Band: Its Literature and Technique*. Boston: Allyn and Bacon, 1961.

Gordon, Col. James. "The Battle and Retreat from Corinth." *Publications of the Mississippi Historical Society* 4 (1901): 63–72.

Great Britain, Army. *The Sounds for Duty and Exercise for the Trumpet and Bugle Horns of His Majesty's Regiments and Corps of Cavalry*. London: Broderip and Wilkinson, 1798.

Greene, Jerome A. *Indian War Veterans: Memories of Army Life and Campaigns in the West, 1864–1898*. New York: Savas Beatie, 2006.

Grinnell, George Bird. *Two Great Scouts and Their Pawnee Battalion: The Experiences of Frank J. North and Luther H. North*. 1928. Reprint, Lincoln: University of Nebraska Press, 1973.

Hammer, Kenneth. *Biographies of the 7th Cavalry, June 25th 1876*. Fort Collins, Colo.: Old Army Press, 1972.

————. *Custer in '76*. Salt Lake City: Brigham Young University Press, 1976.

Harper, Col. Roy B. "Thirteenth Cavalry—Fort D. A. Russell, Wyoming." Regimental Notes. *Cavalry Journal* 31, no. 129 (October 1922): 442–43.

Hazen, Margaret Hindle, and Robert Hazen. *The Music Men: An Illustrated History of Brass Bands in America, 1800–1920*. Washington, D.C.: Smithsonian Institution Press, 1987.

Heitman, Francis B. *Historical Register and Dictionary of the United States Army, from its Organization, September 29, 1789, to March 2, 1903*. 2 vols. Washington, D.C.: Government Printing Office, 1903.

Helbig, Otto. *A History of Music in the U.S. Armed Forces during World War II*. Philadelphia: M. W. Lads, 1966.

Henderson, Hubert. "WW-II Bandsman and Bandleader." Unpublished memoirs.

Hendrickson, Kenneth E., Jr. *The Spanish-American War*. Westport, Conn.: Greenwood Press, 2003.

Henry, Frederick P., ed. *Founders' Week Memorial Volume*. Philadelphia: City of Philadelphia, 1909.

Herbert, Trevor, and Helen Barlow. *Music and the British Military in the Long Nineteenth Century*. New York: Oxford University Press, 2013.

Hinde, Robert. *The Discipline of the Light Horse*. London: Printed for W. Owen, 1778.

History of the Essex Troop, 1890–1925. Newark, N.J.: Essex Troop Armory, 1925.

The History of Fort Myer Virginia: 100th Anniversary Issue, Special Edition of the Fort Myer Post. Fort Myer, Va., June 1963.

A History of U.S. Army Bands, Subcourse Number MU0010. Edition D. Norfolk, Va.: U.S. Army Element, School of Music, 2005.

Honor to the Brave, An Account of the Funeral Obsequies of the Late Captain J. W. Zabriskie, of the 1st Illinois Regiment, Who Was Slain at the Battle of Buena Vista, on the 23d Day of February, 1847. New Brunswick, N.J.: Published by the Committee, 1847. Copy in possession of author.

Hooker, Forrestine C. *Child of the Fighting Tenth: On the Frontier with the Buffalo Soldiers.* Edited by Steve Wilson. New York: Oxford University Press, 2003.

Horsman, Reginald. *Race and Manifest Destiny: The Origins of American Racial Anglo-Saxonism.* Cambridge, Mass.: Harvard University Press, 1981.

Houlton, Honorable William H. "Narrative of the Eighth Regiment." In *Minnesota in the Civil and Indian Wars, 1861–1865.* St. Paul, Minn.: Board of Commissioners, Legislature of Minnesota, Electrotyped and Printed for the State by the Pioneer Press Company, 1890.

Howard, Helen Addison. "Germany's Captured Superhorses." *Western Horseman* 42 (May 1977): 50–52, 146–51.

Hoyt, Epaphras. *Practical Instructions for Military Officers . . . To Which Is Annexed, a New Military Dictionary. . . .* Greenfield, Mass.: John Denio, 1811.

Huey, William G. "Making Music: Brass Bands on the Northern Plains, 1860–1930." *North Dakota History* 54, no. 1 (1987): 3–13.

Hylton, Renne, and Robert K. Wright, Jr. *A Brief History of the Militia and National Guard.* Washington, D.C.: Departments of the Army and the Air Force, Historical Services Division, Office of Public Affairs, National Guard Bureau, August 1993.

Jackson, Kenneth T., Karen Markoe, and Arnold Markoe. *The Scribner Encyclopedia of American Lives.* New York: Scribner's, 1998.

Johnson, Robert and Clarence Buel, eds. *Battles and Leaders of the Civil War: Being for the Most Part Contributions by Union and Confederate Officers.* Vol. 4. 1887. Reprint, New York: Castle Books, Thomas Yoseloff, 1956.

Jones, Katharine M., ed. *Heroines of Dixie: Winter of Desperation.* St. Simons, Ga.: Mockingbird Books, 1988.

Jovovic, Spiridion. "Hoch zu Roß!" *Österreichische Blasmusik* 1 (January 1995): 5–8.

Juno, Irene. "Music Chat from Washington." *Jacobs' Band Monthly* (April 1926): 55–56.

Kalkbrenner, Th. A. *Die Koniglich Preussischen Armee-Märsche.* Leipzig, Ger.: Breitkopf and Härtel, 1896.

Kappey, J. A. *Military Music: A History of Wind-Instrumental Bands.* London: Boosey, 1894.

Kastner, Georges. *Manuel Général de Musique Militaire.* Paris: Typ. F. Didot frères, 1848.

Katcher, Philip. *Union Cavalryman, 1861–1865.* Oxford: Osprey, 1995.

Katz, Friedrich. *The Secret War in Mexico: Europe, the United States, and the Mexican Revolution.* Chicago: University of Chicago Press, 1981.

Kelley, Bruce, and Mark Snell, eds. *Bugle Resounding: Music and Musicians of the Civil War.* Columbia: University of Missouri Press, 2004.

Kenner, Charles L. *Buffalo Soldiers and Officers of the Ninth Cavalry, 1867–1898: Black and White Together*. Norman: University of Oklahoma Press, 2014.

Krause, Herbert, and Gary D. Olson. *Prelude to Glory: A Newspaper Accounting of Custer's 1874 Expedition to the Black Hills*. Sioux Falls, S.Dak.: Brevet Press, 1974.

Lambert, Major Joseph I. *One Hundred Years with the Second Cavalry*. 1939. Reprint, San Antonio, Tex.: Newton Publishing, 1999.

Lanard, Thomas South. *One Hundred Years with the State Fencibles . . . 1813–1913*. Philadelphia: Nields Company, 1913.

Lang, Theodore F., Major, 6th W.Va., Cavalry and Brevet Colonel. *Loyal West Virginia from 1861 to 1865*. Baltimore: Deutsch Publishing, 1895.

Leckie, William H. *The Buffalo Soldiers: A Narrative of the Negro Cavalry in the West*. Norman: University of Oklahoma Press, 1967.

Lefferts, Peter M. "U.S. Army Black Regimental Bands and the Appointments of Their First Black Bandmasters." *Black Music Research Journal* 33, no. 1 (2013): 151–75.

Linehan, John C. "The Fisherville Cornet Band." In *History of Penacook, New Hampshire*, compiled by David Arthur Brown, 247–53. Concord, N.H.: Rumford Press, 1902.

Livingston, Phil, and Ed Roberts. *War Horse: Mounting the Cavalry with America's Finest Horses*. Albany, Tex.: Bright Sky Press, 2003.

Lockwood, Dean Frank C., and Capt. Donald W. Page. *Tucson—The Old Pueblo*. Phoenix: Manufacturing Stationers, 1930.

Lord, Francis A., and Arthur Wise. *Bands and Drummer Boys of the Civil War*. New York: Thomas Yoseloff, 1966.

Maitland, J. A. Fuller, ed. *Grove's Dictionary of Music and Musicians*. New York: MacMillan, 1904.

Mallet, Manesson. *Les Travaux de Mars ou l'Art de la guerre*. Paris, 1691.

Markham, Francis. *Five Decades of Epistles of Warre*. London: Augustine Matthewes, 1622.

Markham, Gervase. "The Souldier's Accidence." In *The Souldiers Exercise, in Three Bookes*. The English Experience, No. 677. Amsterdam: Theatrum Orbis Terrarum, 1974; facsimile of Gervase Markham, "The Souldier's Accidence," in *The Souldiers Exercise: In Three Bookes* (London: Printed by John Norton, for John Bellamy, Hugh Perry, and Henry Overton, 1639).

Marks, Jim. "A Tribute to the First Cavalry Division Band." In "Our Musical Heritage." *Saber* (November/December 1993): 16–17.

Marquis, Albert Nelson. *Who's Who in Chicago and Vicinity: A Biographical Dictionary of Leading Living Men and Women of the City of Chicago and Environs Comprising Cook and Du Page Counties*. Chicago: A. N. Marquis, 1936.

Marshall, Brig. Gen. S. L. A. *Crimsoned Prairie: The Wars between the United States and the Plains Indians during the Winning of the West*. New York: Scribner's, 1972.

Marteinson, John K., Brereton Greenhous, Stephen J. Harris, Norman Hillmer, William Johnston, and William Rawlings. *We Stand on Guard: An Illustrated History of the Canadian Army*. Montreal: Ovale Productions, 1992.

Marteinson, John, with Scott Duncan. *The Governor General's Horse Guards, Second to None.* Toronto: Published for Governor General's Horse Guards Foundation by Robin Brass Studio, 2002.

Martin, J. F. *Martin's World's Fair Album-Atlas and Family Souvenir.* Chicago: C. Ropp, 1892.

Martz, Richard J. "Reversed Chirality in Horns, or Is Left Right? The Horn, on the Other Hand." *Historic Brass Society Journal* 15 (2003): 173–232.

Mayol, Jean Loup, ed. *150 ans de Musique à la Garde Républicaine, Mémoires d'un Orchestre.* Paris: Nouvelle Arche de Noé Editions, 1998.

McCormick, David. "A History of the United States Army Band to 1946." PhD diss., Northwestern University, 1971.

McLynn, Frank. *Villa and Zapata: A History of the Mexican Revolution.* New York: Carroll and Graf, 2001.

"Mechanized Force Becomes Cavalry." *Cavalry Journal* 40, no. 165 (May–June 1931): 5–6.

Meucci, Renato. "Roman Military Instruments and the Lituus." *Galpin Society Journal* 42 (August 1989): 90.

Merriam, Alan. *The Anthropology of Music.* Evanston, Ill.: Northwestern University Press, 1964.

Meyers, Augustus. *Ten Years in the Ranks, U.S. Army.* 1914. Reprint, London: Forgotten Books, 2012.

Michael, John. *Images of America, Fort Myer.* Charleston, S.C.: Arcadia Publishing, 2011.

Montagu, Jeremy. *Timpani and Percussion.* New Haven, Conn.: Yale University Press, 2002.

Morton, J. Sterling. *Illustrated History of Nebraska.* Vol. 2. Lincoln, Neb.: Jacob North, 1907.

"Necessity for Horsed Cavalry under Modern Conditions, Extract from Recent Hearings before the Subcommittee of the Committee on Appropriations, House of Representatives, on the War Department Appropriation Bill, 1938." Reprinted from the *Cavalry Journal*, May–June 1937, in *Cavalry Journal* 37, no. 3 (September 2012): 13, 16.

Nicolle, David. *Medieval Warfare Source Book: Christian Europe and Its Neighbors.* London: Brockhampton Press, 1998.

North, Luther. *Man of the Plains: Recollections of Luther North, 1856–1882.* Edited by Donald F. Danker. Lincoln: University of Nebraska Press, 1961.

Norton, Chauncey S. *"The Red Neck Ties," or, History of the Fifteenth New York Volunteer Cavalry.* Ithaca, N.Y.: Journal Book and Job Printing House, 1891.

Olson, Kenneth. *Music and Musket: Bands and Bandsmen of the American Civil War.* Westport, Conn.: Greenwood Press, 1981.

Oswandel, J. Jacob. *Notes of the Mexican War, 1846–47–48.* Philadelphia, 1885.

Otis, James. *The Boys of '98.* Boston: Dana Estes, 1898.

Paine, J. "Cavalry Bands." *Cavalry Journal, Horse and Mechanized* 20 (July 1930): 345.

Panoff, Peter. *Militärmusik in Geschichte und Gegenwart.* Berlin: Karl Siegismund Verlag, 1938.

Parker, A. A. *Recollections of General Lafayette on His Visit to the United States in 1824 and 1825; with the Most Remarkable Incidents of His Life, From His Birth to the Day of His Death.* Keene, N.H.: Sentinel Printing, 1879.

Piecuch, Jim, ed. *Cavalry of the American Revolution*. Yardley, Pa.: Westholme Publishing, 2012.

Piehler, G. Kurt, ed. *Encyclopedia of Military Science*. Newbury Park, Calif.: Sage Publications, 2013.

Pierce, Edwin H. "What Instrument Shall I Choose?" *Etude* (March 1920): 163–64.

Porter, Horace. *Campaigning with Grant*. Edited by Wayne C. Temple. 1897. Reprint, Bloomington: Indiana University Press, 1961.

Proceedings at the Reception and Dinner in Honor of George Peabody, Esq., of London, by the Citizens of the Old Town of Danvers, October 9, 1856. Boston: Henry W. Dutton, 1856.

Prucha, Francis Paul. *The Sword of the Republic: The United States Army on the Frontier, 1783–1846*. Lincoln: University of Nebraska Press, 1969.

"Public Appreciation for the Achievements of Chief Musician Wade H. Hammond." *Metronome* (1914): 55

Quint, Alonzo H. *The Record of the Second Massachusetts Infantry, 1861–65*. Boston: J. P. Walker, 1867.

Railsback, Thomas C., and John P. Langellier. *The Drums Would Roll: A Pictorial History of U.S. Army Bands on the American Frontier, 1866–1900*. Poole, UK: Arms and Armour Press, 1987.

"Ramsey, Edwin Price, May 9, 1917–March 7, 2013." *Crossed Sabers: A Newsletter of the U.S. Cavalry Association* 13, no. 1 (Summer 2013): 3.

"Reception for Brigade-General Corcoran hosted by Mayor Opdyke and the citizens of New York at Castle Garden." From the series "The Soldier in Our Civil War." *Frank Leslie's Illustrated Newspaper* (6 September 1862): 374–75.

Red Guidon "Soixante Quinze," Being a Complete Illustrated History of B Battery 134th Field Arillery from 1915 to 1919. Akron, Ohio: Red Guidon Association, 1920.

Rehrig, William H. *The Heritage Encyclopedia of Band Music, Composers and Their Music*. Edited by Paul E. Bierley. Vol. 1. Westerville, Ohio: Integrity Press, 1991.

Reschke, Johannes. "Studie zur Geschichte der brandenburgisch-preussischen Herremusik." PhD diss., Friedrich-Wilhelms Universität, Berlin, 1936.

Riben, Hans. "The Musical Instruments in the Swedish State Trophy Collection." In *In Hoc Signo Vinces: A Presentation of the Swedish State Trophy Collection*. Edited by Fred Sandstedt, Lena Engquist Sandstedt, Martin Skoog, and Karin Tetteris. Stockholm: National Swedish Museums of Military History, 2006.

Rivers, Col. William C. "Third Cavalry—Fort Myer, Virginia." Regimental Notes. *Cavalry Journal* 31, no. 126 (January 1922): 101.

Rodenbough, Theophilus F. *From Everglade to Cañon with the Second Dragoons (Second United States Cavalry), An Authentic Account of Service in Florida, Mexico, Virginia, and the Indian Country, Including the Personal Recollections of Prominent Officers, with an Appendix Containing Orders, Reports and Correspondence, Military Records, Etc., etc., etc. 1836–1875*. New York: D. Van Nostrand, 1875.

Sachs, Curt. *The History of Musical Instruments*. New York: Norton, 1940.

Sadie, Stanley, ed. *The New Grove Dictionary of Music and Musicians.* London: MacMillan, 2001.

Sargent, George. "Diary of a Bugler with Company C of the 1st Rhode Island Cavalry and Musician in the Regimental Band from His Enlistment in November 1861 to the Final Confederate Surrender in April 1865." Unpublished manuscript, 2 December 1861. Huntington Library, Art Collections, and Botanical Gardens, San Marino, Calif.

Sawicki, James A. *Cavalry Regiments of the U.S. Army.* Dumfries, Va.: Wyvern Publications, 1985.

Seals, Bob. "In Defense of Honor: General Douglas MacArthur and the Horse Cavalry of 1934." *Cavalry Journal* 32, no. 1 (March 2008): 22–26.

Shiverick, Lt. Col. Nathan C. "The Twelfth Cavalry on the Road." *Cavalry Journal* 31, no. 126 (January 1922): 62–63.

Skelton, William B. *An American Profession of Arms: The Army Officer Corps, 1784—1861.* Lawrence: University Press of Kansas, 1992.

Sklenar, Larry. *To Hell with Honor: Custer and the Little Bighorn.* Norman: University of Oklahoma Press, 2000.

Smart, Ian. "Music on Horseback." Unpublished manuscript, 2000.

Smithers, Don L. "The Hapsburg Imperial Trompeter and Heerpaucker Privileges of 1653." *Galpin Society Journal* 24, (July 1971): 84–95.

———. *The Music and History of the Baroque Trumpet before 1721.* Carbondale: Southern Illinois University Press, 1988.

Smithers, W. D. "The U.S. Cavalry." *Western Horseman* 24, no. 11 (November 1960): 24. Reprinted in *Cavalry Journal* 36, no. 2 (June 2011): 16.

Staff of Fort Myer. *The History of Fort Myer Virginia.* Fort Myer, Va., n.d.

Steffen, Randy. *The Revolution, the War of 1812, the Early Frontier, 1776–1850.* Vol. 1 of *The Horse Soldier, 1776–1943: The United States Cavalryman: His Uniforms, Arms, Accoutrements, and Equipment.* Norman: University of Oklahoma Press, 1977.

Stephan, Wilhelm. *Der Grosser Zapfenstreich.* Bonn, Ger.: Stephan, n.d.

———. "German Military Music: An Outline of its Development." *Journal of Band Research* 9, no. 2 (Spring 1973): 10–21.

Stubbs, Mary Lee, and Stanley Russell Connor. *Armor-Cavalry.* Pt. 1, *Regular Army and Army Reserve.* Washington, D.C.: Office of the Chief of Military History, U.S. Army, 1969.

Sullivan, Jill M. *Bands of Sisters: U.S. Women's Military Bands during World War II.* Lanham, Md.: Scarecrow Press, 2011.

Tarr, Edward H. "Buhl, Joseph David," *The New Grove Dictionary of Music and Musicians,* ed. Stanley Sadie. London: MacMillan, 2001.

———. *East Meets West: The Russian Trumpet Tradition from the Time of Peter the Great to the October Revolution.* Bucina: Historical Brass Society Press, no. 4. Hillsdale, N.Y.: Pendragon Press, 2003.

———. "Further Mandate against the Unauthorized Playing of Trumpets (Dresden: 1736): Introduction and Translation." *Historic Brass Society Journal* 13 (2001): 67–89.

————. *The Trumpet.* London: Batsford, 1988.

Taylor, Frank H. *Philadelphia in the Civil War, 1861–1865: Illustrated from Contemporary Prints and Photographs and from Drawings by the Author.* Philadelphia: The City [of Philadelphia], 1913.

Third Cavalry Museum. *Blood and Steel! The History, Customs, and Traditions of the 3d Armored Cavalry Regiment.* Fort Hood, Tex.: Third Cavalry Museum, 2010–11.

Thompson, Erwin N. *Defender of the Gate: The Presidio of San Francisco, A History from 1846 to 1995.* San Francisco: Golden Gate National Recreation Area, National Park Service, 1995.

Titcomb, Caldwell. "Baroque Court and Military Trumpets and Kettledrums: Technique and Music." *Galpin Society Journal* 9 (June 1956): 58–59.

————. "Carrousel Music at the Court of Louis XIV." In *Essays on Music in Honor of Archibald Thompson Davison by His Associates.* Cambridge, Mass.: Department of Music, Harvard University, 1957.

————. "The Kettledrums in Western Europe: Their History Outside the Orchestra." PhD diss., Harvard University, 1952.

Todd, Frank Morton. *The Story of the Exposition; Being the Official History of the International Celebration Held at San Francisco in 1915 to Commemorate the Discovery of the Pacific Ocean and the Construction of the Panama Canal.* Vol. 3. New York: G. P. Putnam's Sons, 1921.

Toeche-Mittler, Joachim. *Armeemärsche.* Neckargemünd, Ger.: Kurt Vowinckel Verlag, 1966.

————. *Armeemärsch.* Vol. 2, *Sammlung und Dokumentation.* Neckargemünd, Ger.: Kurt Vowinckel Verlag, 1971.

————. *Armeemärsche.* Vol. 3, *Die Geschichte unserer Marschmusik.* Neckargemünd, Ger.: Kurt Vowinckel Verlag, 1975.

Tourte, Robert. *Méthode pour timbales de cavalerie.* Paris: Editions Salabert, 1943.

Turner, Gordon, and Alwyn Turner. *Cavalry and Corps.* Vol. 1 of *The History of British Military Bands.* Staplehurst, UK: Spellmount, 1994.

Turner, James. *Pallas Armata: Military Essays of the Ancient Grecian, Roman, and Modern Art of War. Written in the Years 1670 and 1671.* London: Printed by M. W. for Richard Chiswell, 1683.

Tylden, G. *The Armed Forces of South Africa.* Frank Connock Publication, no. 2. Johannesburg: City of Johannesburg Africana Museum, 1954.

Umhey, Alfred. *Napoleon's Last Grande Armée.* Berkeley, Calif.: Military History Press, 2005.

Urwin, Gregory J. W. *The United States Cavalry: An Illustrated History.* Poole, UK: Blandford Press, 1983.

Utley, Robert. *Custer Battlefield, National Monument, Montana.* Historical Handbook Series 1. Washington, D.C.: National Park Service, 1969.

————, ed. *Life in Custer's Cavalry: Diaries and Letters of Albert and Jennie Barnitz, 1867–1868.* New Haven, Conn.: Yale University Press, 1977.

Vernon, Philip V. ed. *Royal New South Wales Lancers, 1885 to 1985.* Sydney: Royal New South Wales Lancers Centenary Committee, 1986.

Wallace, John, and Alexander McGrattan. *The Trumpet*. New Haven, Conn.: Yale University Press, 2011.

Wathier, R. *Les Timbaliers de la Grande Armée*. Paris: Editions de la Sabretache, 1951.

W. C. B. "Are Army Bands Necessary?" Military Notes. *Journal of the United States Cavalry Association* 25, no. 104 (October 1914): 340–43.

White, William Carter. *A History of Military Music in America*. New York: Exposition Press, 1944.

Whiting, Chester E. *The Baton and the Pendulum*. Clearfield, Pa.: Kurtz Bros., 1963.

———. *The Mounted Cavalry Band—A Cavalryman's Soliloquy*. N.p., n.d.

Whitman, Walt. *Complete Poetry and Collected Prose*. Edited by Justin Kaplan. New York: Library of America, 1982.

Whitwell, David. *The Baroque Wind Band and Wind Ensemble*. The History and Literature of the Wind Band and Wind Ensemble, vol. 3. Northridge, Calif.: Winds, 1983.

———. *The Nineteenth Century Wind Band and Wind Ensemble in Western Europe*. The History and Literature of the Wind Band and Wind Ensemble, vol. 5. Northridge, Calif.: Winds, 1984.

Windolph, Charles. *I Fought with Custer: The Story of Sergeant Windolph, Last Survivor of the Battle of the Little Big Horn as told to Frazier and Robert Hunt*. Edited by Frazier Hunt and Robert Hunt. New York: Scribner's, 1947.

Winn, Col. John S. "Second Cavalry—Fort Riley, Kansas." Regimental Notes. *Cavalry Journal* 31, no. 128 (July 1922): 330.

Wise, Jennings Cropper. *The Long Arm of Lee, or the History of the Artillery of the Army of Northern Virginia, with a Brief Account of the Confederate Bureau of Ordnance*. Vol. 2. Lynchburg, Va.: J. P. Bell, 1915.

Wise, John S. *The End of an Era*. Boston: Houghton, Mifflin, 1899.

Withers, Kristine. "American Mounted Cavalry Operations in World War II." *Cavalry Journal* 32, no. 2 (June 2008): 3–7.

Womack, John. *Zapata and the Mexican Revolution*. New York: Vintage Press, 1970.

Wooster, Robert. *The American Military Frontiers: The United States Army in the West, 1783–1900*. Albuquerque: University of New Mexico Press, 2009.

Young, Otis E. "The United States Mounted Ranger Battalion, 1832–1833." *Mississippi Valley Historical Review* 41, no. 3 (December 1954): 453–70.

Zedler, Johann Heinrich. *Grosses vollständiges Universal-Lexicon*. Halle, Ger., 1732–54.

LAWS, PROCEEDINGS, REGULATIONS, AND OFFICIAL DOCUMENTS

Commonwealth of Massachusetts. *Acts and Resolves Passed by the General Court of Massachusetts, in the Year 1876. . . .* Chap. 205. Boston: Wright and Potter, 1876.

Commonwealth of Massachusetts, Adjutant-General's Office. *Annual Report of the Adjutant-General of the Commonwealth of Massachusetts for the Year Ending December 31, 1878*. Boston: Rand, Avery, 1879.

————. *Annual Report of the Adjutant General of the Commonwealth of Massachusetts for the Year Ending December 31, 1883*. Special Orders No. 70. Boston: Wright and Potter, 1884.

Delaware General Assembly. *Laws of the State of Delaware; From the Second Day of January, One Thousand Eight Hundred and Twenty-Seven, to the Sixteenth Day of February, One Thousand Eight Hundred and Twenty-Nine*. Vol. 7. Dover, Del.: Published by Authority, 1829.

Dominion of Canada. *Sessional Papers*. Vol. 9, *Fourth Session of the Sixth Parliament of the Dominion of Canada, Session 1890*. Vol. 23. Ottawa: Brown Chamberlin, 1890.

Heitman, Francis B. *Historical Register and Dictionary of the United States Army, from Its Organization, September 29, 1789, to March 2, 1903*. Vol. 2. Washington, D.C.: Government Printing Office, 1903.

Library of Congress, Copyright Office. *Catalog of Copyright Entries*. Pt. 3, *Musical Compositions*, n.s., 29 no. 1. Washington, D.C.: Government Printing Office, 1935.

Mossman, Billy C., and M. Warner Stark. *The Last Salute: Civil and Military Funerals, 1921–1969*. Washington, D.C.: Department of the Army, U.S. Government Printing Office, 1974.

National Park Service, U.S. Department of the Interior. "Jefferson National Expansion Memorial." *Museum Gazette* (February 1996): 1.

New York State, Adjutant-General. *Annual Report of the Adjutant-General of the State of New York for the Year 1907*. Vol. 1. Albany, N.Y.: J. B. Lyon Company, 1908.

New York State Senate. Appendix I, "Headquarters Squadron A, National Guard, N.Y., Madison Ave. and 94th St., New York, March 10, 1905." In *Documents of the Senate of the State of New York, One Hundred and Twenty Ninth Session, 1906*. Vol. 4, nos. 5–8, 439–40. Albany: Brandow Printing, 1906.

Price, William R., Major, Eighth U.S. Cavalry, Brevet Colonel, U.S. Army. H.R. Rep. No. 74, 42nd Cong., 3rd Sess., serial 1576, 135.

Rotary International. *Proceedings, Seventeenth Annual Convention of Rotary International*. Denver, Colo., June 14–18, 1926.

"R.A. Mounted Band." Unpublished paper. Royal Artillery Band Archives, Royal Artillery Band Building, Royal Artillery Barracks, n.d., box 14. Woolwich, UK.

U.S. Army. Records of the Adjutant General's Office, 1780s–1917. NARA, RG 94. College Park, Md.

————. *Register of Enlistments in the U.S. Army, 1798–1914*. NARA, Microfilm Publication M233, 81 rolls.

————. *Regulations for the Army of the United States, 1895, with Appendix Separately Indexed, Showing Changes to January 1, 1901*. General Orders, No. 92, II, 1201. Washington, D.C.: Government Printing Office, 1901.

————. *Regulations for the Army of the United States, 1901, with Appendix Separately Indexed, Showing Changes to June 30, 1902*. Paras. 1326 and 1327 Washington, D.C.: Government Printing Office, 1902.

————. *Regulations for the United States Army, 1895*. Washington, D.C.: Government Printing Office, 1895.

———. *Regulations for the United States Army, 1895.* Washington, D.C.: Government Printing Office, 1899.

———. Return of Casualties in 13th Cavalry in Action at Columbus, N.Mex., March 9, 1916, Col. H. J. Slocum, Commanding, Columbus, N.Mex. *Returns from Regular Army Cavalry Regiments, 1833–1916.* NARA, RG 391, Microfilm Publication M744, 16 rolls.

———. Return of the 1st Regiment of Cavalry, Army of the United States, for the month of January 1867, Lt. Col. W[ashington] L[afayette] Elliott, Commanding, Fort Vancouver, Wash. Territory. *Returns from Regular Army Cavalry Regiments, 1833–1916.* NARA, RG 391, Microfilm Publication M744, 16 rolls.

———. Return of the 1st Regiment of Cavalry, Army of the United States, for the month of January 1887, Col. N[athan] A[ugustus] M[onroe] Dudley, Commanding, Fort Custer, Mont. *Returns from Regular Army Cavalry Regiments, 1833–1916.* NARA, RG 391, Microfilm Publication M744, 16 rolls.

———. Return of the 1st Regiment of Cavalry, Army of the United States, for the month of January 1897, Col. Abraham K. Arnold, Commanding, Fort Riley, Kans. *Returns from Regular Army Cavalry Regiments, 1833–1916.* NARA, RG 391, Microfilm Publication M744, 16 rolls.

———. Return of the 1st Regiment of Cavalry, Army of the United States, for the month of July 1905, Major J[oseph] A[lfred] Gaston, Commanding, Fort Clark, Tex. *Returns from Regular Army Cavalry Regiments, 1833–1916.* NARA, RG 391, Microfilm Publication M744, 16 rolls.

———. Return of the 1st Regiment of Cavalry, December 1916, Col. Frederick F. Foltz, Commanding, Douglas, Ariz. *Returns from Regular Army Cavalry Regiments, 1833–1916.* NARA, RG 391, Microfilm Publication M744, 16 rolls.

———. Return of the 2nd Regiment of Cavalry, Army of the United States, for the month of January 1867, Major G[eorge] W. Howland, Commanding, Fort McPherson, Neb. *Returns from Regular Army Cavalry Regiments, 1833–1916.* NARA, RG 391, Microfilm Publication M744, 16 rolls.

———. Return of the 2nd Regiment of Cavalry, Army of the United States, for the month of January 1887, Col. N[elson] B[owman] Sweitzer, Commanding, Fort Walla Walla, Wash. *Returns from Regular Army Cavalry Regiments, 1833–1916.* NARA, RG 391, Microfilm Publication M744, 16 rolls.

———. Return of the 2nd Regiment of Cavalry, Army of the United States, for the month of April 1897, Col. George G. Hunt, Commanding, Fort Wingate, N.Mex. *Returns from Regular Army Cavalry Regiments, 1833–1916.* NARA, RG 391, Microfilm Publication M744, 16 rolls.

———. Return of the 2nd Regiment of Cavalry, Army of the United States, for the month of July 1905, Major Franklin A. Johnson, Commanding, Camp Stotsenburg, Pampanga, Philippine Islands. *Returns from Regular Army Cavalry Regiments, 1833–1916.* NARA, RG 391, Microfilm Publication M744, 16 rolls.

————. Return of the 3rd Regiment of Cavalry, Army of the United States, for the month of January 1867, Major W. B. Lane, Commanding, Fort Marcy, N.Mex. *Returns from Regular Army Cavalry Regiments, 1833–1916*. NARA, RG 391, Microfilm Publication M744, 16 rolls.

————. Return of the 3rd Regiment of Cavalry, Army of the United States, for the month of January 1887, Col. Albert G[allatin] Brackett, Commanding, Fort Davis, Tex. *Returns from Regular Army Cavalry Regiments, 1833–1916*. NARA, RG 391, Microfilm Publication M744, 16 rolls.

————. Return of the 3rd Regiment of Cavalry, Army of the United States, for the month of April 1897, Col. Anson Mills, Commanding, Jefferson Barracks, Mo. *Returns from Regular Army Cavalry Regiments, 1833–1916*. NARA, RG 391, Microfilm Publication M744, 16 rolls.

————. Return of the 3rd Regiment of Cavalry, Army of the United States, for the month of July 1905, Col. Joseph A. Dorst, Commanding, Camp Stotsenburg, Pampanga, Philippine Islands. *Returns from Regular Army Cavalry Regiments, 1833–1916*. NARA, RG 391, Microfilm Publication M744, 16 rolls.

————. Return of the 3rd Regiment of Cavalry, December 1916, Col. Augustus P. Blocksom, Commanding, Mercedes, Tex. *Returns from Regular Army Cavalry Regiments, 1833–1916*. NARA dministration, RG 391, Microfilm Publication M744, 16 rolls.

————. Return of the 4th Regiment of Cavalry, Army of the United States, for the month of January 1867, Major John P. Hatch, Commanding, Fort Mason, Tex. *Returns from Regular Army Cavalry Regiments, 1833–1916*. NARA, RG 391, Microfilm Publication M744, 16 rolls.

————. Return of the 4th Regiment of Cavalry, Army of the United States, for the month of January 1887, Col. William B. Royall, Commanding, Fort Huachuca, Ariz. *Returns from Regular Army Cavalry Regiments, 1833–1916*. NARA, RG 391, Microfilm Publication M744, 16 rolls.

————. Return of the 4th Regiment of Cavalry, Army of the United States, for the month of April 1897, Col. Charles E. Compton, Commanding, Fort Walla Walla, Wash. *Returns from Regular Army Cavalry Regiments, 1833–1916*. NARA, RG 391, Microfilm Publication M744, 16 rolls.

————. Return of the 4th Regiment of Cavalry, Army of the United States, for the month of July 1905, Col. Edgar Z. Steever, Commanding, Presidio of San Francisco, Calif. *Returns from Regular Army Cavalry Regiments, 1833–1916*. NARA, RG 391, Microfilm Publication M744, 16 rolls.

————. Return of the 4th Regiment of Cavalry, December 1916, Col. John F. Guilfoyle, Commanding, Schofield Barracks, Hawaii. *Returns from Regular Army Cavalry Regiments, 1833–1916*. NARA, RG 391, Microfilm Publication M744, 16 rolls.

————. Return of the 5th Regiment of Cavalry, Army of the United States, for the month of January 1867, Col. W[illiam] H[emsley] Emory, Commanding, Sedgwick Barracks, Washington, D.C. *Returns from Regular Army Cavalry Regiments, 1833–1916*. NARA, RG 391, Microfilm Publication M744, 16 rolls.

————. Return of the 5th Regiment of Cavalry, Army of the United States, for the month of January 1887, Col. Wesley Merritt, Commanding, Fort Riley, Kans. *Returns from Regular Army Cavalry Regiments, 1833–1916.* NARA, RG 391, Microfilm Publication M744, 16 rolls.

————. Return of the 5th Regiment of Cavalry, Army of the United States, for the month of April 1897, Col. James F. Wade, Commanding, Fort Sam Houston, Tex. *Returns from Regular Army Cavalry Regiments, 1833–1916.* NARA, RG 391, Microfilm Publication M744, 16 rolls.

————. Return of the 5th Regiment of Cavalry, Army of the United States, for the month of July 1905, Col. Clarence A. Stednian, Commanding, Fort Huachuca, Ariz. Territory. *Returns from Regular Army Cavalry Regiments, 1833–1916.* NARA, RG 391, Microfilm Publication M744, 16 rolls.

————. Return of the 5th Regiment of Cavalry, March 1916, Col. Wilber E. Wilder, Commanding, Lake Itascate, Mex. *Returns from Regular Army Cavalry Regiments, 1833–1916.* NARA, RG 391, Microfilm Publication M744, 16 rolls.

————. Return of the 5th Regiment of Cavalry, December 1916, Col. D. L. Tate, Commanding, Lake Itascate, Mex. *Returns from Regular Army Cavalry Regiments, 1833–1916.* NARA, RG 391, Microfilm Publication M744, 16 rolls.

————. Return of the 6th Regiment of Cavalry, Army of the United States, for the month of January 1867, Col. James Oakes, Commanding, Austin, Tex. *Returns from Regular Army Cavalry Regiments, 1833–1916.* NARA, RG 391, Microfilm Publication M744, 16 rolls.

————. Return of the 6th Regiment of Cavalry, Army of the United States, for the month of January 1887, Col. Eugene A. Carr, Commanding, Fort Bayard, N.Mex. *Returns from Regular Army Cavalry Regiments, 1833–1916.* NARA, RG 391, Microfilm Publication M744, 16 rolls.

————. Return of the 6th Regiment of Cavalry, Army of the United States, for the month of April 1897, Col. Samuel S. Sumner, Commanding, Fort Myer, Va. *Returns from Regular Army Cavalry Regiments, 1833–1916.* NARA, RG 391, Microfilm Publication M744, 16 rolls.

————. Return of the 6th Regiment of Cavalry, Army of the United States, for the month of July 1905, Col. William Staunton, Commanding, Fort Meade, S.Dak. *Returns from Regular Army Cavalry Regiments, 1833–1916.* NARA, RG 391, Microfilm Publication M744, 16 rolls.

————. Return of the 6th Regiment of Cavalry, December 1916, Col. J. A. Gaston, Commanding, Marfa, Tex. *Returns from Regular Army Cavalry Regiments, 1833–1916.* NARA, RG 391, Microfilm Publication M744, 16 rolls.

————. Return of the 7th Regiment of Cavalry, Army of the United States, for the month of January 1867, Col. A[ndrew] J. Smith, Commanding, Fort Riley, Kans. *Returns from Regular Army Cavalry Regiments, 1833–1916.* NARA, RG 391, Microfilm Publication M744, 16 rolls.

————. Return of the 7th Regiment of Cavalry, Army of the United States, for the month of January 1887, Col. James W. Forsyth, Commanding, Fort Meade, Dakota Territory. *Returns from Regular Army Cavalry Regiments, 1833–1916.* NARA, RG 391, Microfilm Publication M744, 16 rolls.

————. Return of the 7th Regiment of Cavalry, Army of the United States, for the month of April 1897, Col. E[dwin] V[ose] Sumner, Fort Grant, Ariz. Territory. *Returns from Regular Army Cavalry Regiments, 1833–1916.* NARA, RG 391, Microfilm Publication M744, 16 rolls.

————. Return of the 7th Regiment of Cavalry, Army of the United States for the month of January 1899, Col. Edwin V. Sumner, Commanding, Vedado, Havana, Cuba. *Returns from Regular Army Cavalry Regiments, 1833–1916.* NARA, RG 391, Microfilm Publication M744, 16 rolls.

————. Return of the 7th Regiment of Cavalry, Army of the United States, for the month of March 1905, Col. Charles Morton, Commanding, Fort Myer, Va. *Returns from Regular Army Cavalry Regiments, 1833–1916.* NARA, RG 391, Microfilm Publication M744, 16 rolls.

————. Return of the 7th Regiment of Cavalry, Army of the United States, for the month of July 1905, Col. Charles Morton, Commanding, Manila, Philippine Islands. *Returns from Regular Army Cavalry Regiments, 1833–1916.* NARA, RG 391, Microfilm Publication M744, 16 rolls.

————. Return of the 7th Regiment of Cavalry, December 1916, Col. Selah R[eeve] H[obbie] Tompkins, Commanding, Colonia Dublan, Mex. *Returns from Regular Army Cavalry Regiments, 1833–1916.* NARA, RG 391, Microfilm Publication M744, 16 rolls.

————. Return of the 8th Regiment of Cavalry, Army of the United States, for the month of January 1867, Col. J[ohn] I[rvin] Gregg, Commanding, Benicia Barracks, Calif. *Returns from Regular Army Cavalry Regiments, 1833–1916.* NARA, RG 391, Microfilm Publication M744, 16 rolls.

————. Return of the 8th Regiment of Cavalry, Army of the United States, for the month of January 1887, Elmer Otis, Commanding, Post of San Antonio, Tex. *Returns from Regular Army Cavalry Regiments, 1833–1916.* NARA, RG 391, Microfilm Publication M744, 16 rolls.

————. Return of the 8th Regiment of Cavalry, Army of the United States, for the month of April 1897, Col. Caleb H. Carlton, Commanding, Fort Meade, S. Dak. *Returns from Regular Army Cavalry Regiments, 1833–1916.* NARA, RG 391, Microfilm Publication M744, 16 rolls.

————. Return of the 8th Regiment of Cavalry, Army of the United States, for the month of July 1905, Col. George S. Anderson, Commanding, Fort William McKinley, Rizal, Philippine Islands. *Returns from Regular Army Cavalry Regiments, 1833–1916.* NARA, RG 391, Microfilm Publication M744, 16 rolls.

————. Return of the 8th Regiment of Cavalry, December 1916, Col. John W. Heard, Commanding, Fort Bliss, Tex. *Returns from Regular Army Cavalry Regiments, 1833–1916.* NARA, RG 391, Microfilm Publication M744, 16 rolls.

————. Return of the 9th Regiment of Cavalry, Army of the United States, for the month of January 1867, Major J[ames] F. Wade, New Orleans, La. *Returns from Regular Army Cavalry Regiments, 1833–1916*. NARA, RG 391, Microfilm Publication M744, 16 rolls.

————. Return of the 9th Regiment of Cavalry, Army of the United States, for the month of January 1887, Col. Edward Hatch, Commanding, Fort McKinney, Wyo. *Returns from Regular Army Cavalry Regiments, 1833–1916*. NARA, RG 391, Microfilm Publication M744, 16 rolls.

————. Return of the 9th Regiment of Cavalry, Army of the United States, for the month of April 1897, Col. David Perry, Commanding, Fort Robinson, Neb. *Returns from Regular Army Cavalry Regiments, 1833–1916*. NARA, RG 391, Microfilm Publication M744, 16 rolls.

————. Return of the 9th Regiment of Cavalry, Army of the United States, for the month of July 1905, Col. Edward S. Godfrey, Commanding, Fort Riley, Kans. *Returns from Regular Army Cavalry Regiments, 1833–1916*. NARA, RG 391, Microfilm Publication M744, 16 rolls.

————. Return of the 9th Regiment of Cavalry, Army of the United States, for the month of March 1911, Col. George S. Anderson, Commanding, Maneuver Division, San Antonio, Tex. *Returns from Regular Army Cavalry Regiments, 1833–1916*. NARA, RG 391, Microfilm Publication M744, 16 rolls.

————. Return of the 9th Regiment of Cavalry, December 1916, Col. Thomas B. Dugan, Commanding, Camp Stotsenburg, Pampanga, Philippine Islands. *Returns from Regular Army Cavalry Regiments, 1833–1916*. NARA, RG 391, Microfilm Publication M744, 16 rolls.

————. Return of the 10th Regiment of Cavalry, Army of the United States, for the month of January 1867, Col. Benjamin Grierson, Fort Leavenworth, Kans. *Returns from Regular Army Cavalry Regiments, 1833–1916*. NARA, RG 391, Microfilm Publication M744, 16 rolls.

————. Return of the 10th Cavalry, Army of the United States, for the month of January 1887, Col. Benjamin H. Grierson, Commanding, Santa Fe, N.Mex. *Returns from Regular Army Cavalry Regiments, 1833–1916*. NARA, RG 391, Microfilm Publication M744, 16 rolls.

————. Return of the 10th Regiment of Cavalry, Army of the United States, for the month of April 1897, Col. John K. Mizner, Commanding, Fort Assiniboine, Mont. *Returns from Regular Army Cavalry Regiments, 1833–1916*. NARA, RG 391, Microfilm Publication M744, 16 rolls.

————. Return of the 10th Regiment of Cavalry, Army of the United States for the month of June 1898, Col. Guy V. Henry, Commanding, Sevilla, Cuba. *Returns from Regular Army Cavalry Regiments, 1833–1916*. NARA, RG 391, Microfilm Publication M744, 16 rolls.

————. Return of the 10th Regiment of Cavalry, Army of the United States for the month of July 1898, Col. Guy V. Henry, Commanding, Camp Hamilton, Santiago, Cuba. *Returns from Regular Army Cavalry Regiments, 1833–1916*. NARA, RG 391, Microfilm Publication M744, 16 rolls.

————. Return of the 10th Regiment of Cavalry, Army of the United States for the month of May 1899, Col. S. M. Whitside, Commanding, Manzanillo, Cuba. *Returns from Regular Army Cavalry Regiments, 1833–1916.* NARA, RG 391, Microfilm Publication M744, 16 rolls.

————. Return of the 10th Regiment of Cavalry, Army of the United States for the month of June 1899, Col. S. M. Whitside, Commanding, Bayanno, Cuba. *Returns from Regular Army Cavalry Regiments, 1833–1916.* NARA, RG 391, Microfilm Publication M744, 16 rolls.

————. Return of the 10th Regiment of Cavalry, Army of the United States, for the month of July 1905, Major Robert D. Read, Commanding, Fort Robinson, Neb. *Returns from Regular Army Cavalry Regiments, 1833–1916.* NARA, RG 391, Microfilm Publication M744, 16 rolls.

————. Return of the 10th Regiment of Cavalry, December 1916, Col. E. W. Evans, Commanding, Colonia Dublan, Mex. *Returns from Regular Army Cavalry Regiments, 1833–1916.* NARA, RG 391, Microfilm Publication M744, 16 rolls.

————. Return of the 11th Regiment of Cavalry, Army of the United States, for the month of July 1905, Col. Earl D. Thomas, Commanding, Fort Des Moines, Iowa. *Returns from Regular Army Cavalry Regiments, 1833–1916.* NARA, RG 391, Microfilm Publication M744, 16 rolls.

————. Return of the 11th Regiment of U.S. Cavalry, for the month of March 1909, Col. James Parker, Commanding, Fort Oglethorpe, Ga. *Returns from Regular Army Cavalry Regiments, 1833–1916.* NARA, RG 391, Microfilm Publication M744, 16 rolls.

————. Return of the 11th Regiment of Cavalry, Army of the United States, for the month of March 1911, Col. James Parker, Commanding, Maneuver Division, San Antonio, Tex. *Returns from Regular Army Cavalry Regiments, 1833–1916.* NARA, RG 391, Microfilm Publication M744, 16 rolls.

————. Return of the 11th Regiment of Cavalry, March 1916, Col. James Lockett, Commanding, Casas Grande, Mex. *Returns from Regular Army Cavalry Regiments, 1833–1916.* NARA, RG 391, Microfilm Publication M744, 16 rolls.

————. Return of the 11th Regiment of Cavalry, December 1916, Col. William J. Nicholson, Commanding, Colonia Dublan, Mex. *Returns from Regular Army Cavalry Regiments, 1833–1916.* NARA, RG 391, Microfilm Publication M744, 16 rolls.

————. Return of the 12th Regiment of Cavalry, Army of the United States, for the month of July 1905, Col. John B. Kerr, Commanding, Fort Oglethorpe, Ga. *Returns from Regular Army Cavalry Regiments, 1833–1916.* NARA, RG 391, Microfilm Publication M744, 16 rolls.

————. Return of the 12th Regiment of Cavalry, March 1916, Col. Horatio G. Sickel, Commanding, Columbus, N.Mex. *Returns from Regular Army Cavalry Regiments, 1833–1916.* NARA, RG 391, Microfilm Publication M744, 16 rolls.

————. Return of the 12th Regiment of Cavalry, December 1916, Col. Horatio G. Sickel, Commanding, Columbus, N.Mex. *Returns from Regular Army Cavalry Regiments, 1833–1916.* NARA, RG 391, Microfilm Publication M744, 16 rolls.

————. Return of the 13th Regiment of Cavalry, Army of the United States, for the month of July 1905, Col. Charles A. P. Hatfield, Commanding, Fort Myer, Va. *Returns from Regular Army Cavalry Regiments, 1833–1916*. NARA, RG 391, Microfilm Publication M744, 16 rolls.

————. Return of the 13th Regiment of Cavalry, December 1916, Col. Henry T. Allen, Commanding, Colonia Dublan, Mex. *Returns from Regular Army Cavalry Regiments, 1833–1916*. NARA, RG 391, Microfilm Publication M744, 16 rolls.

————. Return of the 14th Regiment of Cavalry, Army of the United States, for the month of July 1905, Col. Edward A. Godwin, Commanding, Camp Overton, Mindanao, Philippine Islands. *Returns from Regular Army Cavalry Regiments, 1833–1916*. NARA, RG 391, Microfilm Publication M744, 16 rolls.

————. Return of the 14th Regiment of Cavalry, December 1916, Col. Augustus C. Macomb, Commanding, Del Rio, Tex. *Returns from Regular Army Cavalry Regiments, 1833–1916*. NARA, RG 391, Microfilm Publication M744, 16 rolls.

————. Return of the 15th Regiment of Cavalry, Army of the United States, for the month of July 1905, Col. Edward A. Godwin, Commanding, Camp Overton, Mindanao, Philippine Islands. *Returns from Regular Army Cavalry Regiments, 1833–1916*. NARA, RG 391, Microfilm Publication M744, 16 rolls.

————. Return of the 15th Regiment of Cavalry, December 1916, Col. William H. Hay, Fort William McKinley, Philippine Islands. *Returns from Regular Army Cavalry Regiments, 1833–1916*. NARA, RG 391, Microfilm Publication M744, 16 rolls.

————. Return of the 16th Cavalry, December 1916, Col. William S. Scott, Commanding, Fort Sam Houston, Tex. *Returns from Regular Army Cavalry Regiments, 1833–1916*. NARA, RG 391, Microfilm Publication M744, 16 rolls.

————. Return of the 17th Cavalry, December 1916, Col. Willard A. Holbrook, Commanding, Fort Bliss, Tex. *Returns from Regular Army Cavalry Regiments, 1833–1916*. NARA, RG 391, Microfilm Publication M744, 16 rolls.

————. Return of the 3rd Regiment of Field Artillery, Army of the United States, for the month of August 1908, Col. Lotus Miles, Commanding, Fort Sam Houston, Tex. *Returns from Regular Army Cavalry Regiments, 1833–1916*. NARA, RG 391, Microfilm Publication M744, 16 rolls.

————. Return of the 3rd Regiment of Field Artillery, Army of the United States, for the month of September 1908, Col. Lotus Miles, Commanding, Fort Sam Houston, Tex. *Returns from Regular Army Cavalry Regiments, 1833–1916*. NARA RG 391, Microfilm Publication M744, 16 rolls.

————. Return of the 3rd Regiment of Field Artillery, Army of the United States, for the month of October 1908, Col. Lotus Miles, Commanding, Fort Sam Houston, Tex. *Returns from Regular Army Cavalry Regiments, 1833–1916*. NARA, RG 391, Microfilm Publication M744, 16 rolls.

————. Return of the 3rd Regiment of Field Artillery, Army of the United States, for the month of March 1911, Col. Lotus Miles, Commanding, Maneuver Division, San Antonio, Tex. *Returns from Regular Army Cavalry Regiments, 1833–1916*. NARA, RG 391, Microfilm Publication M744, 16 rolls.

————. *Revised Statues of the United States, Passed at the First Session of the Forty-Third Congress,*
    1873–74. Washington, D.C.: Government Printing Office, 1875.

————. *Revised United States Army Regulations of 1861. With an Appendix Containing the Changes*
    and Laws Affecting Army Regulations and Articles of War to June 25, 1863. Washington, D.C.:
    Government Printing Office, 1863.

U.S. Army, Adjutant-General's Office. "General Orders, No. 88," 25 June 1901. In *General*
    Orders and Circulars, Adjutant General's Office, 1901. Washington, D.C.: Government
    Printing Office, 1902.

U.S. Army, Chief of Infantry, the Chief of Cavalry, and the Army Band. *Band Field Manual:*
    The Band, FM 28–5. Washington, D.C.: Government Printing Office, 1941. NARA,
    RG 287, College Park, Md.

U.S. Army, Music School. *Specialists, Field Music—The Bugles TR 75–5.* Section 1, General,
    3. Washington, D.C.: War Department, 1 November 1928. NARA, RG 287, College
    Park, Md.

U.S. Army. Quartermaster Corps. *Horses and Mules and National Defense.* Compiled by
    Anna Waller. U.S. Army Office of the Quartermaster General, XVIII-3–009, 1958.

U.S. Army, Third Cavalry Public Affairs. *History, Customs, and Traditions of the 3d Armored*
    Cavalry Regiment, 33–2194-B (3d ACR), 2015. Available at http://www.hood.army
    .mil/3D_CR/files/pdfs/BloodAndSteel.pdf.

U.S. Army Heritage and Education Center, Carlisle, Pa., RG 49S-L. Dunston.

U.S. Congress. "Statues at Large, 1879–1875, Vol. 4, 18th–23rd, 1823–1835." *Library of*
    Congress, American Memory, https://memory.loc.gov/ammem/amlaw/lwsllink.html.

U.S. Congress, House of Representatives. Report of House Committee on Military Affairs.
    28 December 1832. *American State Papers: Military Affairs* 5:126.

U.S. House Executive Document 1. Part 2, 53rd Cong., 2nd Sess. Serial 3198, 123.

U.S. Secretary of War. Sec. 2, Act of February 2, 1901 (30 Stat. L., 748). In *The Military*
    Laws of the United States. 4th ed. Washington, D.C.: Government Printing Office, 1901.

————. Sec. 2, Army Reorganization Act of March 2, 1899 (30 Stats., 977). In *The Mili-*
    tary Laws of the United States, Fourth Edition, with Supplemental Showing Changes to March
    4, 1907. Washington, D.C.: Government Printing Office, 1899.

U.S. War Department. *An Act, Establishing Rules and Articles for the Government of the Armies of*
    the United States; with the Regulations of the War Department Respecting the Same. . . . Albany,
    N.Y.: Printed by Websters and Skinners, 1812.

————. *Annual Reports of the War Department for the Fiscal Year Ended June 30, 1901, Report*
    of the Lieutenant-General Commanding the Army, In Five Parts. Pt. 5. Washington, D.C.:
    Government Printing Office, 1901.

————. *Annual Reports, 1907.* Vol. 2. Washington, D.C.: Government Printing Office,
    1907.

————. *The Band: Formations, Movements, Inspections, Etc., Mounted and Dismounted.* Section
    1, 1.f.,g.,h.,j. Training Regulations, No. 130–15. Washington, D.C.: Government
    Printing Office, 15 February 1926. NARA, RG 287, College Park, Md.

―――. *The Band: Organization, Duties and Music Instruments.* Training Regulations, No. 130–5. Washington, D.C.: Government Printing Office, 15 February 1926. NARA, RG 287, College Park, Md.

―――. *Chief of the Militia Bureau, Annual Report.* Washington, D.C.: Government Printing Office, 1925.

―――. General Order 32. 8 July 1845. General Orders, Records of the Adjutant General. NARA, RG 94, College Park, Md.

―――. General Orders, No. 48. *General Orders of the War Department Embracing the Years 1861, 1862 & 1863, Adapted Specially for the Use of the Army and Navy of the United States, Chronologically Arranged in Two Volumes. With a Full Alphabetical Index, by Thos. M. O'Brien & Oliver Diefendorf, Military Attorneys, Leavenworth, Kansas.* Vol. 1. New York: Derby and Miller, 1864.

―――. General Orders. 1908. General Orders, No. 192, issued November 18, 1908: Transfer of colored regiments' white bandmasters to white regiments and assignment of colored bandmasters to colored regiments. CIS index to presidential executive orders and proclamations. Washington, D.C.: Congressional Information Service, 1987. Part 1, 3:1436 (1908–54–27).

―――. *General Regulations for the Army.* Washington, D.C.: Printed by Francis P. Blair, 1834.

―――. *General Regulations for the Army of the United States.* Washington, D.C.: J. and G. S. Gideon, 1841.

―――. Memorandum, Executive Officer, Militia Bureau to Assistant Chief of Staff, G-4 (Logistics), Subj: Answers to Questionnaire for Chief of Staff, 22 November 1927. U.S. Army Heritage and Education Center, Carlisle, Pa. RG168/344a/325.4–Gen.–27.

―――. *Official Army Register for 1908, Published by Order of the Secretary of War in Compliance with Law.* Document No. 312. Washington, D.C.: Adjutant General's Office, War Department, 1907.

U.S. War Department, National Guard Bureau. *Official National Guard Register for 1936.* Washington, D.C.: Government Printing Office, 1936.

―――. *Official National Guard Register for 1939.* Washington, D.C.: Government Printing Office, 1940.

NEWSPAPERS, NEWSLETTERS, AND PROGRAMS

1940 National Guard of the U.S. Naval Militia State of Illinois. 106th Cavalry Collection, Chicago Historical Society.

"3,000 United States Soldiers to Camp Here for Maneuvers at Anniversary and Reunion." *Gettysburg Star and Sentinel,* 18 June 1938.

"All Aboard for Buffalo, Wednesday, October 9, New York State Day at the Pan-American Exposition." *Rome (N.Y.) Citizen,* Tuesday, 1 October 1901.

"Arrival of the Minneswask." *New York Tribune* 58, no. 18,916, Tuesday, 30 August 1898, 1.

"Assist at Organ Concert." 24 March 1934. Unknown Chattanooga, Tenn., newspaper clipping in author's possession.

"At Montauk's Camp." *New York Tribune* 58, no. 18,1916, Tuesday, 30 August 1898.

"August Lederhaus." Obituary Notes. *New York Times*, 26 August 1919.

Black Horse Troop at War. Bulletin no. 1. Chicago: Chicago Black Horse Troop Association, May 1945.

Brady, Erik. "Link to 'Last Stand.'" *USA Today*, 7 November 2002.

———. "Vinatieri Getting a Kick Out of it All." *USA Today*, 7 November 2002.

Bromfield, John D. "Canadians, Hawaiians, First Cavalry and San Mateo Stars to Swing Mallets." *San Francisco Call*, 16 March 1913.

"Condensed News Gathered from all parts of the Country by Telegraph." *Marietta (Ohio) Daily Leader*, 26 August 1896.

"Dedication at Chicago, Arrangements for the Big Military Parade." *New York Times*, 12 October 1892.

"Drum's Band: Its Members Beat the Tattoo upon Each Other." *Brooklyn Daily Eagle*, Monday, 12 May 1890.

Dunlavy, Edwin W., ed. "Beta Iota." Alumni Notes. *Delta* 35, no. 1. Indianapolis, Ind.: Sigma Nu Fraternity, October 1917.

"The End of a Long March, Regular Troops Finish Their Overland Journey." *Washington (D.C.) Morning Times*, Tuesday, 25 May 1897.

"Federal Troops Designated, Largest Number to Parade on Grant Day Seen Together Since the War." *New York Times*, 4 April 1897.

"Federal Troops for the Parade, Special Orders from the Headquarters of the Department of the East." *New York Daily Tribune*, Monday, 19 April 1897.

"Fourth of July." *Sacramento Daily Union*, Friday, 3 July 1863, 1.

Grand Farewell Complimentary Concert by the Eleventh U.S. Cavalry Band, in Gaston Hall—Georgetown College, Wednesday Evening, December 11, 1901, at 8:30 o'Clock, Director, A. Perwein, U.S.A.

"Grant Monument Parade, Assurances of One of the Greatest Military Displays Ever Seen in this City." *New York Times*, 26 March 1897.

"Great Crowd Visits Camp. Many Mexicans from San Antonio See Gen. Carter's Troops. Special to the New York Times." *New York Times*, 13 March 1911.

"Great International Polo Tourney in Sight, Four Crack Teams Entered and Play Starts March 24." *San Francisco Call*, 16 March 1913.

Hirabayashi, Bernice. "Never Too Old to Make Music." *Los Angeles Times*, 14 July 1991.

Illinois College Catalog 2011–2012. Jacksonville: Illinois College, 2011.

"The Inauguration To-Day, Gov. Roosevelt Attended Church Yesterday with Other Dignitaries." *New York Times*, 2 January 1899.

"In Memory of Gen. Grant, Probability that Many Confederate Veterans Will Be in the Parade." *New York Times*, 30 March 1897.

"Laid to Rest at Arlington, General Albert Ordway's Remains Borne to the Grave." *Washington (D.C.) Times*, Thursday, 25 November 1897.

Landrum, Carl. "Nick Musolino Played with Big Band Greats." *Quincy (Ill.) Herald-Whig*, 5 May 1996.

"Major Gregory Buried, Interred in Arlington Cemetery with Full Military Honors." *Washington (D.C.) Morning Times*, Thursday, 5 August 1897, 4.

"Mayor to Review Troop A" in "Plan for Grand Review." *New York Times*, 7 September 1898.

"Mexicans Scared by Fireworks." *Sausalito (Calif.) News*, December 1916.

"Military Gossip." *New York Times*, 13 October 1872.

"Mounted Infantry Inspection." *Brisbane Courier*, Monday, 21 March 1898.

"Mr. Fairbanks Reaches Portland, Visits Grounds Where the Lewis and Clark Exposition Opens To-Day." *New-York Daily Tribune*, 1 June 1905.

"Mr. M'Kinley at Montauk." *New York Times*, 4 September 1898.

New England: The Boston News-Letter, Published by Authority. No. 548 (Monday, October 11–Monday, October 18, 1714).

Ottawa Volunteer Review, 18 July 1870.

"Phillips' Career Spans Cavalry Trooper to Air Force Supplyman." *Air Force Enlisted Widows Home Foundation Newsletter* 21, no. 2 (Spring 1993): 1, 4.

"Route, Formation of World's Fair Fourth of July Military Parade." *St. Louis New Republic*, Tuesday, 28 June 1904.

Schlachtenhaufen, Mark. "Hero Led Last U.S. Army Cavalry Charge." *Edmond (Okla.) Sun*, 4 October 2010. Accessed 25 November 2013, http://www.edmondsun.com/local/x537487919/Hero-led-last-U-S-Army-cavalry-charge.

Schofield Barracks Horse Show, Official Program, 1934. 8 and 9 June 1934.

Simpson, Kirk. "Body of 'The Unknown Soldier' Arrives Home." Associated Press Night Report, Wednesday, 9 November 1921.

Timlin, Gary. "Bunnellite Mounted Up: Here Comes the Kentucky Cavalry!" *News-Tribune* (Flagler Co., Fla.), ca. 1983.

"To Escort Li Hung Chang, Arrival of Four Troops of the Sixth Cavalry." *New York Times*, 27 August 1896.

Venice. "The Second Cavalry Band." Fort Snelling Items. *St. Paul Press*, 22 May 1864, 1.

WEBSITES

"1st Battalion United States Sharpshooters Civil War." New York State Military Museum and Veterans Research Center, NYS Division of Military and Naval Affairs website. Accessed 25 November 2013. http://www.dmna.state.ny.us/historic/reghist/civil/other/1stUSSS/1stUSSS Main.htm.

11th Armored Cavalry's Veterans of Vietnam and Cambodia website. Accessed 25 November 2013. http://www.11thcavnam.com/.

Davis, Tom. "A Chronology of the 1st United States Cavalry: The Diary of Tom Davis." Spanish American War Centennial website. Accessed 25 November 2013. http://www.spanamwar.com/1stUScav.htm.

Digitalt Museum, Stockholm: http://www.digitaltmuseum.se/search?query=puka.

"From Santiago to Manila: Spanish-American War Logistics." Army Logistics University. Accessed 1 January 2015. http://www.almc.army.mil/alog/issues/JulAug98/MS305 .htm.

Harvey, Don. "The Michigan Cavalry Brigade." Michigan in the Civil War website. Accessed 15 February 2003. http://hometown.aol.com/dlharvey/michbrig.htm.

"The History of the 4th U.S. Cavalry Regiment." Official Homepage of Fort Huachuca, Arizona. Accessed 25 November 2013. http://huachuca-www.army.mil/pages/btroop/ history.html.

"History of the United States Army Materiel Command Band." U.S. Army Materiel Command website. Accessed 11 December 2015. http://www.music.army.mil/ organizations/pages/?unit=389AB&p=history.

New York State Military Museum and Veterans Research Center, NYS Division of Military and Naval Affairs. Accessed 25 November 2013. http://www.dmna.state.ny.us/ historic/reghist/civil/other/1stUSSS/1stUSSS Main.htm.

Perwein, Robert, and Charles Holle. "Alexander H. Perwein, 1920." West Point Association of Graduates website. Accessed 25 November 2013. http://apps.westpointaog .org/Memorials/Article/6706/.

Rathvon, William V. "Eyewitness at Gettysburg." 1938 sound recording. Downloaded from National Public Radio, 9 November 2005. Originally aired on *All Things Considered*, 15 February 1999. Accessed 25 November 2013. http://www.npr.org/templates/story/ story.php?storyId=1045619.

"The Royal Artillery Band." British Army website. Accessed 25 November 2013. http:// www.army.mod.uk/music/23942.aspx.

"Vinatieri Archive." National Music Museum website. Accessed 25 November 2013. http:// orgs.usd.edu/nmm/vinatieri.html.

DISCOGRAPHY

Brass Mounted Army, Music of the Old Horse Cavalry, Performed by the California Gold Rush Band, Arrowpoint, Washington, Michigan, 1995.

Custer's Last Band: The Original Music of Felix Vinatieri, Custer's Legendary Bandmaster. Performed by the New Custer Brass Band, Steve Charpié, Leader. America's Shrine to Music Museum, University of South Dakota, Vermillion, S.Dak., 2001.

CORRESPONDENCE AND INTERVIEWS

Dean, Anthony (Eagle and Lyre, Military Music CDs and Publications). E-mail message to author, 19 February 2009; personal communication, 12 March 2010.

Dittmer, Colonel John S. (Ret.). Telephone interview by author, 25 June 2003. Menlo Park, Calif.

Doerner, John A. (chief historian, Little Bighorn Battlefield National Monument, Crow Agency, Mont.). Telephone interview by author, 25 March 2004.

Fear, C. Arthur. Telephone interviews by author, 1 November 2001, 29 March 2003, Evanston, Ill.

Graff, CW4 Aaron (commander of the 1st Cavalry Division Band [successor to the 7th Cavalry band]). E-mail message to author, 12 March 2009, Fort Hood, Okla.

Greger, Chief Warrant Officer Erwin M. (bandleader, commander, Band 1st Cavalry Division). Memo to commanding general, 1st Cavalry Division, APO 201, 28 July 1953. In author's possession.

Henderson, Dr. Hubert. E-mail messages to author, 27 February 2004 and 21 March 2004, Louisville, Ky.

Hoadley, Frank (grandson of Clyde G. Ross). Telephone interview by author, 26 May 2006, Madison, Wis.

Illoway, Chloe (executive director of the Cheyenne Symphony, Cheyenne, Wyo.). Telephone interview by author, 9 June 2006.

Irwin, William H. (1919–2003). Telephone interview by author, 30 July 2001, Chicago.

Ish, Lt. Col. George (Ret.). E-mail message to author, 26 June 2001, Yuma, Ariz.

Kirby, Frank. E-mail messages to author, 24 September 2000 and 6 October 2000.

Kleinendorst, David (president of the Minnesota Farriers Association, Roseville, Minn.). E-mail message to author, 27 February 2003.

Kondratiuk, Col. Leonid (director of historical services of the Massachusetts National Guard). E-mail message to author, 21 May 2003.

Langdon, Elwood. Letters to author, 9 April 2003 and 5 May 2003, Fort Pierce, Fla.

Levykin, Aleksey (director of scientific research, Kremlin Museum). E-mail message to author, 5 February 2008.

Mayer, Dr. Francis N. Telephone interview by author, 25 November 2002, St. Paul, Minn.

Melnyk, Major Les' (Army National Guard historian, National Guard Bureau, Arlington, Va.). E-mail messages to author, 24 April 2003, 20 May 2003, and 13 October 2005.

Ramsden, George. Telephone interview by author, 14 March 2004, Rockport, Mass.

Rankin, Bill. E-mail message to author, 14 April 2003, Caldwell, Idaho.

Ressler, D. Michael (master gunnery sergeant, chief historian, U.S. Marine Band). E-mail message to author, 3 April 2009.

Shaffer, George L. Telephone interview by author, 25 June 2001, Fairfax Station, Va.

Utley, Robert. E-mail messages to author, 3 January 2014 and 25 March 2004, Georgetown, Tex.

Vinatieri, C. Paul. Telephone interview by author, 10 November 2002. Rapid City, S.Dak.

Woodward, Roy. Telephone interview by author, 8 July 1998, Fort Worth, Tex.

Yassel, Chief Warrant Officer Louis S. Interview by Edward M. Coffman. 1 December 1972, Washington, D.C. Copy in author's possession.

Index

Page numbers in *italics* indicate illustrations.
Page numbers followed by *t* indicate tables.